FLORENTINE DRAMA FOR
CONVENT AND FESTIVAL

THE
OTHER VOICE
IN
EARLY MODERN
EUROPE

*A Series Edited by
Margaret L. King and
Albert Rabil, Jr.*

Antonia Pulci

FLORENTINE DRAMA FOR
CONVENT AND FESTIVAL
Seven Sacred Plays

Annotated and translated
by James Wyatt Cook

Edited by James Wyatt Cook and
Barbara Collier Cook

THE UNIVERSITY OF CHICAGO PRESS
Chicago & London

James Wyatt Cook is professor of English at Albion College.

The University of Chicago Press, Chicago 60637
The University of Chicago Press, Ltd., London
© 1996 by The University of Chicago
All rights reserved. Published 1996
Printed in the United States of America
05 04 03 02 01 00 99 98 97 96   1 2 3 4 5

ISBN: 0-226-68516-0 (cloth)
ISBN: 0-226-68517-9 (paper)

Library of Congress Cataloging-in-Publication Data

Pulci, Antonia, 1452–1501.
    [Works.   English.   1996]
    Florentine drama for convent and festival : seven sacred plays / Antonia
Pulci ; annotated and translated by James Wyatt Cook ; edited by James
Wyatt Cook and Barbara Collier Cook.
        p.   cm. — (The other voice in early modern Europe)
    Includes bibliographical references and index.
    ISBN 0-226-68516-0 (cloth   :   alk. paper)
    ISBN 0-226-68517-9 (paper   :   alk. paper)
    1. Pulci, Antonia, 1452–1501—Translations into English. 2.   Religious drama,
Italian—Translations into English.   I. Cook, James Wyatt,
1932–   . II. Cook, Barbara Collier.   III. Title. IV. Series.
PQ4630.P8A23   1996
852'. 3—dc20   96–12766
                                                                         CIP

♾ The paper used in this publication meets the minimum requirements of the
American National Standard for Information Sciences—Permanence of Paper for
Printed Library Materials, ANSI Z39.48-1984.

This translation is for
Leo Wyatt Cook
and
Joshua Gilbert Dauphinais
our third and fourth grandchildren,
who arrived
about the same time as this book.

CONTENTS

THE OTHER VOICE IN EARLY MODERN EUROPE: INTRODUCTION TO THE SERIES

Margaret L. King and Albert Rabil, Jr.

THE OLD VOICE AND THE OTHER VOICE

In western Europe and the United States women are nearing equality in the professions, in business, and in politics. Most enjoy access to education, reproductive rights, and autonomy in financial affairs. Issues vital to women are on the public agenda: equal pay, child care, domestic abuse, breast cancer research, and curricular revision with an eye to the inclusion of women.

These recent achievements have their origins in things women (and some male supporters) said for the first time about six hundred years ago. Theirs is the "other voice," in contradistinction to the "first voice," the voice of the educated men who created western culture. Coincident with a general reshaping of European culture in the period 1300 to 1700 (called the Renaissance or Early Modern period), questions of female equality and opportunity were raised that still resound and are still unresolved.

The "other voice" emerged against the backdrop of a 3,000-year history of misogyny—the hatred of women—rooted in the civilizations related to western culture: Hebrew, Greek, Roman, and Christian. Misogyny inherited from these traditions pervaded the intellectual, medical, legal, religious and social systems that developed during the European Middle Ages.

The following pages describe the misogynistic tradition inherited by early modern Europeans, and the new tradition which the "other voice" called into being to challenge its assumptions. This review should serve as a framework for the understanding of the texts published in the series "The Other Voice in Early Modern Europe." Introductions specific to each text and author follow this essay in all the volumes of the series.

THE MISOGYNIST TRADITION, 500 BCE–1500 CE

Embedded in the philosophical and medical theories of the ancient Greeks were perceptions of the female as inferior to the male in both mind and body. Similarly, the structure of civil legislation inherited from the ancient Romans was biased against women, and the views on women developed by Christian thinkers out of the Hebrew Bible and the Christian New Testament were negative and disabling. Literary works composed in the vernacular language of ordinary people, and widely recited or read, conveyed these negative assumptions. The social networks within which most women lived—those of the family and the institutions of the Roman Catholic church—were shaped by this misogynist tradition and sharply limited the areas in which women might act in and upon the world.

GREEK PHILOSOPHY AND FEMALE NATURE. Greek biology assumed that women were inferior to men and defined them merely as child-bearers and housekeepers. This view was authoritatively expressed in the works of the philosopher Aristotle.

Aristotle thought in dualities. He considered action superior to inaction, form (the inner design or structure of any object) superior to matter, completion to incompletion, possession to deprivation. In each of these dualities, he associated the male principle with the superior quality and the female with the inferior. "The male principle in nature," he argued, "is associated with active, formative and perfected characteristics, while the female is passive, material and deprived, desiring the male in order to become complete."[1] Men are always identified with virile qualities, such as judgment, courage and stamina; women with their opposites—irrationality, cowardice, and weakness.

Even in the womb, the masculine principle was considered superior. Man's semen, Aristotle believed, created the form of a new human creature, while the female body contributed only matter. (The existence of the ovum, and the other facts of human embryology, were not established until the seventeenth century.) Although the later Greek physician Galen believed that there was a female component in generation, contributed by "female semen," the followers of both Aristotle and Galen saw the male role in human generation as more active and more important.

In the Aristotelian view, the male principle sought always to re-

---

1. Aristotle, *Physics*, 1.9 192a20–24 (*The Complete Works of Aristotle*, ed. Jonathan Barnes, rev. Oxford translation, 2 vols. [Princeton, 1984], 1:328).

produce itself. The creation of a female was always a mistake, therefore, resulting from an imperfect act of generation. Every female born
was considered a "defective" or "mutilated" male (as Aristotle's termi-
nology has variously been translated), a "monstrosity" of nature.[2]

For Greek theorists, the biology of males and females was the key
to their psychology. The female was softer and more docile, more apt
to be despondent, querulous, and deceitful. Being incomplete, moreover, she craved sexual fulfillment in intercourse with a male. The
male was intellectual, active, and in control of his passions.

These psychological polarities derived from the theory that the
universe consisted of four elements (earth, fire, air and water), expressed in human bodies as four "humors" (black bile, yellow bile,
blood, and phlegm) considered respectively dry, hot, damp, and cold,
and corresponding to mental states ("melancholic," "choleric,"
"sanguine," "phlegmatic"). In this schematization, the male, sharing
the principles of earth and fire, was dry and hot; the female, sharing
the principles of air and water, was cold and damp.

Female psychology was further affected by her dominant organ,
the uterus (womb), *bystera* in Greek. The passions generated by the
womb made women lustful, deceitful, talkative, irrational, indeed—
when these affects were in excess—"hysterical."

Aristotle's biology also had social and political consequences. If
the male principle was superior and the female inferior, then in the
household, as in the state, men should rule and women must be subordinate. That hierarchy does not rule out the companionship of husband and wife, whose cooperation was necessary for the welfare of
children and the preservation of property. Such mutuality supported
male preeminence.

Aristotle's teacher Plato suggested a different possibility: that
men and women might possess the same virtues. The setting for this
proposal is the imaginary and ideal Republic that Plato sketches in a
dialogue of that name. Here, for a privileged elite capable of leading
wisely, all distinctions of class and wealth dissolve, as do consequently those of gender. Without households or property, as Plato
constructs his ideal society, there is no need for the subordination of
women. Women may, therefore, be educated to the same level as men
to assume leadership responsibilities. Plato's Republic remained imaginary, however. In real societies, the subordination of women remained
the norm and the prescription.

2. Aristotle, *Generation of Animals*, 2.3 737a27–28 (Barnes, 1:1144).

The views of women inherited from the Greek philosophical tradition became the basis for medieval thought. In the thirteenth century, the supreme scholastic philosopher Thomas Aquinas, among others, still echoed Aristotle's views of human reproduction, of male and female personalities, and of the preeminent male role in the social hierarchy.

ROMAN LAW AND THE FEMALE CONDITION. Roman law, like Greek philosophy, underlay medieval thought and shaped medieval society. The ancient belief that adult, property-owning men should administer households and make decisions affecting the community at large is the very fulcrum of Roman law.

Around 450 BCE, during Rome's republican era, the community's customary law was recorded (legendarily) on Twelve Tables erected in the city's central forum. It was later elaborated by professional jurists whose activity increased in the imperial era, when much new legislation, especially on issues affecting family and inheritance, was passed. This growing, changing body of laws was eventually codified in the *Corpus of Civil Law* under the direction of the Emperor Justinian, generations after the empire ceased to be ruled from Rome. That *Corpus*, read and commented upon by medieval scholars from the eleventh century on, inspired the legal systems of most of the cities and kingdoms of Europe.

Laws regarding dowries, divorce, and inheritance most pertain to women. Since those laws aimed to maintain and preserve property, the women concerned were those from the property-owning minority. Their subordination to male family members points to the even greater subordination of lower-class and slave women about whom the laws speak little.

In the early Republic, the *paterfamilias*, "father of the family," possessed *patria potestas*, "paternal power." The term *pater*, "father," in both these cases does not necessarily mean biological father, but householder. The father was the person who owned the household's property and, indeed, its human members. The *paterfamilias* had absolute power—including the power, rarely exercised, of life or death—over his wife, his children, and his slaves, as much as over his cattle.

Children could be "emancipated," an act that granted legal autonomy and the right to own property. Male children over the age of fourteen could be emancipated by a special grant from the father, or automatically by their father's death. But females never could be emancipated; instead, they passed from the authority of their father to a husband or, if widowed or orphaned while still unmarried, to a guardian or tutor.

Marriage under its traditional form placed the woman under her husband's authority, or *manus*. He could divorce her on grounds of adultery, drinking wine, or stealing from the household, but she could not divorce him. She could possess no property in her own right, nor bequeath any to her children upon her death. When her husband died, the household property passed not to her but to his male heirs. And when her father died, she had no claim to any family inheritance, which was directed to her brothers or more remote male relatives. The effect of these laws was to exclude women from civil society, itself based on property ownership.

In the later Republican and Imperial periods, these rules were significantly modified. Women rarely married according to the traditional form, but according to the form of "free" marriage. That practice allowed a woman to remain under her father's authority, to possess property given her by her father (most frequently the "dowry," recoverable from the husband's household in the event of his death), and to inherit from her father. She could also bequeath property to her own children and divorce her husband, just as he could divorce her.

Despite this greater freedom, women still suffered enormous disability under Roman law. Heirs could belong only to the father's side, never the mother's. Moreover, although she could bequeath her property to her children, she could not establish a line of succession in doing so. A woman was "the beginning and end of her own family," growled the jurist Ulpian. Moreover, women could play no public role. They could not hold public office, represent anyone in a legal case, or even witness a will. Women had only a private existence, and no public personality.

The dowry system, the guardian, women's limited ability to transmit wealth, and total political disability are all features of Roman law adopted, although modified according to local customary laws, by the medieval communities of western Europe.

CHRISTIAN DOCTRINE AND WOMEN'S PLACE. The Hebrew Bible and the Christian New Testament authorized later writers to limit women to the realm of the family and to burden them with the guilt of original sin. The passages most fruitful for this purpose were the creation narratives in Genesis and sentences from the Epistles defining women's role within the Christian family and community.

Each of the first two chapters of Genesis contains a creation narrative. In the first "God created man in his own image, in the image of God he created him; male and female he created them." (NRSV, Genesis 1:27) In the second, God created Eve from Adam's rib (2:21–23). Christian theologians relied principally on Genesis 2 for their understanding of the relation between man and woman, interpreting the creation of Eve from Adam as proof of her subordination to him.

The creation story in Genesis 2 leads to that of the temptations in Genesis 3: of Eve by the wily serpent, and of Adam by Eve. As read by Christian theologians from Tertullian to Thomas Aquinas, the narrative made Eve responsible for the Fall and its consequences. She instigated the act; she deceived her husband; she suffered the greater punishment. Her disobedience made it necessary for Jesus to be incarnated and to die on the cross. From the pulpit, moralists and preachers for centuries conveyed to women the guilt that they bore for original sin.

The Epistles offered advice to early Christians on building communities of the faithful. Among the matters to be regulated was the place of women. Paul offered views favorable to women in Galatians 3:28: "There is neither Jew nor Greek, there is neither slave nor free, there is neither male nor female; for you are all one in Christ Jesus." Paul also referred to women as his co-workers and placed them on a par with himself and his male co-workers (Phil. 4:2–3; Rom. 16:1–3; I Cor. 16:19). Elsewhere Paul limited women's possibilities: "But I want you to understand that the head of every man is Christ, the head of a woman is her husband, and the head of Christ is God." (I Cor. 11:3)

Biblical passages by later writers (though attributed to Paul) enjoined women to forego jewels, expensive clothes, and elaborate coiffures; and they forbade women to "teach or have authority over men," telling them to "learn in silence with all submissiveness" as is proper for one responsible for sin, consoling them however with the thought that they will be saved through childbearing (I Tim. 2:9–15). Other texts among the later epistles defined women as the weaker sex, and emphasized their subordination to their husbands (I Peter 3:7; Col. 3:18; Eph. 5:22–23).

These passages from the New Testament became the arsenal employed by theologians of the early church to transmit negative attitudes toward women to medieval Christian culture—above all, Tertullian ("On the Apparel of Women"), Jerome (*Against Jovinian*), and Augustine (*The Literal Meaning of Genesis*).

THE IMAGE OF WOMEN IN MEDIEVAL LITERATURE. The philosophical, legal and religious traditions born in antiquity formed the basis of the medieval intellectual synthesis wrought by trained thinkers, mostly clerics, writing in Latin and based largely in universities. The vernacular literary tradition which developed alongside the learned tradition also spoke about female nature and women's roles. Medieval stories, poems, and epics were also infused with misogyny. They portrayed most women as lustful and deceitful, while praising good housekeepers and loyal wives, or replicas of the Virgin Mary, or the female saints and martyrs. There is an exception in the movement of "courtly love" that evolved in southern France from the twelfth century. Courtly love was the erotic love between a nobleman and noblewoman, the latter usually superior in social rank. It was always adulterous. From the conventions of courtly love derive modern western notions of romantic love. The phenomenon has had an impact disproportionate to its size, for it affected only a tiny elite, and very few women. The exaltation of the female lover probably does not reflect a higher evaluation of women, or a step toward their sexual liberation. More likely it gives expression to the social and sexual tensions besetting the knightly class at a specific historical juncture.

The literary fashion of courtly love was on the wane by the thirteenth century, when the widely read *Romance of the Rose* was composed in French by two authors of significantly different dispositions. Guillaume de Lorris composed the initial 4,000 verses around 1235, and Jean de Meun added about 17,000 verses—more than four times the original—around 1265.

The fragment composed by Guillaume de Lorris stands squarely in the courtly love tradition. Here the poet, in a dream, is admitted into a walled garden where he finds a magic fountain in which a rosebush is reflected. He longs to pick one rose but the thorns around it prevent his doing so, even as he is wounded by arrows from the God of Love, whose commands he agrees to obey. The remainder of this part of the poem recounts the poet's unsuccessful efforts to pluck the rose.

The longer part of the *Romance* by Jean de Meun also describes a dream. But here allegorical characters give long didactic speeches, providing a social satire on a variety of themes, including those pertaining to women. Love is an anxious and tormented state, the poem explains, women are greedy and manipulative, marriage is miserable, beautiful women are lustful, ugly ones cease to please, and a chaste woman, as rare as a black swan, can scarcely be found.

Shortly after Jean de Meun completed *The Romance of the Rose,*

Mathéolus penned his *Lamentations*, a long Latin diatribe against marriage translated into French about a century later. The *Lamentations* sum up medieval attitudes toward women and provoked the important response by Christine de Pizan in her *Book of the City of Ladies*.

In 1355, Giovanni Boccaccio wrote *Il Corbaccio*, another antifeminist manifesto, though ironically by an author whose other works pioneered new directions in Renaissance thought. The former husband of his lover appears to Boccaccio, condemning his unmoderated lust and detailing the defects of women. Boccaccio concedes at the end "how much men naturally surpass women in nobility"[3] and is cured of his desires.

WOMEN'S ROLES: THE FAMILY. The negative perception of women expressed in the intellectual tradition are also implicit in the actual roles that women played in European society. Assigned to subordinate positions in the household and the church, they were barred from significant participation in public life.

Medieval European households, like those in antiquity and in nonwestern civilizations, were headed by males. It was the male serf, or peasant, feudal lord, town merchant, or citizen who was polled or taxed or succeeded to an inheritance or had any acknowledged public role, although their wives or widows could stand on a temporary basis as surrogates for them. From about 1100, the position of property-holding males was enhanced further. Inheritance was confined to the male, or agnate, line—with depressing consequences for women.

A wife never fully belonged to her husband's family or a daughter to her father's family. She left her father's house young to marry whomever her parents chose. Her dowry was managed by her husband and normally passed to her children by him at her death.

A married woman's life was occupied nearly constantly with cycles of pregnancy, childbearing, and lactation. Women bore children through all the years of their fertility, and many died in childbirth before the end of that term. They also bore responsibility for raising young children up to six or seven. That responsibility was shared in the propertied classes, since it was common for a wet-nurse to take over the job of breastfeeding, and servants took over other chores.

Women trained their daughters in the household responsibilities appropriate to their status, nearly always in tasks associated with textiles: spinning, weaving, sewing, embroidering. Their sons were sent

---

3. Giovanni Boccaccio, *The Corbaccio or The Labyrinth of Love*, trans. and ed. Anthony K. Cassell (Binghamton, N.Y.; rev. ed., 1993), 71.

out of the house as apprentices or students, or their training was assumed by fathers in later childhood and adolescence. On the death of her husband, a woman's children became the responsibility of his family. She generally did not take "his" children with her to a new marriage or back to her father's house, except sometimes in artisan classes.

Women also worked. Rural peasants performed farm chores, merchant wives often practiced their husband's trade, the unmarried daughters of the urban poor worked as servants or prostitutes. All wives produced or embellished textiles and did the housekeeping, while wealthy ones managed servants. These labors were unpaid or poorly paid, but often contributed substantially to family wealth.

WOMEN'S ROLES: THE CHURCH. Membership in a household, whether a father's or a husband's, meant for women a lifelong subordination to others. In western Europe, the Roman Catholic church offered an alternative to the career of wife and mother. A woman could enter a convent parallel in function to the monasteries for men that evolved in the early Christian centuries.

In the convent, a woman pledged herself to a celibate life, lived according to strict community rules, and worshipped daily. Often the convent offered training in Latin, allowing some women to become considerable scholars and authors, as well as scribes, artists, and musicians. For women who chose the conventual life, the benefits could be enormous, but for numerous others placed in convents by paternal choice, the life could be restrictive and burdensome.

The conventual life declined as an alternative for women as the modern age approached. Reformed monastic institutions resisted responsibility for related female orders. The church increasingly restricted female institutional life by insisting on closer male supervision.

Women often sought other options. Some joined the communities of laywomen that sprang up spontaneously in the thirteenth century in the urban zones of western Europe, especially in Flanders and Italy. Some joined the heretical movements that flourished in late medieval Christendom, whose anticlerical and often antifamily positions particularly appealed to women. In these communities, some women were acclaimed as "holy women" or "saints," while others often were condemned as frauds or heretics.

In all, though the options offered to women by the church were sometimes less than satisfactory, sometimes they were richly rewarding. After 1520, the convent remained an option only in Roman

Catholic territories. Protestantism engendered an ideal of marriage as a heroic endeavor, and appeared to place husband and wife on a more equal footing. Sermons and treatises, however, still called for female subordination and obedience.

THE OTHER VOICE, 1300–1700

Misogyny was so long-established in European culture when the modern era opened that to dismantle it was a monumental labor. The process began as part of a larger cultural movement that entailed the critical reexamination of ideas inherited from the ancient and medieval past. The humanists launched that critical reexamination.

THE HUMANIST FOUNDATION. Originating in Italy in the fourteenth century, humanism quickly became the dominant intellectual movement in Europe. Spreading in the sixteenth century from Italy to the rest of Europe, it fueled the literary, scientific and philosophical movements of the era, and laid the basis for the eighteenth-century Enlightenment.

Humanists regarded the scholastic philosophy of medieval universities as out of touch with the realities of urban life. They found in the rhetorical discourse of classical Rome a language adapted to civic life and public speech. They learned to read, speak, and write classical Latin, and eventually classical Greek. They founded schools to teach others to do so, establishing the pattern for elementary and secondary education for the next three hundred years.

In the service of complex government bureaucracies, humanists employed their skills to write eloquent letters, deliver public orations, and formulate public policy. They developed new scripts for copying manuscripts and used the new printing press for the dissemination of texts, for which they created methods of critical editing.

Humanism was a movement led by males who accepted the evaluation of women in ancient texts and generally shared the misogynist perceptions of their culture. (Female humanists, as will be seen, did not.) Yet humanism also opened the door to the critique of the misogynist tradition. By calling authors, texts, and ideas into question, it made possible the fundamental rereading of the whole intellectual tradition that was required in order to free women from cultural prejudice and social subordination.

A DIFFERENT CITY. The other voice first appeared when, after so many centuries, the accumulation of misogynist concepts evoked a response from a capable woman female defender: Christine de Pizan. Introducing her *Book of the City of Ladies* (1405), she described how she was affected by reading Mathéolus's *Lamentations:* "Just the sight of this book ... made me wonder how it happened that so many different men ... are so inclined to express both in speaking and in their treatises and writings so many wicked insults about women and their behavior."[4] These statements impelled her to detest herself "and the entire feminine sex, as though we were monstrosities in nature."[5]

The remainder of the *Book of the City of Ladies* presents a justification of the female sex and a vision of an ideal community of women. A pioneer, she has not only received the misogynist message, but she rejects it. From the fourteenth to seventeenth century, a huge body of literature accumulated that responded to the dominant tradition.

The result was a literary explosion consisting of works by both men and women, in Latin and in vernacular languages: works enumerating the achievements of notable women; works rebutting the main accusations made against women; works arguing for the equal education of men and women; works defining and redefining women's proper role in the family, at court, and in public; and describing women's lives and experiences. Recent monographs and articles have begun to hint at the great range of this phenomenon, involving probably several thousand titles. The protofeminism of these "other voices" constitute a significant fraction of the literary product of the early modern era.

THE CATALOGUES. Around 1365, the same Boccaccio whose *Corbaccio* rehearses the usual charges against female nature, wrote another work, *Concerning Famous Women.* A humanist treatise drawing on classical texts, it praised 106 notable women—one hundred of them from pagan Greek and Roman antiquity, and six from the religious and cultural tradition since antiquity—and helped make all readers aware of a sex normally condemned or forgotten. Boccaccio's outlook, nevertheless, is misogynist, for it singled out for praise those women who possessed the traditional virtues of chastity, silence, and obedience. Women who were active in the public realm, for example, rulers and warriors, were depicted as suffering terrible punishments for entering into the masculine sphere. Women were his subject, but Boccaccio's standard remained male.

4. Christine de Pizan, *The Book of the City of Ladies*, trans. Earl Jeffrey Richards; Foreword Marina Warner (New York, 1982), 1.1.1., pp. 3–4.
5. Ibid., 1.1.1–2, p. 5.

Christine de Pizan's *Book of the City of Ladies* contains a second catalogue, one responding specifically to Boccaccio's. Where Boccaccio
portrays female virtue as exceptional, she depicts it as universal. Many
women in history were leaders, or remained chaste despite the lascivious approaches of men, or were visionaries and brave martyrs.

The work of Boccaccio inspired a series of catalogues of illustrious women of the biblical, classical, Christian, and local past: works
by Alvaro de Luna, Jacopo Filippo Foresti (1497), Brantôme, Pierre Le
Moyne, Pietro Paolo de Ribera (who listed 845 figures), and many others. Whatever their embedded prejudices, these catalogues of illustrious women drove home to the public the possibility of female excellence.

THE DEBATE. At the same time, many questions remained: Could a
woman be virtuous? Could she perform noteworthy deeds? Was she
even, strictly speaking, of the same human species as men? These
questions were debated over four centuries, in French, German,
Italian, Spanish and English, by authors male and female, among
Catholics, Protestants and Jews, in ponderous volumes and breezy
pamphlets. The whole literary phenomenon has been called the
querelle des femmes, the "Woman Question."

The opening volley of this battle occurred in the first years of
the fifteenth century, in a literary debate sparked by Christine de
Pizan. She exchanged letters critical of Jean de Meun's contribution
to the *Romance of the Rose* with two French humanists and royal secre-
taries, Jean de Montreuil and Gontier Col. When the matter became
public, Jean Gerson, one of Europe's leading theologians, supported
de Pizan's arguments against de Meun, for the moment silencing the
opposition.

The debate resurfaced repeatedly over the next two hundred
years. *The Triumph of Women* (1438) by Juan Rodríguez de la Camara (or
Juan Rodríguez del Padron) struck a new note by presenting arguments
for the superiority of women to men. *The Champion of Women* (1440–42)
by Martin Le Franc addresses once again the misogynist claims of *The
Romance of the Rose*, and offers counterevidence of female virtue and
achievement.

A cameo of the debate on women is included in the *Courtier*, one
of the most-read books of the era, published by the Italian Baldassare
Castiglione in 1528 and immediately translated into other European
vernaculars. The *Courtier* depicts a series of evenings at the court of
the Duke of Urbino in which many men and some women of the
highest social stratum amuse themselves by discussing a range of lit-

erary and social issues. The "woman question" is a pervasive theme throughout, and the third of its four books is devoted entirely to that issue.

In a verbal duel, Gasparo Pallavicino and Giuliano de' Medici present the main claims of the two traditions—the prevailing misogynist one, and the newly emerging alternative one. Gasparo argues the innate inferiority of women and their inclination to vice. Only in bearing children do they profit the world. Giuliano counters that women share the same spiritual and mental capacities as men and may excel in wisdom and action. Men and women are of the same essence: just as no stone can be more perfectly a stone than another, so no human being can be more perfectly human than others, whether male or female. It was an astonishing assertion, boldly made to an audience as large as all Europe.

THE TREATISES. Humanism provided the materials for a positive counterconcept to the misogyny embedded in scholastic philosophy and law, and inherited from the Greek, Roman and Christian pasts. A series of humanist treatises on marriage and family, education and deportment, and on the nature of women helped construct these new perspectives.

The works by Francesco Barbaro and Leon Battista Alberti, respectively *On Marriage* (1415) and *On the Family* (1434–37), far from defending female equality, reasserted women's responsibilities for rearing children and managing the housekeeping while being obedient, chaste, and silent. Nevertheless, they served the cause of reexamining the issue of women's nature by placing domestic issues at the center of scholarly concern and reopening the pertinent classical texts. In addition, Barbaro emphasized the companionate nature of marriage and the importance of a wife's spiritual and mental qualities for the well-being of the family.

These themes reappear in later humanist works on marriage and the education of women by Juan Luis Vives and Erasmus. Both were moderately sympathetic to the condition of women, without reaching beyond the usual masculine prescriptions for female behavior.

An outlook more favorable to women characterizes the nearly unknown work *In Praise of Women* (ca. 1487) by the Italian humanist Bartolommeo Goggio. In addition to providing a catalogue of illustrious women, Goggio argued that male and female are the same in essence, but that women (reworking from quite a new angle the Adam and Eve narrative) are actually superior. In the same vein, the Italian humanist Maria Equicola asserted the spiritual equality of men and women in *On Women* (1501). In 1525, Galeazzo Flavio Capra (or Capella) published his work *On the Excellence and Dignity of Women*. This humanist tradition of treatises defending the worthiness of women culminates in the work of Henricus Cornelius Agrippa *On the Nobility and Preeminence of the Female Sex*. No work by a male humanist more succinctly or explicitly presents the case for female dignity.

THE WITCH BOOKS. While humanists grappled with the issues pertaining to women and family, other learned men turned their attention to what they perceived as a very great problem: witches. Witch-hunting manuals, explorations of the witch phenomenon, and even defenses of witches are not at first glance pertinent to the tradition of the other voice. But they do relate in this way: most accused witches were women. The hostility aroused by supposed witch activity is comparable to the hostility aroused by women. The evil deeds the victims of the hunt were charged with were exaggerations of the vices to which, many believed, all women were prone.

The connection between the witch accusation and the hatred of women is explicit in the notorious witch hunting manual, *The Hammer of Witches* (1486), by two Dominican inquisitors, Heinrich Krämer and Jacob Sprenger. Here the inconstancy, deceitfulness, and lustfulness traditionally associated with women are depicted in exaggerated form as the core features of witch behavior. These inclined women to make a bargain with the devil—sealed by sexual intercourse—by which they acquired unholy powers. Such bizarre claims, far from being rejected by rational men, were broadcast by intellectuals. The German Ulrich Molitur, the Frenchman Nicolas Rémy, the Italian Stefano Guazzo coolly informed the public of sinister orgies and midnight pacts with the devil. The celebrated French jurist, historian, and political philosopher Jean Bodin argued that, because women were especially prone to diabolism, regular legal procedures could properly be suspended in order to try those accused of this "exceptional crime."

A few experts, such as the physician Johann Weyer, a student of Agrippa's, raised their voices in protest. In 1563, he explained the witch phenomenon thus, without discarding belief in diabolism: the devil deluded foolish old women afflicted by melancholia, causing them to believe that they had magical powers. Weyer's rational skepticism, which had good credibility in the community of the learned, worked to revise the conventional views of women and witchcraft.

WOMEN'S WORKS. To the many categories of works produced on the question of women's worth must be added nearly all works written by women. A woman writing was in herself a statement of women's claim to dignity.

Only a few women wrote anything prior to the dawn of the modern era, for three reasons. First, they rarely received the education that would enable them to write. Second, they were not admitted to the public roles—as administrator, bureaucrat, lawyer or notary, university professor—in which they might gain knowledge of the kinds of things the literate public thought worth writing about. Third, the culture imposed silence upon women, considering speaking out a form of unchastity. Given these conditions, it is remarkable that any women wrote. Those who did before the fourteenth century were almost always nuns or religious women whose isolation made their pronouncements more acceptable.

From the fourteenth century on, the volume of women's writings crescendoed. Women continued to write devotional literature, although not always as cloistered nuns. They also wrote diaries, often intended as keepsakes for their children; books of advice to their sons and daughters; letters to family members and friends; and family memoirs, in a few cases elaborate enough to be considered histories.

A few women wrote works directly concerning the "woman question," and some of these, such as the humanists Isotta Nogarola, Cassandra Fedele, Laura Cereta, and Olimpia Morata, were highly trained. A few were professional writers, living by the income of their pen: the very first among them Christine de Pizan, noteworthy in this context as in so many others. In addition to *The Book of the City of Ladies* and her critiques of *The Romance of the Rose*, she wrote *The Treasure of the City of Ladies* (a guide to social decorum for women), an advice book for her son, much courtly verse, and a full-scale history of the reign of king Charles V of France.

WOMEN PATRONS. Women who did not themselves write but encouraged others to do so boosted the development of an alternative tradition. Highly placed women patrons supported authors, artists, musicians, poets, and learned men. Such patrons, drawn mostly from the Italian elites and the courts of northern Europe, figure disproportionately as the dedicatees of the important works of early feminism.

For a start, it might be noted that the catalogues of Boccaccio and Alvaro de Luna were dedicated to the Florentine noblewoman Andrea Acciaiuoli and to Doña María, first wife of King Juan II of Castile, while the French translation of Boccaccio's work was commissioned by Anne of Brittany, wife of King Charles VIII of France. The humanist treatises of Goggio, Equicola, Vives, and Agrippa were dedicated, respectively, to Eleanora of Aragon, wife of Ercole I d'Este, duke of Ferrara; to Margherita Cantelma of Mantua; to Catherine of Aragon, wife of King Henry VIII of England; and to Margaret, duchess of Austria and regent of the Netherlands. As late as 1696, Mary Astell's *Serious Proposal to the Ladies, for the Advancement of Their True and Greatest Interest* was dedicated to Princess Ann of Denmark.

These authors presumed that their efforts would be welcome to female patrons, or they may have written at the bidding of those patrons. Silent themselves, perhaps even unresponsive, these loftily placed women helped shape the tradition of the other voice.

THE ISSUES. The literary forms and patterns in which the tradition of the other voice presented itself have now been sketched. It remains to highlight the major issues about which this tradition crystallizes. In brief, there are four problems to which our authors return again and again, in plays and catalogues, in verse and in letters, in treatises and dialogues, in every language: the problem of chastity; the problem of power; the problem of speech; and the problem of knowledge. Of these the greatest, preconditioning the others, is the problem of chastity.

THE PROBLEM OF CHASTITY. In traditional European culture, as in those of antiquity and others around the globe, chastity was perceived as woman's quintessential virtue—in contrast to courage, or generosity, or leadership, or rationality, seen as virtues characteristic of men. Opponents of women charged them with insatiable lust. Women themselves and their defenders—without disputing the validity of the standard—responded that women were capable of chastity.

The requirement of chastity kept women at home, silenced them, isolated them, left them in ignorance. It was the source of all other impediments. Why was it so important to the society of men, of whom chastity was not required, and who, more often than not, considered it their right to violate the chastity of any woman they encountered?

Female chastity ensured the continuity of the male-headed household. If a man's wife was not chaste, he could not be sure of the legitimacy of his offspring. If they were not his, and they acquired his property, it was not his household, but some other man's, that had endured. If his daughter was not chaste, she could not be transferred to another man's household as his wife, and he was dishonored.

The whole system of the integrity of the household and the

transmission of property was bound up in female chastity. Such a requirement only pertained to property-owning classes, of course. Poor women could not expect to maintain their chastity, least of all if they were in contact with high-status men to whom all women but those of their own household were prey.

In Catholic Europe, the requirement of chastity was further buttressed by moral and religious imperatives. Original sin was inextricably linked with the sexual act. Virginity was seen as heroic virtue, far more impressive than, say, the avoidance of idleness or greed. Monasticism, the cultural institution that dominated medieval Europe for centuries, was grounded in the renunciation of the flesh. The Catholic reform of the eleventh century imposed a similar standard on all the clergy, and a heightened awareness of sexual requirements on all the laity. Although men were asked to be chaste, female unchastity was much worse: it led to the devil, as Eve had led mankind to sin.

To such requirements, women and their defenders protested their innocence. More, following the example of holy women who had escaped the requirements of family and sought the religious life, some women began to conceive of female communities as alternatives both to family and to the cloister. Christine de Pizan's city of ladies was such a community. Moderata Fonte and Mary Astell envisioned others. The luxurious salons of the French *précieuses* of the seventeenth century, or the comfortable English drawing rooms of the next, may have been born of the same impulse. Here women might not only escape, if briefly, the subordinate position that life in the family entailed, but they might make claims to power, exercise their capacity for speech, and display their knowledge.

THE PROBLEM OF POWER. Women were excluded from power: the whole cultural tradition insisted upon it. Only men were citizens, only men bore arms, only men could be chiefs or lords or kings. There were exceptions which did not disprove the rule, when wives or widows or mothers took the place of men, awaiting their return or the maturation of a male heir. A woman who attempted to rule in her own right was perceived as an anomaly, a monster, at once a deformed woman and an insufficient male, sexually confused and, consequently, unsafe.

The association of such images with women who held or sought power explains some otherwise odd features of early modern culture. Queen Elizabeth I of England, one of the few women to hold full regal authority in European history, played with such male/female images—positive ones, of course—in representing herself to her subjects. She was a prince, and manly, even though she was female. She was also (she claimed) virginal, a condition absolutely essential if she was to avoid the attacks of her opponents. Catherine de' Medici, who ruled France as widow and regent for her sons, also adopted such imagery in defining her position. She chose as one symbol the figure of Artemisia, an androgynous ancient warrior-heroine, who combined a female persona with masculine powers.

Power in a woman, without such sexual imagery, seems to have been indigestible by the culture. A rare note was struck by the Englishman Sir Thomas Elyot in his *Defence of Good Women* (1540), justifying both women's participation in civic life and prowess in arms. The old tune was sung by the Scots reformer John Knox in his *First Blast of the Trumpet against the Monstrous Regiment of Women* (1558), for whom rule by women, defects in nature, was a hideous contradiction in terms.

The confused sexuality of the imagery of female potency was not reserved for rulers. Any woman who excelled was likely to be called an Amazon, recalling the self-mutilated warrior women of antiquity who repudiated all men, gave up their sons, and raised only their daughters. She was often said to have "exceeded her sex," or to have possessed "masculine virtue"—as the very fact of conspicuous excellence conferred masculinity, even on the female subject. The catalogues of notable women often showed those female heroes dressed in armor, armed to the teeth, like men. Amazonian heroines romp through the epics of the age—Ariosto's *Orlando Furioso* (1532), Spenser's *Faerie Queene* (1590–1609). Excellence in a woman was perceived as a claim for power, and power was reserved for the masculine realm. A woman who possessed either was masculinized, and lost title to her own female identity.

THE PROBLEM OF SPEECH. Just as power had a sexual dimension when it was claimed by women, so did speech. A good woman spoke little. Excessive speech was an indication of unchastity. By speech, women seduced men. Eve had lured Adam into sin by her speech. Accused witches were commonly accused of having spoken abusively, or irrationally, or simply too much. As enlightened a figure as Francesco Barbaro insisted on silence in a woman, which he linked to her perfect unanimity with her husband's will and her unblemished virtue (her chastity). Another Italian humanist, Leonardo Bruni, in advising a noblewoman on her studies, barred her not from speech, but from public speaking. That was reserved for men.

Related to the problem of speech was that of costume, another, if silent, form of self-expression. Assigned the task of pleasing men as their primary occupation, elite women often tended to elaborate costume, hairdressing, and the use of cosmetics. Clergy and secular moralists alike condemned these practices. The appropriate function of costume and adornment was to announce the status of a woman's husband or father. Any further indulgence in adornment was akin to unchastity.

THE PROBLEM OF KNOWLEDGE. When the Italian noblewoman Isotta Nogarola had begun to attain a reputation as a humanist, she was accused of incest—a telling instance of the association of learning in women with unchastity. That chilling association inclined any woman who was educated to deny that she was, or to make exaggerated claims of heroic chastity.

If educated women were pursued with suspicions of sexual misconduct, women seeking an education faced an even more daunting obstacle: the assumption that women were by nature incapable of learning, that reason was a particularly masculine ability. Just as they proclaimed their chastity, women and their defenders insisted upon their capacity for learning. The major work by a male writer on female education—*On the Education of a Christian Woman*, by Juan Luis Vives (1523)—granted female capacity for intellection, but argued still that a woman's whole education was to be shaped around the requirement of chastity and a future within the household. Female writers of the next generations—Marie de Gournay in France, Anna Maria van Schurman in Holland, Mary Astell in England—began to envision other possibilities.

The pioneers of female education were the Italian women humanists who managed to attain a Latin literacy and knowledge of classical and Christian literature equivalent to that of prominent men. Their works implicitly and explicitly raise questions about women's social roles, defining problems that beset women attempting to break out of the cultural limits that had bound them. Like Christine de Pizan, who achieved an advanced education through her father's tutoring and her own devices, their bold questioning makes clear the importance of training. Only when women were educated to the same standard as male leaders would they be able to raise that other voice and insist on their dignity as human beings morally, intellectually, and legally equal to men.

THE OTHER VOICE. The other voice, a voice of protest, was mostly female, but also male. It spoke in the vernaculars and in Latin, in treatises and dialogues, plays and poetry, letters and diaries and pamphlets. It battered at the wall of misogynist beliefs that encircled women and raised a banner announcing its claims. The female was equal (or even superior) to the male in essential nature—moral, spiritual, intellectual. Women were capable of higher education, of holding positions of power and influence in the public realm, and of speaking and writing persuasively. The last bastion of masculine supremacy, centered on the notions of a woman's primary domestic responsibility and the requirement of female chastity, was not as yet assaulted—although visions of productive female communities as alternatives to the family indicated an awareness of the problem.

During the period 1300 to 1700, the other voice remained only a voice, and one only dimly heard. It did not result—yet—in an alteration of social patterns. Indeed, to this day, they have not entirely been altered. Yet the call for justice issued as long as six centuries ago by those writing in the tradition of the other voice must be recognized as the source and origin of the mature feminist tradition and of the realignment of social institutions accomplished in the modern age.

We would like to thank the volume editors in this series, who responded with many suggestions to an earlier draft of this introduction, making it a collaborative enterprise. Many of their suggestions and criticisms have resulted in revisions of this introduction, though we remain responsible for the final product.

ACKNOWLEDGMENTS

I want to acknowledge gratefully the help and kindness of several individuals and organizations. First, I want to thank my coeditor of the English texts, Barbara Collier Cook, whose patient and disciplined reading called my attention to several lapses I might otherwise have missed and who suggested many helpful emendations. Elissa B. Weaver has been exceedingly generous with her time, her scholarly acumen, and her advice. She consulted the Florentine archives for me when I was unable to go myself, locating Antonia Pulci's will (wills, really; there are several versions) and the tax records that made possible her definitive identification of the Tanini as Antonia's birth family. She also arranged for microfilms of the Miscomini collection of 1490 and conducted a line-by-line comparison between my 1514 Florentine text (printer unknown) of *La rappresentatione di Santa Domitilla* and that in Miscomini, and she has been constantly accessible via e-mail to answer my questions and to act as a sounding board for my ideas.

Konrad Eisenbichler guarded against my imperfect command of fifteenth-century Italian idioms, spending three delightful days with me as we read the English version aloud against the Italian. The anonymous readers who so carefully combed the text also offered numerous helpful suggestions that vastly improved the translation. In addition, I am grateful to Albert Rabil, Jr., and Margaret L. King, first for including this translation in their series, and second for their guidance and their useful feedback on the penultimate version of my introduction to it.

I am also grateful to the staffs at the Newberry Library, the British Library, and the Warburg Institute—especially, at the latter, Nicholas Mann—for their interest and support. The Albion College

Faculty Development Committee and the Hewlett-Mellon Faculty Development Fund made possible my work in the British Library and the Warburg Institute. The Associated Colleges of the Midwest and the Great Lakes Colleges Association and their advisory committee on the Newberry Library Interdisciplinary Program in the Humanities made possible an extended period of time at the Newberry Library, where the bulk of the translation was done. Thanks also to Mark Musa, whose expressed interest in what I was doing hurried me along.

Finally, I also wish to acknowledge the hurriedly conscripted thespians who convinced me of the power of Pulci's plays to hold an audience. These include my colleagues among the Fellows of the Newberry Library, who presented a unisex-cast, closet-drama version of bits and pieces of these plays before a meeting of the Newberry Fellows Seminar in the spring of 1994. Especially I owe a debt of gratitude to Tom Oosting, professor of theater at Albion College, who found time and resources to cast, direct and produce a readers'-theater version of one of these plays, and to the Albion College drama students and colleagues—particularly Carol Gaffke, Sandra Schultz, and Patricia Visser—who performed the English-language premier of *St. Theodora* in the Albion College Black Box in the spring of 1995.

J. W. C.
Albion, Michigan
September 19, 1995

FLORENTINE DRAMA FOR
CONVENT AND FESTIVAL

Seven Sacred Plays

ANTONIA PULCI AND
HER PLAYS

THE OTHER VOICE, THE NOBLER DEED,
THE WOMANLY CONCERN

A gratuitous and invidious misogyny sometimes appears in writing about the lives of saints (hagiography). Sometimes misogyny even typifies the personal writings of nuns. The perception of women as the weaker and less rational vessel, responsible for the Fall, and more subject to sin, pervades even the work of such a figure as St. Teresa of Avila, the Spanish religious mystic (1515–82).[1]

In none of Antonia Pulci's (1452–1501) plays, however, do examples of such misogyny appear. On the contrary, Pulci's female saints and her secular women are typically more intelligent, more rational, more constant in their purposes, more compassionate, and more emotionally stable than their male counterparts. In their respective plays Pulci's heroines, and even her minor female characters, are presented as the proactive forces who themselves change and who produce change. Once Saints Theodora, Domitilla, and Guglielma have embarked on courses of action, they follow through. They are good at predicting the consequences of their actions, and they accept those consequences unflinchingly.

Though *St. Guglielma*, for instance, has been an obedient wife and daughter (and though she has good reason to regret both), she nevertheless assumes responsibility for the spiritual welfare both of the brother-in-law who attempted to seduce her and the husband who undervalued her. The secular Rosana instructs her beloved Ulimentus in his duty to his parents even though by following her advice he op-

---

1. See especially *The Life of Teresa of Jesus: The Autobiography of St. Teresa of Avila,* trans. and ed. by E. Allison Peers (Garden City, N.Y.: Image Books, 1960). See also St. Teresa of Avila, *Moredas (The Interior Castle),* trans. by Kiernan Cavanaugh and Otilio Rodriguez (New York: Paulist Press, c. 1979).

poses her own best interests. Inspired by God, Donna Iacopa (a minor
Roman character bearing the name of Pulci's mother) appears on the
scene with funeral necessities for St. Francis. Saints Domitilla and
Theodora face martyrdom more than willingly.

Even though women who are other than Christian and less than
good—pagans, false friends, and prostitutes—do appear in Pulci's
plays, their misapprehensions and vices arise from their choices, circumstances, and rearing, never from innate weaknesses associated
with their gender. Her female characters' propensity to act in ways
that match their reasoned words and her own regular refusal to allow
those characters to conform to anti-female stereotypes or to express
derogatory views about women mark her drama distinctively with another voice. And Antonia Pulci's voice, Christine de Pizan's apart, is
one of the earliest to be raised in Renaissance Europe.[2]

Beyond this principled refusal to pander to popular antifeminist
attitudes, another aspect of Pulci's plays that identifies them with an
emergent European female consciousness appears in her frequent
heightening of realism through the expression of "womanly concerns." Apart from her activity as a playwright—an enterprise in
which, as a woman, she was perhaps unique in her place and time—
Pulci pursued a not atypically bifurcated career, first as a wife and primary care-giver to her nieces (she never had children of her own), and
later as a Augustinian tertiary and as the founder of an order, the sisters of Santa Maria della Misericordia.[3] Many situations that Pulci
developed in her plays reflect these womanly concerns and her piety
as well.

Often her principal character is a woman, as in *St. Domitilla, St.
Guglielma, St. Theodora,* and *Rosana.* The situations some of these women
encounter parallel those that Pulci had to deal with in her own life—
often so closely that one is hard pressed to resist seeing in her plots
thinly veiled displacements of her own experience and circumstances.
The relations between fathers and daughters, sisters and brothers,
husbands and wives, lovers and beloveds, and mothers and children of-

---

2. In the last twenty years, the works of Christine De Pizan have become widely
available. See her *Ditié de Jehanne d'Arc,* ed. Angus J. Kennedy and Kenneth Varty,
Medium Aevum Monographs, n.s. 9 (Oxford: Society for the Study of Medieval
Languages and Literature, 1977); *The Book of the City of Ladies,* trans. Earl Jeffrey Richards
(New York: Persea, 1982); and *The Treasure of the City of Ladies, Or the Book of the Three Virtues,*
trans. Sarah Lawson (Hammondsworth: Penguin, 1985).

3. Giuseppe Richa, *Notizie istoriche delle chiese fiorentine,* vol. 5 (Florence: Pietro Gaetano
Viviani, 1757), 249.

ten emerge thematically. Guglielma, for example, though she would prefer a religious life, is pressured by her parents into marrying the King of Hungary, and Domitilla and Theodora, likewise, though they resist the pressure, are bullied by uncles, would-be husbands, and rulers in an effort to break their wills. Antonia Pulci's brother, Nicolò Tanini, as we shall see, encouraged her to remarry after her husband, Bernardo Pulci, died. The choice between marriage or convent faced virtually every young woman in Renaissance Italy;[4] Pulci herself faced it—certainly after the death of her husband, and presumably before her marriage as well.

After Guglielma becomes the queen of Hungary, she encourages her recently converted husband to go on pilgrimage to the Holy Land and to take her along. The king tells her that she, instead, must stay at home and run the kingdom. The king is hardly out of sight before Guglielma's brother-in-law attempts to seduce her; she successfully resists. This is, of course, already in the fifteenth century a stock dramatic situation traceable to the deutero-canonical story of Susanna (Sus.:1–64), whom Mary D. Garrard calls the "archetype of innocence and purity, first threatened and then miraculously saved."[5] Pulci's handling of the story's consequences, however, is anything but conventional and reflects both her sensitivity to the issues of psychology and power implicit in the situation as well as her careful thinking about them as issues confronting women.

Guglielma, though she is the queen and the regent, finds herself almost totally silenced and disempowered by her brother-in-law's attempt. Such silencing and disempowerment, of course, remain frustrating realities that often confront women in their interactions with powerful men. The queen dares not tell the court lest the kingdom be thrown into confusion. She decides to wait to speak out until her husband returns:

> I will keep still, woe, now how great a wrong
> That he's attempted to seduce the queen!

4. Margaret L. King, *Women of the Renaissance* (Chicago: University of Chicago Press, 1991), 82–83.

5. Mary D. Garrard, *Artemesia Gentileschi, The Image of the Female Hero in Italian Baroque Art* (Princeton, NJ: Princeton University Press, 1989), 187. Deutero-canonical writings are those preserved as scriptural by the Roman-Catholic dispensation but considered apocryphal by Protestants. In the version of the scriptures that Antonia Pulci would have known, the story occurs in the book of Daniel. For the story of "Susanna and the Judgement of Daniel," see *The New Jerusalem Bible* (New York: Doubleday, 1966), 1447–49. For a discussion of Susanna as hero and icon, see Garrard, 183–204.

The king's great majesty has been disgraced.
My court will be in turmoil if I speak—
O God, you're my defender, you my guide;
Susanna was, I know, preserved by you;
I don't know what I ought to do or say;
I shall keep silent till the king returns.

(*St. Guglielma,* lines 231–38)

Unfortunately, the brother gets to the king first and accuses her of loose and treacherous behavior. Without consulting Guglielma, the king believes his brother's accusation and condemns her to death—a sentence from which no human appeal seems possible. Pulci also makes clear the projective psychological mechanism by which the rejected brother attributes to Guglielma his own treachery and lasciviousness. Her purity, he decides, is a sham; surely she has deceived his brother with others, and so she deserves to die:

I know for sure that only on account
Of fear does she appear so brusque and pure
To one who'd tempt her, put her to the test,
For being false is nothing new to her.
Let's see how much that heaven of hers will care,
For I shall find a way to be avenged;
I'll pay you back for that, know what you may,
And I am sure that you'll regret it soon.

(*St. Guglielma,* lines 239–46)

Clearly, Pulci recognized and articulated the tendency of every would-be rapist or ardent seducer to attribute his own desires to his victim, and she perceived the fine line between the seducer's lust and the violence implicit in his threat.

Other womanly concerns, like the dangers associated with child-bearing, the grief that comes with child rearing, and the jealousy of husbands, are frequently treated in Pulci's plays. From a literary perspective, these concerns are directly traceable to the hagiographies from which much of the matter of Pulci's plays was drawn, and to the advice of advocates of the superiority of celibacy over marriage, like St. Jerome and his followers. Pulci sets them, however, in the context of her characters' often difficult decision making, and moves them from the level of abstract argument to that of human and specifically feminine problems.

Concern over the grief associated with child rearing appears both in *St. Francis,* and in the less securely attributed *Rosana.* In both plays parents express the disappointment they feel at the way their children have turned out. Perhaps Pulci found in such arguments some consolation that she and Bernardo had produced no offspring.

Certainly Queen Rosana's lament over her childless condition and her litany of attempted remedies—baths, herbs, medicines, physicians, prayers, and charms—might well be a reflection of Antonia Pulci's disappointment at her own experience of childlessness, if this less securely attributed play indeed is hers (*Rosana I,* lines 177–84).

The expected subordination of women to male family members is another issue that Pulci treats. The power of brothers over sisters appears in *St. Anthony the Abbot.* In one of a number of striking anachronisms that conflate early Christian Egypt and fifteenth-century Florence in this play, Anthony convinces his sister that she should enter the convent of the Murate in Florence—the reverse of Pulci's personal situation since she had to convince her brother that she preferred the religious life. The allusion to the Murate also serves to identify the play with the Pulci family; Bernardo wrote a poem of 206 octaves on the passion of Christ and addressed it, together with a letter, to Sister Annalena de' Tanini in that convent.[6]

St. Anthony overcomes his sister's initial objections with sweet and pious reasons, and eventually she willingly, if rather abruptly, accedes. More interestingly, during Anthony's temptations, a demon accuses him of having forced her into the convent instead of fulfilling his brotherly responsibility of finding her a husband, and the devil imagines that, unhappy there with no prospect of marriage, the sister returns to secular life where, forced into prostitution in order to survive, she loses her soul.

This scenario—a choice between convent or brothel—was all too possible for unmarried women in fifteenth- and early sixteenth-century Florence. Women needed substantial dowries to marry, and even well-to-do Florentine families often could not muster the resources to assure appropriate matches for all their daughters. Despite efforts by the community to address this problem—like establishing a bank, the *monte di dote,* where money could accumulate to provide dowries—many young women found themselves destined from birth to the certain

6. Francesco Flamini, *La lirica toscana del rinascimento anteriore ai tempi del Magnifico* (Pisa: T. Nistri, 1891), 244.

prospect of the religious life or, failing that, to the life of the cour-
tesan. Beatrice del Sera, a nun writing in the sixteenth century, expresses the regret that nuns feel at their involuntary withdrawal from
the world—a regret that her editor, Elissa Weaver, convincingly finds
autobiographical.[7] Unlike del Sera, of course, Pulci voluntarily chose
the convent, and in drama as in life, she displayed her interest in
communities of women.

Three sorts of female communities appear in her plays: the convent, the brothel, and the seraglio. Convents figure prominently in
St. Guglielma and in *St. Theodora*. In the former, Guglielma finds refuge
with a community of nuns when, though she is thought to have been
executed, she has fled Hungary. She lives happily in the community
as a lay sister until she is restored to her husband and becomes the
means for a general familial reconciliation. While dwelling in seclu-
sion and disguise, Guglielma acquires a reputation for abilities conso-
nant with the healing and counselling occupations that claimed the
attention of many of the religious women of Italy who lived indepen-
dently as *pinzochere* (uncloistered women who had donned the habit
and committed themselves to a religious life without taking vows)—
about whom more will follow.

St. Theodora, whose heroine, like St. Domitilla, also lives as a kind
of *pinzochera*—in her case as a virgin dedicated to Christ and dwelling
in her own home—opens with a playlet within a play in which two
novices threaten to refuse to act in the evening's performance because they feel they have been denied access to the most desirable
costumes. The sweet reason and kindness with which their superiors
help them perceive their mistake and soothe their ruffled feathers
contrasts markedly with a later scene set in a brothel. There two prostitutes, played by the same two sisters, accuse each other of thievery
and worse, insult one another grossly, and achieve a rapprochement
only under the threat of one to kill and eat the hen of the other.
The scenes from the seraglio in *Rosana* reveal an indolent obsession
among the denizens of the harem with clothes and with pleasing
men.

Domitilla, Guglielma, Rosana, and Theodora all become the ob-
jects of unwelcome masculine attentions—a concern of women
throughout history. The Emperor Domitian and his dependent,
Aurelianus, try to force St. Domitilla to marry. The governor of Syria

7. See Elissa Weaver, ed., Introduction to *Amor di Virtù: Commedia in cinque atti*, by
Beatrice del Sera, *Classici Italiani Minori* vol. 17 (Ravenna: Longo Editore, 1990), 46–50.

twice unsuccessfully woos Theodora—first for himself and then for another. On her first refusal he condemns her to a life of prostitution, on her second to death. Guglielma's brother-in-law attempts to seduce her, and only the intervention of a providential indisposition prevents Rosana from becoming his concubine. Pulci does not flinch from confronting this aspect of womanly concerns.

In *St. Domitilla*, the protagonist, a niece of Domitian, the Roman emperor, is dissuaded from marriage and persuaded to assume the habit by her Christian servants. (She chooses, as does Theodora, and as Pulci apparently did between 1487 and 1500, to dwell in the familial home even though she has assumed the veil.) Again, all the usual arguments of the writers of hagiography appear—most of them deriving ultimately from the writings of St. Jerome and St. Ambrose.[8] Domitilla, who has been happily looking forward to her marriage, has been resisting the arguments. Then her servants switch their tactics and begin describing the instability of husbandly affections, and the dangers of a husband's groundless jealousy. This theme, though still a hagiographical one, Pulci treats most feelingly, moving it from the level of priestly harangue to womanly concern. It is just these arguments treating jealousy that Domitilla finds most telling:

> My mother suffered, as I well recall,
> So many torments throughout all her life;
> Because of her husband's jealousy alone
> Bore very great distress; and if I were
> To think that I would follow such a path,
> The garments of the world I'd never don,
> Though I don't think my spouse Aurelian
> Would act like this because he is so kind."
>
> (*St. Domitilla*, lines 153–60)

The prospective behavior of husbands once they acquired power over their wives was a perennial concern of European women for whom divorce was rarely if ever an option. Conceivably Antonia Pulci— whose own father had, on one occasion at least, ill-treated her mother with his infidelity—appeals here to her own experience in

---

8. See Saint Jerome, "Letter 47; To Desiderius," W. H. Fremantle, *et al.* trans., *The Principal Works of St. Jerome*, A Select Library of Nicene and Post-Nicene Fathers, vol. 6 (Grand Rapids, MI: Wm. B. Eerdmans Co. 1954, 65–79). See also Saint Ambrose, "Epistle 63 [to the Church of Vercellae]," H. de Romistin, trans., *The Principal Works of St. Ambrose*, A Select Library . . . , vol. 10 (1955), 457–464.

putting such a sentiment into the mouth of her heroine. Similarly in
St. Francis, Francis's mother is the object of her husband's scorn and
verbal abuse, and the dialogue that Pulci assigns to the mother makes
clear that her emotional investment is principally in her child, not in
her jealous and abusive husband.

> Sweet son, I feel surpassing sorrow that
> I see you being punished in this way,
> Your father's action grieves me greatly for,
> Because of you, I feel life drain away.
> You know, indeed, I have no one but you,
> And so I am resolved to set you free.
>
> (*St. Francis,* lines 153–58)

As will appear below, *St. Theodora* and *Rosana* are less securely at-
tributable to Antonia Pulci than are the other plays. Yet among the
arguments that suggest they are very likely hers is the appearance in
them of precisely the sorts of womanly concerns that occupied Pulci's
attention in the plays of certain attribution. In the first part of
Rosana, particularly, Queen Rosana's distress at her childlessness,
though not an uncommon literary issue and certainly a frequent concern for women, nevertheless parallels Pulci's personal situation. That
fact together with *Rosana*'s treatment of other issues that interest
Pulci, like conversion to Christianity and amity between spouses,
move me to include the play in her canon.

Steadfast freedom from misogyny, committed female characters of
heroic energy, great intelligence, unshakable though credible virtue,
and situations reflecting womanly concerns all contribute to "the
other voice"—the voice of an emergent, European female consciousness as it manifests itself in Antonia Pulci's plays.

BIOGRAPHY

Paul Colomb de Batines, the earliest and still in some ways the
most reliable bibliographer of *sacre rappresentazioni,* said that Antonia
Pulci was born a Tanini.[9] Francesco Flamini, however, confidently as-

---

9. In *Bibliografia delle antiche rappresentazioni sacre e profane* (Firenze: Per la Società Tipografica,
1852), 14–15.

serted that she was "of the house of" Gianotti and fussed that he couldn't imagine what gave rise to the Tanini notion.[10] The great nineteenth-century editor of *sacre rappresentazioni* Alessandro D'Ancona agreed with Flamini.[11] As recently as 1992 Georges Ulysse, in his "A Pair of Writers: The Sacred Plays of Bernardo and Antonia Pulci," says that she was born "Antonia Gianotti."[12] Her contemporary, Brother Antonio Dulciati *fiorentino*, in a memorandum concerning her, however, identifies her as a Tanini. This memorandum is cited by Richa (249 ff.), and Elissa Weaver, working on the problem in Florentine archives, has unravelled the origin of the confusion and found definitive evidence in the tax records that Antonia was a Tanini.[13]

Born Antonia, daughter of Francesco d'Antonio di Giannotto Tanini and Iacopa da Roma in 1452 (Richa 249), she was the daughter of a Florentine family whose fortunes as bankers were beginning to rise. Francesco fathered seven children, five in wedlock and two illegitimately. Besides Antonia, he and Iacopa had Girolama (b. 1448), Niccolò (b. 1460), Gostanza (b. 1463), Cornelia (b. 1464), Tita (b. 1465), and Lucrezia (b. 1466). His illegitimate offspring were Giulio (b. 1429), who was sired before Francesco's marriage to Iacopa, and Lizabetta, who was born out of wedlock in the same year as Cornelia (1464). This fruitful sequence was terminated in 1467 by Francesco's death.

The family's circumstances clearly permitted Antonia to receive a careful literary and religious education. Judging from the texts of her

---

10. Flamini says: "Che la moglie di Bernardo fosse dei Tanini è un errore entrato non so come nella storia letteraria, e restatovi poi a lungo." [That the wife of Bernardo was of the house of Tanini is an error that has crept, I don't know how, into literary history and then remained there for a long time] (238). The real error, however, was one that Flamini helped perpetuate.

11. Alessandro D'Ancona, ed., *Sacre rappresentazioni dei secoli XIV, XV e XVI* (Florence: Le Monnier, 1872), vol. 3, 199.

12. "Un Couple D'Ecrivains: Les *sacre rappresentazioni* de Bernardo et Antonia Pulci," *Les femmes écrivains en Italie au Moyen Âge et à la Renaissance* in Actes du colloque international Aix-en-Provence, 12–14 novembre 1992 (Aix-en-Provence: Universitè de Provence, 1994), 178.

13. Elissa Weaver has generously supplied and given me permission to publish these details concerning the Tanini family—details she discovered in the tax records (*catasti*) of Florence in connection with her book on convent drama, forthcoming from Cambridge University Press. The details confirm the account of the family given by Brother Antonio Dulciati *fiorentino* in the sixteenth-century memorandum and quoted in Richa. The relevant Florentine tax records are: ASF Catasto 78 c. 536r; 407 c. 260 v.; 497 c. 274; 822 c. 657 v.; 837 c.24 r; and 924 c. 564 v., *quartiere* S. Giovanni, *gonfalone* Leon d'oro.

plays and the examples that occur there concerning exchanging money (*St. Francis*) and assaying gold (*St. Anthony the Abbot*), at least a portion of the early part of that education was probably much like that described by Paul F. Grendler as typical of the curriculum of independent *abbaco* schools to which the merchant classes sent their sons (and a lucky few—around ten percent—their daughters), though Pulci herself was more likely to have been tutored at home than to have attended classes at one of the *abbaco* schools.[14]

These schools "taught vernacular reading and writing, commercial mathematics, and accounting, instead of Latin grammar and literature" (Grendler 163). At the heart of this essentially commercial curriculum was the *Liber abbaci* of Leonardo Fibonacci (from around 1170 to after 1240)—"an encyclopedia of practical mathematics" (Grendler 164). In addition, however, in their neighborhood schools or at the homes of wealthier families, *abbaco* masters taught double-entry bookkeeping and "how to read a series of secular and religious vernacular books and how to write in Italian" (Grendler 166).

Arguing convincingly that the curriculum of these schools was essentially stable throughout Italy from the fourteenth through the late sixteenth centuries, Grendler cites typical vernacular texts that were frequently taught. One was *The Flower of Virtue*, which contains "forty short chapters . . . each devoted to a single virtue or vice." A second was *Epistles and Gospels that are read throughout the year at mass*, including "well-known sermons, parables, and scenes from the life of Christ, plus important passages from Paul's letters" (167). *The Lives of the Holy Fathers* was a third. This contained a collection of lives of the desert fathers of Egypt (including St. Anthony) by Saint Athanasius (295–373) that, with later additions, had been translated first into Latin and later into Italian. Beyond this, the curriculum included *The Golden Legend* (composed 1260–67) of Jacopo di Verrazzo (Jacobus de Voragine), and translated into Italian as *A Collection of Legends of the Saints*. The chivalric romances with their stories of knights and ladies appeared as well.[15]

The hagiographical matter of some of Pulci's plays reflects a close

---

14. Grendler, "What Piero Learned in School: Fifteenth-Century Vernacular Education" in *Piero della Francesca and His Legacy*, ed. by Marilyn Aronberg Levin, Studies in the History of Art, 48, Center for Advanced Study in the Visual Arts, Symposium Papers XXVIII (Washington: National Gallery of Art, 1995), 161–74.

15. The titles of these works respectively appear in Grendler (167) as follows: *Fior di virtù; Epistole e Evangeli che si leggono tutto l'anno all messa; Le vite dei Santi Padri; Legenda Aurea; Leggendario dei santi.*

familiarity with aspects of the vernacular books in this curriculum. The first book of *The Lives of the Holy Fathers*, for example, is devoted to the life of Saint Anthony the Abbot, and Pulci's *Saint Anthony* seems to draw heavily upon chapters 7, 8, 9, 16, and 23.[16] A life of St. Anthony appears in *A Collection of Legends* as well.[17] The *Epistles and Gospels* contains the story of the Prodigal Son (Luke 15), which was to be read on the Saturday following the second Sunday of *Quaresima* (Lent, the forty days before Easter) and another version of the St. Anthony story.[18]

Grendler's examples of the non-commercial aspects of this curriculum come largely from Venice. One may be sure that a Florentine variation on this program of study, or a variation introduced by an individual Tuscan tutor, would include the great Florentine vernacular poets Dante and Petrarch. Certainly Antonia Pulci's plays reveal in their intertextual echoes her intimate knowledge of both.[19] The polished composition of her drama also demonstrates her absolute mastery of the principal forms of Italian verse—especially *ottava rima* (an eleven-syllable-per-line [hendecasyllabic], eight-line stanza, rhyming ABABABCC), but also of *terza rima* (hendecasyllabic, interlinking three-line stanzas rhyming ABA, BCB, CDC—the form of Dante's *Divine Comedy*) and *rima baciata* ("kissed rhyme," or rhymed couplets).

St. Domitilla's discussion with her uncle the emperor concerning the ancient Roman poets on the subject of virginity (*St. Domitilla*, lines 449–56), suggests that both Domitilla and her creator are well-read in at least that aspect of classical literature.

For a fifteenth-century Florentine woman of her class to have received the training to make possible such accomplishment, though

16. *Le Vite de' Santi Padri insieme col prato spirituale, Descritte da San Girolamo, S. Athanasio, & da molti altri antichi Santi Padri* (Venice: Presso Pietro Milocco, 1644).

17. *Legendario di Jacobus di Voragine*. MS Newberry 24: Bartolemeo di Trento (?), 13th c., 27 recto. This tiny manuscript with its almost microscopic and sometimes illegible text is intriguing. On its final flyleaf there appears in a careful fifteenth-century Tuscan hand a Latin prayer: *O gloriosa donna excelza supra sidera/ qui recreavit provide/ O gloriosa donna* ("O glorious Lady, make [me] ready for Him who has restored [me] again to life, O glorious Lady"). There follows what may be the drawing of an inkwell (apparently the writer's pen ran dry), and the drawing of the head of a woman wearing what may be a religious veil. Beside the inkwell is written the name "Antonia."

18. *Epistole et Evangelii, et Letioni* (Florence: *Appresso i Giunti*, 1551). Reproduces the woodcuts of a 1495 edition. The story of the prodigal son occurs in chapter 21, and St. Anthony's story in chapter 27.

19. Cross-references to the Italian vernacular poets appear in the notes to the texts of the plays.

remarkable, was not altogether surprising. Bequests of books in the wills of women suggest a considerable degree of literacy among the Florentine merchant class, and, as many had been tutored at home, cultured women often composed letters and poems.[20] What makes Antonia Pulci's work most unusual is the combination of skill, output, and apparent professionalism that characterized it.

During her eighteenth year she married Bernardo Pulci. Bernardo was a member of the Florentine literary clan that enjoyed the friendship and sometimes the patronage of Lorenzo de' Medici and his family. Bernardo's brother Luigi, a boon companion of the young Lorenzo's colorful recreational activities, wrote among other works the epic poem *Morgante Maggiore* that had been commissioned by Lorenzo's mother Lucrezia Tornabuoni de' Medici. Bernardo's brother Luca, who had the misfortune to die a pauper in the *Stinche*—the debtor's prison of Florence—had earlier written *La Giostra di Lorenzo de' Medici,* a poem commemorating the tournament staged to celebrate Lorenzo's coming of age.

Bernardo himself is known to have written two *sacre rappresentazioni: Barlaam and Josaphat,* and *The Angel Raphael.* On the death of Cosimo de' Medici in 1464, Bernardo composed a poem in *terza rima* in commendation of Cosimo as the father of his country. He also wrote a long *ternario* (a poem in triplets) in praise of the Virgin, sonnets lamenting scandals at the papal court in Rome, and a *ternario* in the mode of visions in which he commends poverty and condemns wealth. Apparently both Bernardo and Antonia Pulci shared pious and rather ascetic religious values—including the value of poverty to virtuous living.

At least early on in their marriage, Bernardo's own poverty, though he and his wife may have considered it a mark of virtue, was nonetheless dangerously pressing. In 1466, before his union with Antonia, Bernardo and Luigi had had to ask their friends for help to satisfy Luca's debts with the bank after his business failed. On Luca's death in the year of Antonia's marriage (1470), the responsibility for caring for his surviving children fell partly to Luigi and partly to Bernardo and Antonia. The couple's financial resources at this time were extremely meager, and the additional mouths to feed strained their limited means.[21]

20. Lorenzo de' Medici's mother, Lucrezia Tornabuoni, provides a case in point. See Franco Pezzarossa, *I poemetti sacri di Lucrezia Tornabuoni* (Florence: Olschki, 1978).

21. Florentine tax records containing information about the married life of Bernardo

It may well be the case that, casting about for ways to survive financially, the Pulcis hit upon the idea of writing sacred dramas for popular performance and for publication in the burgeoning Florentine printing industry. Such an enterprise suited both their talents and their piety. If this is indeed the case, Antonia and Bernardo represent the very first instance on record of a wife and husband collaborating as professional writers for a literary market.

The necessities that seem to have pressed them to write were relieved when Bernardo was able to secure steady, responsible employment. In 1471 Luigi had appealed on Bernardo's behalf to Lorenzo de' Medici for help, but help was not immediately forthcoming. Bernardo's financial difficulties continued until 1476, when with Lorenzo's intervention he acquired the office of chamberlain of the district of Mugello. This office he held until the first of March 1477, when it seems his health constrained him to give it up. He was ill for three years. Some time before 1484 he was placed in charge of procuring provisions for the officials of the Florentine and Pisan universities, and he enjoyed the comfortable emoluments of this office until his death in 1487.[22]

Following Bernardo's passing, Antonia Pulci's brother Nicolò Tanini encouraged her to remarry, as I noted above, but moved by her piety and surely by the value she assigned to a more independent existence, she preferred to enter the religious life.[23] For several years—from Bernardo's death until 1500—she apparently lived the life of an uncloistered Augustinian sister, or as a *pinzochera*.

Pinzochere, as I earlier noted, were women who dressed in religious garb and committed themselves to a life of Christian good works and charity but who, instead of entering an established community of nuns, chose to live either in their own homes, as Antonia Pulci did, or in less formal communities with other women, as Pulci seems also to have done. Sometimes nominally under the control of male religious superiors, *pinzochere* were in fact often their own arbiters. The resultant freedom they achieved from the control of husbands, fa-

---

and Antonia Pulci may be found in Catasto 1480 Campioni, Part I, c. 64 v., *quartiere S. Croce, gonfalone Carro.*

22. Francesco Flamini, "Vita e Liriche di B. Pulci," in *Il Propugnatore*, n.s. vol. 1 (Bologna: G. Romagnoli, 1888), 239.

23. My principal sources for biographical details about Antonia Pulci following Bernardo's death are Richa, *Notizie*, 5.249–57, and a copy of Antonia Pulci's will. The three revisions of Pulci's will can be found in ASF *Notarile Antecosimiano* 9535, ff. 66r–67v, 70v, and 72v–74r.

thers, brothers, priests, and confessors sometimes proved difficult for
their contemporaries to rationalize. Italians found no comfortable
category to which they might consign such females without males,
and this uneasiness expressed itself culturally in jokes about the perceived androgyny of the *pinzochere*, and in a dance called the *pinzochera*,
in which women and men exchanged roles.[24]

Though pinzochere became the object of sometimes scurrilous
humor, and though their independence contravened certain social
norms, they constituted, nevertheless, a very considerable proportion
of the Florentine population in the fifteenth century. "By the beginning of the sixteenth century," Katherine Gill tells us, open
monasteries for women "peppered almost every Italian town. . . . " She
continues: "Some consisted of nuns who, although they had pro-
fessed solemn vows, did not observe strict enclosure and had not observed it for as long as anyone could remember; these regarded the
freedom to exit as a right acquired by custom. Others had acquired license by petitioning the papacy and receiving an exemption for the
obligation of enclosure. Finally, there were communities of laywomen
who took no solemn vows and who might or might not have a formal
ecclesiastical tie in the form of accountability to a monastic order, a
bishop or the papacy" (Gill 16).

Often, Gill resumes, the women who belonged to these communities were middle-class. The communities themselves were regularly
associated with one or more charitable or even semiprofessional enterprises. Strikingly, Gill cites David Herlihy, who classifies *pinzochere*
("uncloistered religious") as working (class) women in fifteenth-century Florence. [25] The combined numbers of *pinzochere* and *commesse* (the

24. Katherine Gill, addressing popular attitudes toward *pinzochere*, cites "a long didactic
poem, *Reggimento e costumi di donna* , written by Francesco da Barberino in the early
trecento, [that] expresses strong doubts about whether any woman can become a
pinzochera, a domestic recluse, or a *conversa* without succumbing either to the temptation
of exercising religious authority or to the temptation of lust. Gill, "Open Monasteries
for Women in Late Medieval and Early Modern Italy: Two Roman Examples," in Craig
A.Monson, ed., *The Crannied Wall: Women, Religion, and the Arts in Early Modern Europe* (Ann
Arbor: Univ. of Michigan Press, 1995), 15–48, note 26. Gill also observes that, in the
genre of Renaissance "sexy songs," the lyrics of "The Pinzochere Who Have Been to
Rome" declare the skill of the Florentine *pinzochere* in cosmetics, midwifery, and magical
healing. The singers boast of secret knowledge by which they can accomplish amazing
feats and influence people. The song also suggests that the *pinzochere* have assumed
this social posture in order to sport an undeserved mask of respectability (Gill 27).

25. David Herlihy, *Opera Mulieria: Women and Work in Medieval Europe* (New York: Mcgraw-
Hill, 1990), table 7.1, "Occupations of Female Household Heads in Florentine
Tuscany, 1427," 159.

female dependents of religious houses, very like *pinzochere*), Gill notes, "exceed the largest occupational category, that of servants. Their average taxable incomes are surpassed only by innkeepers and wool merchants, and are about the same as furriers. Midwifery and medicine are two of the fields in which Herlihy surmises the Florentine *pinzochere* worked.[26]

Antonia Pulci might have objected to being called a *pinzochera* on grounds of status, on grounds of the term's sexually ambiguous overtones, and, because the French equivalent of *pinzochere*, the Beguines, had been suppressed in the thirteenth century, even on grounds of religious heterodoxy.[27] She might well have preferred *ammantellata*—a woman who wore the mantle or cloak of, in her case, an Augustinian sister while living privately. We have every reason to suppose, however, that following Bernardo's death in 1487, Antonia chose to attach herself to the class of independent religious women, however labeled. It seems clear that she shared quarters with some of the women who lived as Augustinian tertiaries—sisters of the third order. According to Neel tertiaries comprised a kind of "shadow order" of the Augustinian establishment, but they were not typically enclosed (Neel 321). Their dress, however, distinguished them: "Augustinian nuns customarily wore 'the gonella,' or gown, the scapular, the mantle of black cloth, the white veil and the black veil."[28]

During the period following Bernardo's death, like her heroine St. Guglielma, Antonia Pulci chose to live the life of an Augustinian tertiary without subscribing to the vows that would have cut her off from the world. Thirteen years after his death, however, she and at least some of her companions elected to take more formal vows and, according to Richa (250), to become officially an order of Augustinian sisters. Perhaps in anticipation of her death, she elected at this time to withdraw from the world as founder of the order of Santa Maria della Misericordia.

After that enclosure, the word *pinzochera* would have ceased to apply to the cloistered women, though it still might have been appropriate for any who had not been enclosed. In a letter to the order Pulci founded, dated at Forlì, October 11, 1506, Pope Julius II addressed the

26. Gill, 16–17; see also Herlihy, 162–66. Herlihy's data reflect the situation in the year 1427. Very likely the situation had not changed substantially by the 1490s.

27. See Carol Neel, "The Origin of the Beguines," in *Signs* 14.2 (1989): 321–41.

28. Mary Martin McLaughlin, "Creating and Recreating Communities of Women: The Case of Corpus Domini, Ferrara, 1406–1452," *Signs* 14.2 (1989): 298.

nuns of Santa Maria della Misericordia as "Beloved daughters in
Christ, of the *ammantellate*, or of the Florentine *pinzochere*, of the order
of St. Augustine, greetings and apostolic blessings. . . ."[29] Ambiguity
is implicit in the Latin adverb *seu* (a form of *sive* here translated "or,"
though it could be construed with the force of "or rather"). Here "or"
can either suggest that the Latin *pinzocheris* restates *mantellatis*, or it
can discriminate between the two terms. The ambiguous usage implies
that the pope, and presumably his contemporaries, did not make as
sharp a distinction between *ammantellate* and *pinzochere* as modern
scholarship sometimes draws.

After Bernardo's death, Antonia Pulci continued to write and to
oversee the production of plays as long as her health permitted, and
perhaps received from their printing, if not from their production,
some funds with which to finance the charitable enterprises of the
community she founded. She would not, however, have had to depend
on whatever income such efforts produced to underwrite her charitable activities.

Because Antonia Pulci had borne no children, the dowry remained
intact that her family would have paid Bernardo Pulci upon her bearing
a child (a payment that would have relieved the couple's early penury).
The money eventually passed into her *de facto* control, and with these
funds she determined to found her order and acquire an edifice to
house it. Accordingly, on the first Tuesday of January in the year
1500, at the Convent of Santa Maria di San Gallo outside the San
Gallo gate, she formally took the habit of an Augustinian sister from
the hands of Brother Antonio Dulciati *fiorentino*, Prior of the Convent.
That same Brother Antonio, as I noted above, later wrote a memorandum concerning Antonia Pulci, and Giuseppe Richa quotes it in his
discussion of the nuns of Santa Maria della Misericordia. I include a
lengthy portion of it here because it is little known:

> Francesco Tanini, a Florentine citizen had for his wife Dona
> Iacopa of Rome, to whom was born one male child named
> Niccolò, who is still living, and six female children, of whom
> three were married in Florence and one in Pisa to persons of
> similar condition. One of these three was named Antonia who
> was the wife of Bernardo Pulci, a Florentine gentleman with
> whom she lived exceedingly happily seventeen years, after

29. Cited in Richa, 251: *Dilectis in Christo filiabus mantellatis, seu pinzocheris florentinis, ord. S.
Augustini, salutem, & apopolticam benedictionem.*

which Bernardo passed to the other life. And although Niccolò
Tanini, her brother, tried to persuade her to contract a second
marriage, she nevertheless, so inspired by God, wished to embrace the religious life, and with such a resolution did so on the
first Tuesday of January in 1500, at the Convent of Santa Maria
di San Gallo outside the gate of the same name, and occupied
by the Eremite Brothers of St. Augustine of the congregation
of Lombardy. . . . There, then, the devout Antonia took the
habit of St. Augustine at the hands of Brother Antonio
Dulciati *fiorentino*, Prior of the Convent, to serve God in the
observation of that rule, and with her dowry having purchased a
house from Domenico Alamanni outside that same San Gallo
gate, almost opposite the monastery of Lapo in the Borgo San
Marco on the road that leads to Fiesole, Antonia was enclosed
in that house with some women the 26th of February of 1500,
the last Thursday of Carnival season, under the spiritual rule of
those religious [monks], and the names of her companions were:
Sister Caterina di Domenico di Biagio, Sister Settimia di Luca
di Domenico, Sister Maria di Giovanni Pennini, Sister
Alessandra di Agostino, Sister Maria di Niccolò Ciatti, and Maria
Battista da Cotignola servigiale, and Monna di Antonio del
Candanti Antonia. And there she died . . . the 26th of
September 1501 on a Sunday . . . and was buried nearby in the
church of the above-mentioned Friars in the Chapel of Santa
Monica, [at the Church of the Eremite Friars of St. Augustine
of the Congregation of Lombardy the next day] in keeping with
her will, notarized by Ser Giovanni di Domenico di Bartolommeo
da Tizzano. . . . Notwithstanding the death of the founder,
forty other women took the habit of the Augustinian
Ammantellate. [Translation mine][30]

---

30. *"Francesco Tanini Cittadino Fiorentino ebbe per Moglie Dona Iacopa da Roma, dalla quale nacque un
Figlio mascio per nome Niccolò, che ancor vive, ed ebbe sei Figliole femmine, delle quali ne furono maritate tre
in Firenze, ed una in Pisa con Persone di eguale condizione. Una di queste tre si chiamò Antonia, la quale fu
moglie di Bernardo de' Pulci Gentiluomo Fiorentine, con cui visse in somma pace anni 17, dopo che i quali
Bernardo passò ad altra vita. E benchè Niccolò Tanini suo fratello la persuadesse a contrarre lei le seconde
nozze, non ostante, così inspirata da Dio, volle abbracciare lo stato Religioso, e con una tale risoluzione si
condusse il primo Martedì di Gennaro del 1500. al Convento di S. Maria di S. Gallo fuori della Porta di tal
nome, abitato da i Frati Eremiti di S. Agostino della Congregazione di Lombardia. . . ." In esso adunque prese
la devota Antonia l'Abito di S. Agostino per le mani di Frate Antonio Dulciati Fiorentino Priore del
Convento per servire a Dio nell' osservanza di quell' Istituto, e colla sua dote avendo comprata una casa da
Domenico Alamanni fuori della medesima Porta a S. Gallo, quasi dirimpetto al Monastero di Lapo nel Borgo
di S. Marco, in sulla via, che conduce a Fiesole, in essa casa si racchiuse Antonia con alcune Donne il dì 26*

One is hard-pressed to know what word besides "founder" to apply to Pulci's role within the order she established. Her dictation and frequent (three) revisions of her will during the period between the founding of the order and two weeks before her death suggests that she may have been a sick woman when she finally decided to seek official status for her order. If that is so, it lessens the probability that she would have been named prioress, for it seems unlikely that someone ill would have been entrusted with administrative responsibility.

At the same time, a parallel case reported by Mary Martin McLaughlin seems to suggest that authority over the community accompanied control of its purse strings, in which case "prioress" would not, in Pulci's case, be altogether a misnomer (243–341). McLaughlin reports that a Ferrarese woman, Bernardina Sedazzari, founded a community of devout lay-women, which she dedicated to the "Body of Christ and the Visitation of the Blessed Virgin Mary." Bernardina died in 1425. Her will named Lucia Mascheroni her sole heir. When another member of the community, Ailisia de Baldo, began to assert authority over the sisters, Mascheroni sued under the terms of Sedazzari's will for control of the foundation. Both ecclesiastical and secular authorities ruled that Sedazzari had the right to bequeath the "monastery" as property and exercise jurisdiction over its members, and confirmed the rights of her heir to do likewise—though the Solomonic decision in this case also vested authority over the other sisters in the rival de Baldo (McLaughlin 293–95).

In Pulci's case, the founder made her fellow sisters her heirs in common, thereby freeing them to organize as seemed appropriate or as they were able to negotiate with the Augustinians under whose aegis they now functioned. The case of Sedazzari and the demographic data reported by Margaret L. King that documents the rapid increase in the number of Florentine female religious communities between 1427 and 1552 make clear that for an unmarried woman or a widow to invest the capital represented by her dowry in founding a religious community was not at all uncommon in Pulci's day or earlier (King 83).

Febbraro del 1500. Giovedi giorno di Berlingaccio, sotto lo spiritual governo di quei Religiosi, ed i nomi delle Compagne sono: Suor Caterina di Domenico di Biagio, Suor Settimia di Luca di Domenico, Suor Maria di Gio. Pennini, Suor Alessandra di Agostino, Suor Maria di Niccolò Ciatti, e Maria Battista da Cotignola Servigiale, e Monna di Antonio del Cadanti Antonia, e la di lei morte . . . il 26 di Settembre del 1501 in Domenica, e che nel di ap presso avesse sepoltura nella Chiesa di i suddetti Frati nella Cappella di S. Monaca, conforme al suo testamento rogato da Ser Giovanni di Domenico di Bartolommeo da Tizzano. . . . [N]on ostante la morte della Fondatrice presero l' Abito di Ammantellate Agostiniane 40. altre Donne . . . (Richa 249–51).

In founding her community, then, Antonia Pulci exercised an option widely available to pious women of even quite modest means in Renaissance Italy.

LITERARY ANTECEDENTS

The genre in which Antonia and Bernardo Pulci had chosen to write was popular in its origins and had become a pan-European phenomenon. As early as the tenth century, liturgical tropes (bits of scripture acted out in the chancels of churches, often on holidays) had been performed. Well known to English readers are the famous cycles of mystery plays—the Wakefield, Towneley, York, and Chester cycles—that were performed from the thirteenth to the sixteenth centuries in cities throughout England on Corpus Christi day (the ninth Thursday after Easter). Of these, some have recently been resurrected by societies of players in universities—most notably perhaps under the auspices of the Records of Early English Drama (REED) project at the University of Toronto. Less well known, perhaps, is an Easter play written between 1363 and 1376 by Katherine of Sutton, prioress of the convent of Barking (Middlesex). This liturgical drama was written for performance by nuns and friars.[31]

Miracle plays associated with the wonders done by saints seem to have captured the popular imagination in France, and an anonymous Easter play that was written and performed at the convent of Origny-Saint Benoît appears in a late thirteenth-, early fourteenth-century manuscript.[32]

A northern antecedent of Antonia Pulci was Hrosvita von Gandersheim (c. 935-c. 973), a German abbess who wrote six plays in Latin. These were adaptations or imitations of the comedies of Terence, and seem to have been read aloud and accompanied with

---

31. Katharine Sutton's work was first published by K. Young in *The Harrowing of Hell in Liturgical Drama, Transactions of the Wisconsin Academy of Sciences, Arts, and Letters*, 16 (1910), 888–947. The manuscript in which they appear, the *Barking Ordinarium*, contains three works by Sutton: the *Dispositio Crucis*, the *Elevatio Crucis*, and the *Visitatio Sepulchri*. The entire manuscript was published in two volumes by the Henry Bradshaw Society and edited by J. B. L. Tolhurst (London: 1927–28). See also N. Cotton, *Women Playwrights in England 1363–1750* (Lewisburgh, Pa., Bucknell University Press: 1980), 27–28 (cited in Weaver, *Amor* 21).

32. For the text of the *Ludus Paschalis* of Origny-Saint Benoît and a discussion of it, see K. Young in *The Drama of the Medieval Church* (Oxford: Clarendon Press, 1933) vol. 1, 411–50 and 684–87 (cited in Weaver, *Amor* 20).

mime.[33] Hildegard von Bingen (1098–1179) wrote both the text and music for a sacred play, the *Ordo Virtutem*, that she and some of her sisters performed in their monastery.[34] In the Germanic tradition, too, morality plays, like *Everyman* (*Jedermensch*), continue to be performed regularly in Austria to this day.

It seems likely that the survival of plays by female authors of sacred drama like Hrosvita von Gandersheim, Hildegard von Bingen, Katherine of Sutton, Antonia Pulci and the sixteenth-century Beatrice del Sera, and the survival, too, of exemplars of anonymous works written for performance by and for cloistered communities of women, points to an ongoing tradition of performance of such drama in convents that prepared the public for women to be active in this genre both as authors and as performers.

In Italy, sacred plays or representations were performed in various regions throughout the country. Though originally a form developed by and for the people and consequently often very colloquial in their language and rough in their syntax and versification, in the last decades of the fifteenth century these plays captured the imaginations of members of the Tuscan intelligentsia. That interest coincided with intense activity in the emergent Italian vernacular literary tradition and with a rapidly expanding printing industry and the insatiable public appetite for its products. The fascination with sacred drama coincided, too, with an ongoing efflorescence of lay initiatives typified by St. Francis and his followers, both male and female, whose object was to live simply, do penance, and imitate Christ (Gill 18).

All this happened as well at a moment of growing religious zeal that was soon to be exploited and intensified by the Ferrarese friar Girolamo Savonarola (1452–98). The circumstances, then, were propitious for the Tuscan development of the genre of *sacre rappresentazioni* from a sub-literary popular phenomenon into a sub-species of high literary art—particularly with respect to its poetic quality. Several Tuscan writers penned sacred plays in passable Italian vernacular verse. Among them were Bernardo Pulci himself, Antonio Alamanni, Castellano de' Castellani, and Feo Belcari. Even Lorenzo de' Medici

33. Weaver (*Amor* 20) cites a modern edition: *Hrotsvithae Opera*, ed. by H. Homeyer (Vienna: Schoningh, 1970). Some of Hrosvita's plays have been translated into English by H. J. W. Tillyard, *Plays of Roswitha* (London: Faith Press, 1923).

34. See Peter Dronke's chapter on Hildegard von Bingen in *Women Writers of the Middle Ages* (Cambridge: Cambridge University Press, 1984), 144–201. For the text with music, see Dronke, ed., *Harmonia Mundi Editions with Text of Hildegard von Bingen's* Ordo virtutem (Oxford: Oxford University Press, 1970) (cited in Weaver, *Amor* 20).

made a contribution with his *rappresentazione, The Play of Saints John and Paul*—a confraternity play written for his son Giulio with, as Nerida Newbiggin has so trenchantly remarked, "a part for every kid."[35] If Lorenzo's effort constitutes a detour in the course of an otherwise illustrious literary career, Antonia Pulci's work, by contrast, brings *sacre rappresentazioni* near their apogee of poetic and dramatic excellence.

ANALYSIS

I have spoken above about the strength of characterization of Pulci's female characters and about her mastery of several sorts of Italian verse. A part of the strength of that characterization, not only of the female but of the male characters as well, arises from her innovative use of dialogue within the framework provided by *ottava rima* stanzas. In the plays of Feo Belcari, for instance, the speeches of the characters are almost always the same length as the stanza. Pulci by contrast achieves a kind of conversational verisimilitude by breaking the stanza among several speakers or by allowing a single speaker to continue for more than one stanza.

She also occasionally reinforces the effects of tonal shifts by moving from one sort of stanza to another. The prayers uttered by St. Guglielma, for instance, move from *ottava* into *terza rima*, the stanza of Dante's *Comedy*, which Pulci evidently considered the higher style. Similarly, on one occasion, in the prologue to *St. Theodora* when the matter is light, the playwright employs the *settenario*, a shorter, seven-syllable line, rhymed in the couplets of *rima baciata*. As the rhyming resources of the Italian language are much richer than those of English, and as I have chosen to represent Pulci's Italian rhyme with English blank verse, I have tried to reflect the movement between *ottava* and *terza rima* with tonal shifts and the instance of *rima baciata* with line length.

An unusual realism also marks Pulci's characters. Speaking about that realism in the context of Pulci's play of *St. Francis*, Franco Cardini observed that, in the beginning of the play, Francis is presented as a Florentine banker of Pulci's time, impatient with the requests of the

35. "The Politics of the *'sacra rappresentazione'* in Lorenzo's Florence" (paper presented at the Warberg Institute, Univ. of Warwick Conference on Lorenzo, May 31, 1992). See also Konrad Eisenbichler, "Confraternities and Carnival: the Context of Lorenzo de' Medici's Rappresentazione di SS. Giovanni e Paolo," in *Comparative Drama* 27:1, 1993, 128–140.

poor for alms.[36] Georges Ulysse has also noted the humanity of her
saints as opposed to the stereotypes of the hagiographic tradition and
has called attention to character traits that Pulci seems to share with
her stage creations—with *St. Francis*, a refusal to be dominated and a
contempt for wealth, and, with Guglielma, a scorn for excess. About
Pulci's realism Ulysse remarks that she has the ability to present contemporary life and to represent several facets of a personality. The
prodigal son, Ulysse notes, is not the same when he is with his gambling companions, his father, his brother, or the cashier (Ulysse 189).

A healthy and credible skepticism also appears in her portrayals of
non-Christian characters. Before her conversion, St. Domitilla's
Christian servants do not easily win her to their point of view.
Indeed, they are presented as sanctimonious busybodies at first, and I
suspect that Pulci's audience would not find them any more convincing than Domitilla initially does. Not all the pagans are won over.
Three Ethiopians visiting St. Anthony in the desert refuse baptism
with dignity, saying that they were reared in the religion of their
country and had always lived with justice. In this scene, Pulci not
only heightens realism by having virtuous pagans reject conversion,
she also reflects an essential aspect of fifteenth-century debate between traditional Christians and Humanists.

It is virtually unimaginable that Antonia Pulci was unaquainted at
least with vernacular aspects of the humanistic discussion that arose
with the renewed Florentine interest in the authors of ancient
Greece and Rome. Before 1466, as Stefano Carrai has demonstrated, a
precocious Bernardo Pulci had completed the first known vernacular
translation of the *Eclogues* of Virgil and dedicated it to Lorenzo de'
Medici. Her brothers- in-law as well were deeply involved in vernacular
projects based upon the ancient authors.[37] Surely, given her literary
bent, Antonia Pulci would have read her husband's work and likely
that of her brothers-in-law too. Beyond that, however, hints that she
was acquainted with some of the issues that interested the humanists
appear in several places in her plays.

---

36. In "La Figura di Francesco D' Assisi nella *Rappresentatione di sancto Francesco* di Antonia
Pulci," *Il francescanesimo e il teatro medievale*. Atti del Convegno Nazionale di Studi, San
Miniato, 8–10 Ottobre 1982 (Castelfiorentino: Società Storica della Valdelsa, 1984),
201.

37. Stefano Carrai, "Lorenzo e l'umanesimo volgare dei fratelli Pulci," in Bernard
Toscani, ed., *Lorenzo De' Medici, New Perspectives*, Proceedings of the International
Conference held at Brooklyn College and the Graduate Center of the City University
of New York, April 30-May 2, 1992 (New York: Peter Lang, 1993), 1–21.

I have already mentioned the dignified Ethopians of *St. Anthony*, and how St. Domitilla reveals her own and her creator's familiarity with the Roman poets as she debates the issue of virginity with her uncle, the emperor Domitian. Beyond these instances, the arguments that both Aurelianus in *St. Domitilla* and especially Quintianus in *St. Theodora* employ in their attempts to woo the saints as their spouses suggest a familiarity with the fifteeth-century humanist discussion of Epicurean doctrine.

Familiarity with such issues may account for a part of the realism with which Pulci draws her characters. Her ancient Roman villains display considerable depth of characterization. Detached cruelty aside, the Roman emperor Domitian in *St. Domitilla*, and the governor Quintianus in *St. Theodora* seem rational and sensible beside the in-flamed and seemingly self-destructive zeal of the Christians who in-sist on being persecuted. Put succinctly, while Pulci's human villains are villainous enough, they are also complex and, because complex, they appear as credible, three-dimensional characters.

Even her allegorical figures, like the seven deadly sins in *The Prodigal Son* and in *Saint Anthony the Abbot* can evoke both our dislike and our sympathy. As a writer, Pulci displays the ability to provide us with a double view of the persons she introduces to us.

In both *St. Francis* and *St. Guglielma* Pulci presents the poor as moved by multiple motives to seek alms. Some accept charity with convincing Christian gratitude; others rush cynically to get in on the action while they can. The King of Hungary's seneschal, who has re-sponsibility for distributing the alms, takes a very dim view of the pro-ceedings and seems convinced that the alms seekers are all simply loafers who take advantage of their more fortunate betters. From this technique of presenting double visions, considerable merriment arises.

Antonia Pulci regularly displays a piquant sense of humor. Sometimes, as above, it appears in her development of situations, but it often expresses itself in word play and punning. She employs, for instance, a kind of Boccaccian class humor that assigns peculiar names like "Hedgehog" or "Curly" (*Randellino*), or "Priest's Cap" (*Beretta*) to the prodigal son's gambling companions, and titles like "father of the donkey," (*padre dell'asino*)—a drover in *St. Francis*—to per-sons of the urban lower classes and the peasantry. Similarly, one of the prostitutes in *St. Theodora* has for her *nom de guerre* "Madam Acconcia"—Madam Fix-it, Dress-up, or Serviceable. This linguistic playfulness reveals her characters' personality traits or, sometimes, the comparative degree of seriousness that she wants her audience to attribute to her *dramatis personae.*

Pulci's playfulness—a quality missing from the plays of her husband Bernardo—contributes to an engaging variety in the matter of her plays. Such variety, like the gambling scenes in *The Prodigal Son,* ordering breakfast for the king and poking fun at the ignorance and pomposity of physicians in *St. Guglielma,* and the impatience of the executioner in *St. Domitilla,* create a level of audience interest higher than unrelieved piety might achieve. It may also reflect an acquaintance with variety *(varietas)* as a formal device of rhetoric, and if so, suggests another facet of her education.

As a dramatist, she also displays a flair for spectacle. Angels probably flew in *St. Guglielma.* St. Francis goes naked to his grave while still alive, and Aurelianus in *St. Domitilla* dances himself to death—all on stage.

Recognizing the difficulties that beset a too-biographical reading of the works of a literary artist, I nevertheless think that close familiarity with a considerable body of her work does give rise to a reasonably accurate portrait of the personality of the woman who wrote them. She was clearly self-confident, a doer as well as a dreamer, a formidable debater, and something of a perfectionist. In the early editions of her plays, I have never found a mismetered line. The same cannot be said for some of the impressionistic readings and "corrections" of those same lines by her nineteenth-century editors or for some of the very corrupt sixteenth-century editions from which I had to work early on.

She thought and felt deeply about religious matters, about the difficulties that women faced in her world, and about ways either to cope with or avoid those difficulties. She had a fine eye for irony, a good sense of humor that may have included, as I shall shortly maintain, a capacity for enjoying a laugh at her own expense, an ability to get along well with people, and an abiding appreciation for the people she cared about—as naming as her heirs her *consorelle*—her fellow sisters—suggests.

She was interested in exotic places, for she sets scenes in Babylon *(St. Francis),* Egypt *(St. Anthony the Abbot),* England and Hungary *(St. Guglielma),* Caesarea *(Rosana),* and Syria *(St. Theodora).* The tone of the passages she assigns her principal characters when they pray also attests to her deep religious feelings, and many of the situations in her plays as well as the details we know of her life and bequests attest to her charity and generosity. Though her mother had perhaps suffered from her father's philandering, Pulci herself—apparently blessed with a happy first marriage (Richa 249)—avoided the dangers of male domination that might be associated with a second. To display appropriately the grounds on which some of the details of that personality analysis rests, I must turn now to the question of the attribution of her plays. This question, like that of her family connection, is sorely vexed.

THE PULCI CANON

That four plays were Antonia Pulci's we can be very certain: *St. Guglielma, St. Domitilla,* and *St. Francis* all bear the attribution *Composta per Mona Antonia donna di Bernardo Pulci,* "Written by Madam Antonia, wife of Bernardo Pulci." Though no manuscript versions and no printed editions are known to survive that antedate the 1490 collection of *rappresentazioni* edited by Antonio Miscomini and preserved in the *Biblioteca Nazionale* in Florence, the attribution itself and a notation of 1483 as the date of composition of *St. Domitilla* make clear that she wrote at least those three plays before Bernardo's death in 1487.[38] A fourth, *The Prodigal Son,* also bears the identification. Its earliest surviving edition, however, seems to date from Florence about the year 1550, and the printer is unknown. Nevertheless, no one has raised serious questions about Antonia Pulci's authorship of this play, and, though it seems her weakest effort, I think it almost certainly hers. After Bernardo Pulci's death, identifying the author as his wife would no longer have been appropriate, and perhaps identifying the author at all would, after she decided on a religious life, have struck Pulci as prideful.

For seemingly later plays, in any case, we are dependent on a tradition of attribution and internal correspondences with the plays of unquestioned provenance. Not surprisingly, then, much disagreement persists about the other plays sometimes assigned to her. Both Colomb de Batines and Alfredo Cioni also attribute *St. Anthony the Abbot* to her. [39] Although it lacks the identifying *"composta da . . . ,"* it does appear in the Miscomini collection and in another edition of

---

38. Franco Cardini agrees that the expression "donna di Bernardo Pulci" would be inappropriately applied to a widow (198). The caption at the beginning of *St. Domitilla* in the Miscomini collection gives the date of composition of that play as 1483.

39. Colomb de Batines, 23; Alfredo Cione, *Bibliografia delle Sacre Rappresentazioni* (Florence: Sansoni Antiquariato, 1961), 86.

about 1490 (Florence: Bartolomeo de Libri). Its anachronistic reference to enclosing the sister of an Egyptian monk in the Florentine monastery of the Murate identifies it generally with convent drama or with drama written for performance by Florentine confraternities, and improves the likelihood that, at such an early date, Antonia Pulci wrote it—possibly completing it after Bernardo's death. Certain other anachronisms in the play identify its author with the Medici circle—particularly a joke about the pharmacist Bisticci, which was the nickname of the Medici dynasty's founder who was also a pharmacist.

Colomb de Batines also assigns her *Ioseph Figliuolo di Jacob,* though that is probably a confusion arising from the similarity of her name with that of another playwright, Antonio Pucci. *Susana [sic]* occasionally appears attributed to Pulci in library holdings—I have seen it so attributed in the British Library—but I have not been able to determine on what grounds and have reluctantly elected to exclude it from this volume, although a reference to the Susanna story that appears in *St. Guglielma* makes the attribution tempting.

Rosana, a play in two parts, has enough thematic material in common with the plays securely attributed to her—orientalism, an interest in communities of women, a concern with the disappointments that children bring, a competent woman making crucial decisions, and particularly the moving discussion of the woes of childlessness in Part I—that I consider it a likely enough candidate for inclusion here. D'Ancona reports and Cioni confirms that *Rosana* appeared in a now lost fifth volume of the Magliabecchiana collection, and its early date makes Pulci's authorship seem to me very likely.[40]

Another St. Francis play, *How St. Francis Converted Three Thieves,* has also sometimes been offered as a possibility, but again, not enough evidence has been adduced to warrant its inclusion here.

St. Theodora, however, I am almost completely convinced was written for performance by the sisters of the convent Pulci founded—though conceivably by an anonymous successor writing in the manner of Antonia Pulci or by a posthumous collaborator who finished what she had begun. The probabilities seem to favor Pulci's having written at least a part of it herself, perhaps in the fourteen months between her having occupied the house she bought from Alamanni and her

---

40. D'Ancona, vol. 3, 361. See also Cioni 86. Cioni refers us to an unpublished ms. of Francesco Cionacci (Magliabechiana, classe VIII, n. 9) in which Cionacci discusses the history, verse forms, and staging of *Sacre rappresentazioni* and a now lost fifteenth or early sixteenth-century collection that contained *Rosana.*

death the following year. Georges Ulysse suggests that, because the first surviving edition dates from 1554 and contains a caption using the words "commedia" and "tragedia" in a theatrical sense, the play may belong to an epoch later than Pulci's life (Ulysse 180). Given, however, that Dante two centuries earlier uses both terms in their theatrical sense in *Convivio* 1.5.8, this suggestion, couched as a question, bears little weight if Ulysse means that such theatrical meanings did not attach to the terms as early as the fifteenth century. If, however, Ulysse means that the application of those terms specifically to *sacre rappresentazioni* was a later development, the objection becomes more arguable.

The 1554 edition of the play bears the epigram "Brought to light again" after the title, *Saint Theodora, Virgin and Martyr*.[41] This suggests a provenance earlier than the edition. Other circumstances potentially identify *St. Theodora* with Pulci's convent. In his discussion of the subsequent history of the "Monache della Misericordia [The Sisters of Charity]," Richa quotes portions of a letter written to the Florentine ecclesiastical authorities by Pope Clement VII on July 29, 1528. In the letter, thirty-two current sisters of the order are named, among them "Sister Angelica, abbess, and Sister Hyppolita, vicar of the monastery of St. Clement, Florence, of the regular canonical order of St. Augustine, both sisters in the flesh and the daughters of Leonardo Strozzi of Ferrara."[42] The letter goes on to restore to the sisters Angelica and Hyppolita Strozzi—now, twenty-seven years after the death of the foundress, the abbess and the vicar of their order—their dowries, amounting to 155 florins. The pope also gives the Sisters of Charity twenty large gold florins. *St. Theodora* opens with an exchange between two novices named Angela and Hippolyta, who are miffed because they think they have been discriminated against in the choice of costumes for the evening's play. Here is a substantial bit of that opening dialogue:

Sister Angela says:
> It's still true, after all,
> A woman who's arrogant
>> Always gets everything
> The way that she has done.

---

41. *S. Theodora: Vergine et Martire. Di nuovo mandata in Luce* (Florence: 1554).

42. *Soror Angelica Abbatissa, & Soror Hyppolita Vicaria Monasterii S. Clementis de Flor. Ordinis Canonicorum Regularium S. Augustini, ambo Sorores carnales, & filiae Lionardi de Strozzis de Ferraria.*

        This convent as it seems   5
    Exists for her alone.
        But I desire to have
    A little fun with her.

Sister Hippolyta:
        Ah, wait a bit and see,
    We are two malcontents!   10
        I have my mind so full
    Of wrath and of disdain,
        That I must be confessed.
    My lines I'd like to shred,
        For they don't make good sense.   15

Sister Angela:
    You'll have a thousand reasons;
        Since all our speech is in
    Eight lines or seven lines;
        Those things we have to say—
    If they want them attired   20
        In only three or four;
    That's fine, Our duty is
        To be cast out
    And then be ridiculed
        By all the convent's nuns.   25

Sister Hippolyta:
    If I stay in this mood
        It's them I'll ridicule,
    For they will stay to watch
        And give me the delight
    Of turning up my nose at them;   30
        I want to mock them all.

Sister Angela:
    I'm not so sure of this;
        I am a bit afraid
    The prior might be enraged.

Sister Hippolyta:
    Don't get exited, Angela;   35
        That doesn't matter much;

Our poor old man will stay
    Close by the fire and won't
Trouble his brain about
    Whatever we may say.   40

                     (*St. Theodora*, lines 1–40)

Angela, of course, was a very common name, and Hippolyta not uncommon. Nevertheless, the names occurring as a set both in a play traditionally associated with Antonia Pulci and in a document detailing the history of the order she founded raises some intriguing possibilities. It is conceivable that the sisters Strozzi joined the convent as teen-age novices shortly after its founding in 1500, and, possibly based on a factual incident in the life of the community, found themselves and the incident set up to engage the interest of the audience and to establish the coming contrast when the same two novices perform the parts of the prostitutes, Acconcia and Minoccia—an identity made unmistakable by the device of a hood one of them chooses to wear—and to provide a bit of innocent fun for the community, including jokes about the prior. Moreover, I think this raises the possibility as well that the "arrogant woman" about whom the first eight lines complain may be none other than the founder-playwright Antonia Pulci herself, in a kind of self-satirizing, cameo reference.

Other scenarios are certainly possible. The play could have been written after the Strozzi sisters had become figures of authority, and the fun at their expense as novices could have been retrospective. The play could have been written by Antonia Pulci without the novice's prologue and without the Minoccia-Acconcia scenes, and these added later—which would account for the application of "comedy and tragedy" to a *rappresentazione* written so early. And, of course, the play might have been written later by someone else entirely for performance at another convent, and the names of the sisters entirely coincidental.

Nonetheless, *St. Theodora*'s unmistakable association with convent drama, the fact that the names in the play appear as a set both there and in Pope Clement's letter, and the circumstance that the persons named in the play may be identifiable with members of Pulci's order seem to me to improve the chances that the tradition of attributing the play to her is correct. If it is correct, the play confirms her tendency to borrow both characters and incident directly from life, displacing them appropriately and deploying them in the service of her art.

Quite apart from external considerations, however, comparing *St. Theodora* with *St. Domitilla*, we find parallel treatment of pagan attitudes toward Christians and similar attributes of self-confidence and constancy in the heroines. The protagonists' living arrangements as consecrated women living privately match Pulci's own between 1476 and 1500. As in *St. Francis*, and *St. Guglielma*, we find parallel instances of class humor—Crispus and Faustus from *St. Theodora* are Pulcian Dogberrys and Bottoms—and parallel intensity of tone in the prayers. The poetry also seems to display a similar level of mastery.

PERFORMANCE

Sacre rappresentazioni, argues Cesare Molinari, constituted one aspect of a series of Florentine public spectacles that included pageants and processions and that celebrated saints' days and public occasions.[43] Generally these plays were staged by confraternities and, as we have seen, by convents. Confraternities were organizations of laymen, often associated with churches or religious foundations. Their purposes were devotional and social, and, as Konrad Eisenbichler and others have demonstrated, often political as well (Eisenbichler 128–40). Sometimes the plays they staged seem to have been principally intended for their members and sometimes for the Florentine general public.

With respect to Antonia Pulci's plays specifically, some of them—*St. Anthony the Abbot, St. Francis*, and *The Prodigal Son*, with their masculine heroes and preponderance of male characters—may have been written for performance in confraternities before the death of Bernardo. The others, except perhaps for *Rosana* seem instead to have been created with the expectation that they would be performed by women for audiences of women. In the case of *Rosana*, if the prologue is coeval with the rest of the text, the audience was expected to be male and female, adult and juvenile, since fathers, mothers, and children are addressed by the speaker heralding the play.

Costuming seems to have been quite elaborate, as both the texts of the plays and contemporary woodcuts attest. Actors in the confraternities seem to have been drawn from the ranks of the younger men and boys, and, in the convents, from among the novices. Though when men took women's roles in the confraternities, no eyebrows

43. *Spettacoli fiorentini del Quattrocento* (Venice: Neri Pozza Editore, 1961), 1–2.

seem to have been raised, when men's parts were played by women cross-dressed as men, nuns' male religious superiors sometimes found the practice scandalous enough to try (ineffectually) to forbid it (Weaver, *Amor* 23). The plays were apparently sometimes performed in churches, sometimes in the squares before churches, and sometimes on raised platforms in refectories (using scenery that could vary from extremely simple to very elaborate, depending on the depth of the pockets of the sponsoring organization), and sometimes, perhaps, in procession on pageant wagons. [44]

Some evidence suggests that over time a considerable arsenal of architectural scenery accumulated in Florence during the second half of the fifteenth century, and that scenery was probably loaned. A temple in which St. Guglielma is depicted in a contemporary woodcut as praying matches descriptions of a temple that appeared in other plays. Palaces, houses, and a mountain may have been represented by architectural scenery as well (Molinari 67–99).

Changes in venue seem to have been represented by architectural constructions, by painted backdrops, or even by chairs labeled with the names of the locales (Molinari 67–115). These designated places, or *luoghi deputati* as they were called, appeared together simultaneously on the stage, obviating the need for changes of scenery and providing the actress-nuns or young actors with the ability to move almost instantly from Rome to Cesarea or from Assisi to Babylon, making for an approximation of the sorts of effects that cinematography can give us today or that the multiple acting areas of the Shakespearian apron stage made possible.

Contributing to the possibilities for spectacle was the existence of an apparatus that made people appear to fly, and Molinari suggests, as I earlier noted, that it may have been used in connection with the appearance of angels in *St. Guglielma* (35–54). Contemporary or near-contemporary woodcuts and paintings give some idea of the possibilities for staging (see Molinari, figs. 1–46), while stage directions suggest that music (both vocal and instrumental) and dancing embellished the productions. Two examples of this occur at the wedding celebrations of St. Guglielma and in the banquet celebrating the return of the Prodigal Son.

Audiences for the plays performed by and for members of the

---

44. The whole question of the possibility of production on pageant wagons is explored in the introduction to *Nuovo corpus di sacre rappresentazioni fiorentine,* ed. Nerida Newbigin (Bologna: Commissione per I Testi di Lingua, 1983), xxviii–xxxix.

confraternities sometimes included both men and women. Men and boys participated fully in the lives of these organizations. The women and girls of their families, though considered sisters of the confraternities, generally participated only in theory. At celebrations for feast days, fifteenth-century women seem to have been invited as infrequently as once a year.[45] As *Rosana* anticipates a mixed audience, and as the play requires two successive days to perform, it may have been performed for the feast of San Giovanni Battista [St. John the Baptist], which regularly lasted two days or longer.

For plays presented at convents, nuns, their female relatives, and women from the communities and their minor children composed the audience. Men were prohibited, though it appears that occasionally some contrived to sneak in.[46]

AFTERMATH

Pulci's contributions to the genre of the *sacra rappresentazione*, although artistically distinguished, came near what Molinari perhaps mistakenly thought to be the end of the period of the greatest general popularity of the form. That popularity peaked, as he thought, about the middle of the fifteenth century.

Any lack of interest in this genre, however, does not seem to have extended to the convent, where the composition and staging of such plays not only continued to lend variety and interest to the lives of cloistered women, as the work of Beatrice del Sera suggests, but also spilled over into the lay community.

The sheer demographics of convent life in Renaissance Florence account in part for the sustained claustral activity in sacred drama. Margaret L. King reports that "in Florence, female convents increased from five in the mid-trecento to forty-seven in 1552, while the number of nuns in each soared to approximately seventy-three. . . . [From] 440 in 1428–29 . . . [the number] swelled to 3,419 [13 percent of the female population of Florence] . . . by . . . 1552."[47]

---

45. See Ronald F. E. Weissman, *Ritual Brotherhood in Renaissance Florence* (New York: Academic Press, 1982).

46. Elissa Weaver, seminar presented to Fellows of the Newberry Library, Nov.19, 1994.

47. *Women*, 83. King draws these statistics from Richard C. Trexler, "Le Célebat à fin du Moyen Age: les rèligieuses de Florence," *Annales: ESC* 27:1329–50, and from Julius Kirchner and Anthony Molho, "The Dowry Fund and the Marriage Market in Early Quattrocento Florence," *JMH* 50:403–38.

To serve this expanding audience, an active community of play-wrights succeeded Antonia Pulci in Florence. Many of these were male; Weaver names Antonio Alamanni, Giovan Maria Cecchi (1518–87, the most famous of the writers of sacred comedy), Giovanni Rucellai (1475–1525), and others less well known (*Amor* 29–34). Some of these writers were laymen, and others were friars. Unlike most of their female counterparts, their names have come down to us.

In the convents, too, certain sisters, often those responsible for overseeing novices, were appointed *drammaturghe*—nuns responsible both for writing plays and for dramatic production. Thus Pulci also had female successors in Florentine convents. Most if not all of these remain, at least for the moment, anonymous. In Florence, elsewhere in Italy, and in France as well, the tradition of sacred drama to which Pulci had made her contribution in the fifteenth century continued and expanded through the sixteenth and seventeenth centuries, sometimes moving beyond the walls of the convent and into the dramatic mainstream (Weaver, *Amor* 31).

The printing history of Pulci's plays—the Miscomini collection of 1490 and the survival of later examples of individual editions of the plays, often roughly printed but frequently containing woodcuts whose originals clearly dated from a period earlier than the editions they embellished—demonstrates a continued popular interest in *reading* the plays, at least, if not in their production. The plays associated with the lives of saints, however, were undoubtedly performed on the days dedicated to the saints' veneration. These days, of course, rolled around annually with the liturgical cycle, and it strikes me as extremely unlikely that the plays were written for a single performance.

Pulci's plays continued to be printed intermittently for 300 years, and Alessandro D'Ancona assured their survival along with other examples of the genre by collecting many of them in a ninteenth-century edition. While I have not found documentary evidence of the continued claustral production of Pulci's plays, in the printed editions one finds vestigial suggestions of production. Stage directions, for example, vary slightly from one edition to another. This, of course, may simply result from editorial decisions, but it may also suggest that convents other than that of the sisters of Santa Maria della Misericordia later performed Pulci's plays from printed editions. Moreover, the corrupt condition of the text, particularly of several sixteenth-century editions, suggests the possibility that they were printed from scripts that had been used for performance and, as scripts often are, modified to suit the exigences of production.

In the 1490 edition of the Miscomini collection a marginal note in an early sixteenth-century hand (on f. B7 v.) accompanies the text of *St. Domitilla*, and identifies by the names "Eufrosina and Teodora" characters unnamed in the printed text. This may be an editorial correction (even authorial?), or it may suggest that the Miscomini itself was used as the source of an acting version.

As not only nuns but also women and children from the neighborhoods in which convents were located comprised the audiences for the production of convent drama,[48] it may well be that seeing the young novices acting and playing the roles of men as well as women predisposed a portion of the public to accept actresses on the secular stage as it developed in the sixteenth century. It may also have prepared the literary public to accept the poetic productions of such a writer as the sixteenth-century actress and poet Isabella Andreini.[49]

From the perspective of literary history, one discovers some irony in the fate of Antonia Pulci's plays over the centuries. At the hands of the compilers of histories of theater, Antonia Pulci's work, though generally considered praiseworthy, has regularly rated at most only a sentence or two. The work of Bernardo, on the other hand, though he wrote only two known plays as compared with the five that Antonia Pulci certainly wrote and the two others (three, if one counts the two parts of *Rosana* separately) that she probably wrote, has generally commanded at least a paragraph, and at least one monograph is devoted to his life and work.

Having compared the plays that Bernardo wrote with those of Antonia, I find her to be not only more productive, but also the more accomplished playwright. We see in this state of affairs an instance of the long-established tendency of the literary establishment to seek its norms in the work of male writers and to consider the work of female writers anomalous, with the consequent literary institutionalization of a patriarchal canon.

48. Weaver, seminar, Nov.19, 1994.

49. See Isabella Andreini, *Fragmenti di alcune scritture della Signora Isabella Andreini, comica gelosa e academica intenta* (1627; Venice: Presso G. B. Combi, 1989). See also Anna Elizabeth MacNeil, "Music and the Life and Work of Isabella Andreini: Humanistic Attitudes toward Music, Poetry and Theater during the Late Sixteenth and Early Seventeenth Centuries" (Ph.D. diss., University of Chicago, 1994).

PRINCIPLES OF THIS TRANSLATION

Translation is at best a risky enterprise. One tries to echo the language, style, and tone of one's source. Inevitably, though, emphases will shift in moving from one language to another, and translators must have a clear idea of the compromises they are willing to make—what they will sacrifice to keep and what strikes them as too important to lose. As in my other verse translations from Italian,[50] I have elected to represent the Italian rhymed hendecasyllabic line and stanza with English blank verse equivalents, or the shorter lines with fewer iambs. This has been a choice made by other translators from Italian to English, from Edmund Spenser to Mark Musa. One loses, of course, the rhyme of the original. Because it is a language whose inflections typically end in vowels, Italian has approximately four times as many rhyming possibilities as English. Thus, though it is certainly possible to arrive at good English rhymed versions of Italian poems, as Thomas Bergin's translations of selections from Petrarch demonstrate, over the course of a long poem, trying to preserve rhyme can force ingenuities and infidelities to the text at the cost of other poetic values. Given the comparative paucity of rhyming resources in English as compared with those in Italian, I find it possible to approximate better the Italian's tonal qualities if I am not constrained by the necessity of rhyming ingenuities and the consequent loss both of lexicon and inference that they often impose.

Forced to choose between representing the literal meaning of a word or phrase or catching its underlying concept, I regularly opt for the concept. Forced to a similar choice between literal representation of the Italian tense sequence or one that rings true as English idiom, I regularly choose the latter. This sometimes results, for example, in the representation as English future tenses of the Italian subjunctive—a mood alive and well in Italian though dead in English except in condition-contrary-to-fact clauses. My goal has been to make the plays readable and even performable as English verse. At the same time, the English text is a highly literal representation of the Italian.

The Italian texts that I have chosen to translate and, in the case of those taken from incunables, to edit, have been the earliest ones

---

50. *The Autobiography of Lorenzo de' Medici: A Commentary on My Sonnets* (Binghamton, NY: Center for Medieval and Renaissance Texts, 1994), and Francesco Petrarca, *Petrarch's Songbook: Rerum Vulgarium Fragmenta* (Binghamton, NY: Center for Medieval and Renaissance Texts, 1995).

that have been accessible to me. I originally transcribed the Italian from the earliest editions available in the British and Newberry Libraries, and have subsequently corrected those transcriptions to conform to the versions included in the 1490–93 collection of Miscomini.

For the plays not in the Miscomini collection, I have used the following editions: the text of *San Antonio Abate* from which I worked is that printed by Iacopo Chiti (Florence 1552). That of *St. Theodora* is the one printed in Lucca in 1557, which D'Ancona also used. I compared this text with the emendations of D'Ancona and have tried to follow the earlier one except where something was clearly wrong; in such cases I followed D'Ancona. As no incunable version of the two parts of *Rosana* was available to me, I have relied exclusively on D'Ancona's edition for that text. To the best of my knowledge, this is the first time that the plays by and attributed to Antonia Pulci have been published together in any language.

SUGGESTIONS FOR FURTHER READING

Primary Works

Alberti, Leon Battista (1404–72). *The Family in Renaissance Florence.* Trans. Renée Neu Watkins. Columbia, SC: University of South Carolina Press, 1969.

Ambrose, Saint (340–97). "Epistle 63 [to the Church of Vercellae]," in *The Principal Works of St. Ambrose.* Trans. H. de Romistin. A Select Library of Nicene and Post-Nicene Fathers. 2nd series, vol. 10. Grand Rapids, MI: Wm. B. Eerdmans Publishing Company, 1955, 457–64.

Andreini, Isabella (1562–1604). *Fragmenti di alcuni scritture della Signora Isabella Andreini, comica gelosa e academica intenta.* 1627. Presso G. B. Combi, 1989.

Ariosto, Ludovico (1474–1533). *Orlando Furioso.* Trans. Barbara Reynolds. 2 volumes. New York: Penguin Books, 1975–77.

Astell, Mary (1666–1731). *The First English Feminist: Reflections on Marriage and Other Writings.* Ed. and intro. Bridget Hill. New York: St. Martin's Press, 1986.

Barbaro, Francesco (1390–1454). *On Wifely Duties.* Trans. Benjamin

Kohl. In Kohl and R. G. Witt, eds., *The Earthly Republic.* Philadelphia: University of Pennsylvania Press, 1978, 179–228. See especially the preface and book 2.

Baring-Gold, Sabine. *The Lives of the Saints.* 16 vols. Edinburgh: J. Grant, 1914.

Boccaccio, Giovanni (1313–75). *Concerning Famous Women.* Trans. Guido A. Guarino. New Brunswick, NJ: Rutgers University Press, 1963.

————. *Corbaccio or The Labyrinth of Love.* Trans. Anthony K. Cassell. Second revised edition. Binghamton, NY: Medieval and Renaissance Texts and Studies, 1993.

Bruni, Leonardo (1370–1444). "On the Study of Literature (1405) to Lady Battista Malatesta of Montefeltro," in *The Humanism of Leonardo Bruni: Selected Texts.* Trans. and intro. Gordon Griffiths, James Hankins, and David Thompson. Binghamton: Medieval and Renaissance Texts and Studies, 1987, 240–51.

Castiglione, Baldassare (1478–1529). *The Courtier.* Trans. George Bull. New York: Viking Penguin, 1967.

Cioni, Alfredo. *Bibliografia delle Sacre Rappresentazioni.* Florence: Sansoni Antiquario, 1961.

Colomb de Batines, Paul. *Bibliografia delle antiche rappresentazioni sacre e profane.* Florence: Per la Società Tipografica, 1852.

D'Ancona, Alessandro, ed. *Sacre rappresentazioni dei secoli XIV, XV e XVI.* 3 vols. Florence: Le Monnier, 1872.

Dante Alighieri (1265–1321). *The Divine Comedy. The Portable Dante.* Ed. trans., and intro. Mark Musa. New York: Penguin Books, 1995.

de Lorris, William, and Jean de Meun. *The Romance of the Rose.* Trans. Charles Dahlbert. Princeton: Princeton University Press, 1971; reprint, University Press of New England, 1983.

de' Medici, Lorenzo. *The Autobiography of Lorenzo de' Medici: A Commentary on My Sonnets.* Trans. and intro. James Wyatt Cook. Binghamton, NY: Center for Medieval and Renaissance Texts, vol. 129, 1994.

de Navarre, Marguerite (1492–1549). *The Heptameron.* Trans. P. A. Chilton. New York: Viking Penguin, 1984.

de Pizan, Christine (1365–1431). *Ditiè de Jehanne d'Arc.* Ed. Angus J. Kennedy and Kenneth Varty. *Medium Aevum* Monographs, n.s. 9. Oxford: Society for the Study of Medieval Languages and Literature, 1977.

————. *The Book of the City of Ladies*. Trans. Earl Jeffrey Richards. New York: Persea, 1982.

————. *The Treasury of the City of Ladies*. Trans. Sarah Lawson. New York: Viking Penguin, 1985. Also trans. and intro. Charity Cannon Willard. Ed. and intro. Madeleine P. Cosman. New York: Persea Books, 1989.

de Voragine, Jacobus (Iacopo di Verazzo, ca. 1229–98). *The Golden Legend*. Ed. and trans. William Granger Ryan and Helmut Pippenger. New York: Arno Press, 1969.

Del Sera, Beatrice (1515–85). *Amor di Virtú: Commedia in cinque atti*. Ed. Elissa Weaver. Classici Italiani Minori, vol. 17. Ravenna: Longo Editore, 1990.

Elyot, Thomas (1490–1546). *Defence of Good Women: The Feminist Controversy of the Renaissance*. Ed. Diane Bornstein. Facsimile Reproductions. New York: Delmar, 1980.

Epistole et Evangelii, et Letioni. Florence: Appresso i Giunti, 1551.

Erasmus, Desiderius (1467–1536). *The Praise of Folly*. Trans. Craig R. Thompson. Chicago: University of Chicago Press, 1965.

————. *Erasmus on Women*. Ed. Erika Rummel. Toronto: University of Toronto Press, 1996.

Fior di virtù historiato. Utilissimo a' Fanciulli, e ad ogni fedel Christiano. Bologna: 1551(?).

Flamini, Franco. *La lirica toscana del rinascimento anteriore ai tempi del Magnifico*. Pisa: T. Nistri, 1891.

Herlihy, David. *Opera Mulieria: Women and Work in Medieval Europe*. New York: Mcgraw-Hill, 1990.

Jerome, Saint (345–420). "Letter 47; To Desiderius." *The Principal Works of Saint Jerome*. Trans. W. H. Fremantle, et al. A Select Library of Nicene and Post-Nicene Fathers. 2nd series, vol. 2. Grand Rapids MI: W. B. Eerdmans Co., 1954, 65–79.

Kempe, Margery (1373–1439). *The Book of Margery Kempe*. Trans. Barry Windeatt. New York: Viking Penguin, 1986.

King, Margaret L., and Albert Rabil, Jr. *Her Immaculate Hand: Selected Works by and about the Women Humanists of Quattrocento Italy*. Binghamton, NY: Medieval and Renaissance Texts and Studies, vol. 20, 1983.

Klein, Joan Larsen, ed. *Daughters, Wives, and Widows: Writings by Men* about *Women and Marriage in England, 1500–1640*. Urbana: University of Illinois Press, 1992.

Knox, John (1505–72). *The Political Writings of John Knox: The First Blast of the Trumpet against the Monstruous Regiment of Women and Other Selected Works*. Ed. Marvin A. Breslow. Washington: Folger Shakespeare Library, 1985.

Kors, Alan C., and Edward Peters, eds. *Witchcraft in Europe, 1100–1700: A Documentary History*. Philadelphia: University of Pennsylvania Press, 1972.

Krämer, Heinrich, and Jacob Sprenger. *Malleus Maleficarum* (ca. 1487). Trans. Montague Summers. London: The Pushkin Press, 1928; reprint, New York: Dover, 1971. The "Hammer of Witches" is a convenient source for all the misogynistic commonplaces on the eve of the sixteenth century, and an important text in the witch craze of the following centuries.

Le Vite de' Santi Padri insieme col prato spirituale, Descritte da San Girolamo. S. Athanasio, e da molti altri antichi Santi Padri. Venice: Pietro Milocco, 1644.

Legendario di Jacobus di Voragine. Ms. Newberry 24: Bartolemeo di Trento (?): thirteenth century.

Molinari, Cesare. *Spettacoli fiorentini del Quattrocento*. Venice: Neri Pozza Editore, 1961.

Petrarch, Francis. *Petrarch's Songbook: Rerum Vulgarium Fragmenta*. Trans. James Wyatt Cook. Intro. Germaine Warkentin. Binghamton, NY: Center for Medieval and Renaissance Texts, vol. 151, 1995.

Richa, Giuseppe. *Notizie istoriche delle chiese fiorentine*, vol. 5. Florence: Pietro Gaetano Viviani, 1757.

Rhodes, Dennis E. *Gli Annali Tipografici Fiorentini del XV Secolo*. Pref. Roberto Ridolfi. Florence: Leo S. Olschki Editore, 1988.

Spenser, Edmund (1552–99). *The Faerie Queene*. Ed. Thomas P. Roche, Jr. with the assistance of C. Patrick O'Donnell, Jr. New Haven: Yale University Press, 1978.

Teresa of Avilla, Saint (1515–82). *The Life of Teresa of Jesus: The Autobiography of St. Teresa of Avila*. Trans. and ed. E. Allison Peers. Garden City, NY: Image Books, 1960.

———. *Moradas (The Interior Castle)*. Trans. Kiernan Cavanaugh and Otilio Rodriguez. New York: Paulist Press, ca. 1979.

Vives, Juan Luis (1492–1540). *The Instruction of the Christian Woman*. Trans. Rycharde Hyrde. London, 1524, 1557.

von Bingen, Hildegard. *Harmonia Mundi Editions with Text of Hildegard von Bingen's Ordo Virtutem*. Ed. Peter Dronke. Oxford: Oxford University Press, 1970.

Weyer, Johann (1515–88). *Witches, Devils and Doctors in the Renaissance: Johann Weyer, De praestigiis daemonum*. Ed. George Mora with Benjamin G. Kohl, Erik Midelfort, and Helen Bacon. Trans. John Shea. Binghamton: Medieval and Renaissance Texts and Studies, 1991.

Wilson, Katharina M., ed. *Medieval Women Writers*. Athens, GA: University of Georgia Press, 1984.

———. *Women Writers of the Renaissance and Reformation*. Athens, GA: University of Georgia Press, 1987.

Wilson, Katharina M., and Frank J. Warnke, eds. *Women Writers of the Seventeenth Century*. Athens, GA: University of Georgia Press, 1989.

Secondary Works: Antonia Pulci and Florentine History

Cardini, Franco. "La Figura di Francesco D' Assisi nella *Rappresentatione di sancto Francesco* di Antonia Pulci, *Il francescanesimo e il teatro medievale*." Atti del Convegno Nazionale di Studi, San Miniato, 8–10 ottobre 1982. Castelfiorentino: Società Storica della Valdelsa, 1984.

Carrai, Stefano. "Lorenzo e L'umanismo volgare dei fratelli Pulci." In *Lorenzo De' Medici: New Perspectives*, ed. Bernard Toscani. Studies in Italian Culture, vol. 13. New York: Peter Lang, 1993.

Dronke, Peter. "Hildegard von Bingen." In *Women Writers of the Middle Ages*. Cambridge: Cambridge University Press, 1984, 144–201.

Eisenbichler, Konrad. "Confraternities and Carnival: The Context of Lorenzo de' Medici's *Rappresentazione di SS. Giovanni e Paolo*." *Comparative Drama* 27:1, 1993, 128–40.

Gill, Katherine. "Open Monasteries for Women in Late Medieval and Early Modern Italy: Two Roman Examples." In *The Crannied Wall: Women, Religion, and the Arts in Early Modern Europe*. Ed. Craig R. Monson. Ann Arbor: University of Michigan Press, 1995, 15–48.

Grendler, Paul F. *Schooling in Renaissance Italy: Literacy and Learning, 1300–1600*. Baltimore: Johns Hopkins University Press, 1989. See especially chapter eleven, "Learning Merchant Skills," 306–29.

———. "What Piero Learned in School: Fifteenth-Century Vernacular Education." In *Piero della Francesca and His Legacy*. Ed.

Marilyn Aronberg Levin. Studies in the History of Art 48. Center for Advanced Study in the Visual Arts, Symposium Papers XXVIII. Washington: National Gallery of Art, 1995, 161–74.

Kirschner, Julius, and Anthony Molho. "The Dowry Fund and the Marriage Market in Early Quattrocento Florence." JMH 50: 403–38.

McLaughlin, Mary Martin. "Creating and Recreating Communities of Women: The Case of Corpus Domini, Ferrara, 1406–52." *Signs* 14.2 (1989): 293–320.

Neel, Carol. "The Origin of the Beguines." *Signs* 14.2 (1989): 321–41.

Newbigin, Nerida, ed. *Nuovo Corpus di sacre rappresentazioni fiorentine.* Bologna: Commissione per i Testi di Lingua, 1983, xxviii–xxxix.

Rusconi, Roberto, ed. *Il movimento religioso femminile e francescanesimo nel secolo XIII.* Atti del Convegno internazionale, Assisi, 11–13 ottobre 1979. Assisi: Società internazionale di studi francescani, 1980.

———. *Il movimento religioso femminile in Umbria nei secoli XIII-XIV.* Atti del Convegno internazionale di studio nel ambito delle celebrazione per L'VIII centenario della nascità di S. Francesco d'Assisi, Citta di Castello, 27–29 ottobre 1982. Quaderni de Centro per il Collegamento degli Studi Medievali e Umanistici nell'Università de Perugia, vol. 12. Florence and Perugia: Regione dell'Umbria e La Nuova Editrice, 1984.

Trexler, Richard C. "Le Célebat à fin du Moyen Age: le règieuses de Florence." *Annales*: ESC 27: 1329–50.

Ulysse, Georges. "Les femmes écrivains en Italie au Moyen Âge et à la Renaissance." *Actes du colloque international Aix-en-Provence, 12–14 novembre 1992.* Aix-en-Provence: Universitè de Provence, 1994.

Weaver, Elissa. "The Convent Wall in Tuscan Drama." In *The Crannied Wall: Women, Religion, and the Arts in Early Modern Europe.* Ed. Craig A. Monson. Ann Arbor: University of Michigan Press, 1995, 73–86.

Weissman, Ronald F. E. *Ritual Brotherhood in Renaissance Florence.* New York and London: Academic Press, 1982.

Secondary Works: The Misogynist Tradition

Bloch, R. Howard. *Medieval Misogyny and the Invention of Western Romantic Love.* Chicago: University of Chicago Press, 1991.

Clark, Elizabeth A. *Ascetic Piety and Women's Faith: Essays on Late Ancient Christianity.* Lewiston, NY: Edwin Mellen Press, 1986.

Dixon, Suzanne. *The Roman Family*. Baltimore: Johns Hopkins University Press, 1992.

Gardner, Jane F. *Women in Roman Law and Society*. Bloomington: Indiana University Press, 1986.

Horowitz, Maryanne Cline. "Aristotle and Woman." *Journal of the History of Biology* 9 (1976): 183–213.

Lerner, Gerda. *The Creation of Patriarchy*. New York: Oxford University Press, 1986.

Lochrie, Karma. *Margery Kempe and Translations of the Flesh*. Philadelphia: University of Pennsylvania Press, 1992.

Maclean, Ian. *The Renaissance Notion of Woman: A Study of the Fortunes of Scholasticism and Medical Science in European Intellectual Life*. Cambridge: Cambridge University Press, 1980.

Okin, Susan Moller. *Women in Western Political Thought*. Princeton: Princeton University Press, 1979.

Pagels, Elaine. *Adam, Eve, and the Serpent*. New York: Harper Collins, 1988.

Pomeroy, Sarah B. *Goddesses, Whores, Wives, and Slaves: Women in Classical Antiquity*. New York: Schocken Books, 1976.

Sommerville, Margaret R. *Sex and Subjectivity: Attitudes to Women in Early-Modern Society*. London: Arnold, 1995.

Tetel, Marcel. *Marguerite de Navarre's Heptameron: Themes, Language & Structure*. Durham, NC: Duke University Press, 1973.

Treggiari, Susan. *Roman Marriage: Iusti Coniuges from the Time of Cicero to the Time of Ulpian*. Oxford: Oxford University Press, 1991.

Walsh, William T. *St. Teresa of Avila: A Biography*. Rockford, IL: TAN Books & Publications, 1987.

Warner, Marina. *Alone of All Her Sex: The Myth and the Cult of the Virgin Mary*. New York: Knopf, 1976.

Secondary Works: The Other Voice

Beilin, Elaine V. *Redeeming Eve: Women Writers of the English Renaissance*. Princeton: Princeton University Press, 1987.

Benson, Pamela Joseph. *The Invention of Renaissance Woman: The Challenge of Female Independence in the Literature and Thought of Italy and England*. University Park: Pennsylvania State University Press, 1992.

Davis, Natalie Zemon. *Society and Culture in Early Modern France*. Stanford:

Stanford University Press, 1975. See especially chapters 3 and 5.

Ferguson, Margaret W., Maureen Quilligan, and Nancy J. Vickers, eds. *Rewriting the Renaissance: The Discourses of Sexual Difference in Early Modern Europe.* Chicago: University of Chicago Press, 1987.

Herlihy, David. "Did Women Have a Renaissance? A Reconsideration." *Medievalia et Humanistica,* n.s. 13 (1985): 1–22.

History of Women in the West, A. Vol. 1, *From Ancient Goddesses to Christian Saints.* Ed. Pauline Schmitt Pantel. Cambridge, MA: Harvard University Press, 1992.

———. Vol. 2, *Silences of the Middle Ages.* Ed. Christiane Klapisch-Zuber. Cambridge: Harvard University Press, 1992.

———. Vol. 3, *Renaissance and Enlightenment Paradoxes.* Ed. Natalie Zemon Davis and Arlette Farge. Cambridge: Harvard University Press, 1993.

Hull, Suzanne W. *Chaste, Silent, and Obedient: English Books for Women, 1475–1640.* San Marino, CA: The Huntington Library, 1982.

Jordan, Constance. *Renaissance Feminism: Literary Texts and Political Models.* Ithaca: Cornell University Press, 1990.

Kelly, Joan. "Did Women Have a Renaissance?" In *Women, History and Theory.* Chicago: University of Chicago Press, 1984. Also in Renate Bridenthal, Claudia Koonz, and Susan M. Stuard, eds. *Becoming Visible: Women in European History.* 2nd ed. Boston: Houghton Mifflin, 1987, 175–202.

———. "Early Feminist Theory and the *Querelle des Femmes.*" In *Women, History and Theory.*

Kelso, Ruth. *Doctrine for the Lady of the Renaissance.* Foreword by Katharine M. Rogers. Urbana: University of Illinois Press, 1956, 1978.

King, Margaret L. *Women of the Renaissance.* Foreword by Catharine R. Stimpson. Chicago: University of Chicago Press, 1991.

Laqueur, Thomas. *Making Sex: Body and Gender from the Greeks to Freud.* Cambridge, MA: Harvard University Press, 1990.

Lerner, Gerda. *Creation of Feminist Consciousness, 1000–1870.* New York: Oxford University Press, 1994.

Maclean, Ian. *Woman Triumphant: Feminism in French Literature, 1610–1652.* Oxford: Clarendon Press, 1977.

Matter, E. Ann, and John Coakley, eds. *Creative Women in Medieval and Early Modern Italy.* Philadelphia: University of Pennsylvania Press,

1994. (Sequel to Monson's collection)

Monson, Craig A., ed. *The Crannied Wall: Women, Religion, and the Arts in Early Modern Europe.* Ann Arbor: University of Michigan Press, 1992.

Rose, Mary Beth, ed. *Women in the Middle Ages and the Renaissance: Literary and Historical Perspectives.* Syracuse: Syracuse University Press, 1986.

Stuard, Susan M. "The Dominion of Gender: Women's Fortunes in the High Middle Ages." In Renate Bridental, Claudia Koonz, and Susan M. Stuard, eds., *Becoming Visible: Women in European History.* 2nd ed. Boston: Houghton Mifflin, 1987, 153–72.

Wiesner, Merry E. *Women and Gender in Early Modern Europe.* Cambridge: Cambridge University Press, 1993.

Willard, Charity Cannon. *Christine de Pizan: Her Life and Works.* New York: Persea Books, 1984.

Wilson, Katharina, ed. *An Encyclopedia of Continental Women Writers.* New York: Garland, 1991.

Women Writers in English 1350–1850: 30 volumes projected, 8 published through 1995. Oxford: Oxford University Press.

THE PLAY OF SAINT FRANCIS
COMPOSED BY LADY ANTONIA,
WIFE OF BERNARDO PULCI

[Someone speaks the prologue.]

    O Jesus, my Redeemer from on high,
If any prayer of mine you have approved,
Now for your charity, for your great love,
Set your sweet fire within my breast so I
Can show most fervently to everyone,
The pious story and great miracles
Of Francis, your high servant, your elect.   8
Attend devoutly all you with hearts sincere.
    And, Virgin Mary, you, elect in heaven,
Who's seated at the right hand of your Son,
Inflame and set alight my fantasy
With your good counsel and your aid divine
So that, unfraught with peril, my small boat
Can reach the harbor; for all sinners you
Are the firm and steadfast column, and you are
The queen and lady of heaven and of earth.[1]   16
    Because it would require too long to tell
His every miracle and holy life,
I therefore wish to show a part of it,

---

1. This stanza borrows from Petrarch the images of the small boat reaching harbor and the phrasing of the characterization of the Virgin. The earliest known editions of *St. Francis* are the Miscomini edition of 1490 and another printed by Bartolemeo de Libri about the same time. Cioni lists only one sixteenth-century edition, that printed in Florence by the Giunti in 1559. The life of St. Francis was widely known and circulated both as oral tradition and as hagiography. The incidents in Pulci's version are not those of *The Golden Legend*. Visitors to Assisi today will hear many of the same stories from the tour guides.

Portray his righteous, boundless charity,
The way he chose to scorn the world to have
Repose at his departure, caring not
For any pleasure of the world because he had
Devoted every thought of his to God.   24

While St. Francis is at his desk, a poor man comes and asks for alms, and St. Francis, being busy, chases him away:
Good sir, a little charity for God,
Let this decrepit fellow thank you for.

St. Francis says:
Do not disturb me; ah, go you with God,
Do you not see how busy I am now?

The poor man says to St. Francis:
O me, unfortunate, I should be dead,
For I am treated thus by everyone;
Lord of heaven, pity take on me,
Give to me my true well-being at least.   32

St. Francis says to himself:
O stingy one, why did you drive away
That feeble pauper with such wrath intense
When you should feel just pity, seeing him?
Forgive me Jesus, my sweet Lord, for that.

St. Francis says to the poor man:
Take this, companion dear and brother good,
For I have greatly erred in ousting you.

The poor man says:
For me, may God reward you, my good sir,
Since, afterwards, I cannot pay you back.   40

Going to St. Damian's, St. Francis falls on his knees before the crucifix and says:
O righteous Lord, who on the cross was nailed
For me, your precious blood immaculate
I see pour down to wash me clean again,
An undeserving sinner, mean and vile.

The crucifix says to St. Francis:
> My temple's fallen, Francis, into ruin
> Indeed; rise up at once and set it right;
> Put into practice what I say to you,
> For you shall be the doer of much good.　　　　48

Having heard the crucifix speak, St. Francis comes to and says to himself:
> Such sweetness great I feel within my heart,
> O boundless God, I cannot speak of it,
> For, with no grief, are you surpassing Joy;
> The sweet gifts of your words you've made me hear.
> I shall restore your temple eagerly—
> I shall because I wish to heed just you.
> Pray, let me travel only in your way,
> And let my will remain therein content.　　　　56

St. Francis, having gone home, secretly gets money together and goes to St. Damian's and, once there, tells the priest of that church how he wants to restore it and offers him the money:
> May God prolong your life, O priest. I wish
> To speak together with you, if you please,
> For I long urgently to build again
> This church of God, thus fallen into ruin,
> Because it is my Lord's commandment that
> This temple by my hands shall be rebuilt.
> This money, Father, take from me and see
> This temple reconstructed with it, please.　　　　64

Refusing the money, the priest says to him:
> My son, oh, if your father only knew
> That you would wish to do a thing like this
> And that I took this money from you, he
> Would certainly deprive me of my life.
> Don't even think that I would keep it here,
> For undertaking such an enterprise.
> I'm very grateful for your company,
> But I don't want this money; take it hence!　　　　72

St. Francis throws the money away and says to himself:
> I set no value, my sweet Lord, upon
> Whatever riches this vain world may own;

True Lover of my soul, I only wish
To follow you and for your Love endure
Each harshness; make me the victor in
This enterprise. Your sweetness set within
My heart; I'll throw away this money for
My only longing is to follow you.   80

A friend goes to St. Francis's father and speaks thus:
Be advised that I just found your son
Who had a lot of money with him, and
I went behind him, and I followed him,
So I could find out what he meant to do—
To leave this money at St. Damian's
Because he wished to reconstruct that church.
What I have seen I tell you willingly,
Because you've always been my closest friend.   88

The father of St. Francis says:
Oh wretched me! Alas, what you have said!
It's just enough to be the death of me!
This wayward, cursèd son of mine! No cause
Has he, indeed, to treat me in this way!
If I can find him, I give you my word
That I shall beat him, and without restraint;
I'll make him give my money back to me,
And, like a rogue, send him away from me.   96

While searching for St. Francis, his father says:
Where shall I find again this villain who
Has robbed me of my money? who for me
Was in an evil hour born? I shall perhaps
Soon cure you of this woeful madness,
Ungrateful for so many benefits,
You'd throw away what I have sweated for!
Just wait until I get my hands on you;
For all your foolish thoughts, you'll get your due.   104

Hidden in a ditch and seeing his father coming, St. Francis, addressing God, says:
O Jesus, righteous Lord, defend me as
You did your Jacob when from Esau and
His awful wrath you rescued him, and as

You Daniel saved, so kindle me with your
Sweet love, for each chaste thought of mine
Is fixed on you. I pray that you'll become
My shield, and be my escort and my guide,
Sweet Lord, in whom my heart sets all its trust.   112

*Coming forth from the ditch, St. Francis turns toward Asissi, and, as he walks, to
himself says this:*
Wretch, why now are you staying hidden thus?
Why aren't you pleased to come forth from this place?
Not to be found in this life is your rest,
So why then fear your father's threats,
And why do you remain so anxious? I
Desire to go and find him, face to face,
So he may do with me what pleases him;
I only seek, my Lord, to find your peace.   120

*St. Francis, having arrived at the piazza of Assisi and being thought a fool, was
scorned by many, and one, seeing him ill dressed and throwing filth and stones at him,
says this:*
He certainly must be a lunatic;
You wretched oaf! From what place have you sprung?

Another likewise scorns him and says:
Do you enjoy thus being wrapped in rags?
And have you of your senses taken leave?

A friend of St. Francis's father says that he will go and tell the father:
His father has, alas, looked everywhere
For him in these days since he fled; now that
He's here I shall go and report to him,
For he, I know, will make him leave this place.   128

And when he has come before St. Francis's father, he says:
Know that your son's in the piazza now,
And everyone's amused at him because
He is behaving like a lunatic,
And many folk line up to gawk at him.

St. Francis's father says:
If this club doesn't break within my hands,

I'll make him pay for such a grievous lapse.
Ah woe, this sin's unfortunate for me.
My money first, my honor now, I've lost.   136

The father, having found St. Francis in the square, and pushing him into the house,
says to him:
You fool and lunatic, I've caught you now.
Ah cursèd be the day that you were born,
For although you're my son, you've ruined me.
With much care and expense I reared you up;
With such a treatment shall I pay you back
That you will fall down prostrate at my feet.
You get inside you ugly little thief,
My goods and your brains, too, you've fooled away.   144

His father imprisons him and says:
Since you have brought this evil on yourself,
And fortune wishes that it should be thus,
This prison will remain your home as long
As my life shall endure. Now get inside,
And take my curses with you; here you may,
Together with your madness, pine away.

And addressing his servants, he says:
But bread and water, nothing let him have;
And do not bring me any news of him.   152

St. Francis's mother goes to the prison, and, opening the cage for him, says:
Sweet son, I feel surpassing sorrow that
I see you being punished in this way;
Your father's action grieves me greatly for,
Because of you, I feel life drain away.
You know, indeed, I have no one but you,
And so I am resolved to set you free.
Be careful that your father does not find
You, son, for he's exceedingly enraged.   160

Having come out of prison, St. Francis says to his mother:
O, do not grieve for me, my mother sweet,
For by this human life I set no store,
Nor by the threats my father makes to me.
So quickly do we all depart from here,

I only think about things joyful and
About surpassing glory infinite;
As much as I'm derided in the world,
So much shall I be welcomed up in heaven.   168

St. Francis's father returns home, and finding that his mother has let him flee, speaks to
her and departs in search of him:
　　　Alas that you have played the fool, gone mad,
　　　Is this the help that you would give to me?
　　　Do you not think about the shame you've caused?
　　　Oh, woe is me that you have let him go!
　　　You see that he has bankrupted my house,
　　　It would be right to make you search for him;
　　　If I can find him, since you love him so,
　　　With violent rage I'll tear him into bits!   176

St. Francis, seeing his enraged father coming toward him, says:
　　　Though Father's coming, I won't be afraid,
　　　Because my Lord has so inflamed me and
　　　Has made my mind feel so secure that I
　　　Am not concerned though I may tortured be.

Approaching St. Francis, his father says:
　　　Beware if you would make a fool of me!
　　　At my unlucky hour were you born!
　　　You scoundrel, let me have my money back,
　　　And only keep your madness for yourself.   184

Giving him his money, St. Francis says to his father:
　　　I do not value riches, Father, nor
　　　The gold or silver of this wretched world.
　　　I think but on the lofty sweetness of
　　　My Lord who is in the eternal choir
　　　Up there where all the highest joys abide,
　　　Where every treasure, surely, one can find;
　　　Take here the money I return to you
　　　Because I mean to follow my Lord now.   192

St. Francis's father leads him before the bishop to make him renounce his inheritance,
and says:
　　　Since you intend to disobey me thus,

With me I'd have you to the bishop come,
And in his presence wish to have you say
How you no longer count yourself my son.

St. Francis says to his father:
I'm very happy thus to come with you,
And every pact and contract I shall make
With you that I'll no more be called your son.
For serving Jesus is my sole desire.   200

Having come before the bishop, St. Francis's father explains that he wants to disinherit him:
May the true God, Reverend Father, always be
With you. Please understand my wish,
For I desire to disinherit him,
Truly the cause of every woe of mine,
Because, to me, he's always wayward been
And wicked. Let the consequence of that
Content him, since my fortune wants it thus;
Explain to us how thus it may be done.   208

St. Francis agrees and, first addressing his father, speaks to the bishop thus:
I'm happy to relinquish everything
Both good paternity and all my rights,
My whole inheritance I would refuse,
Since this is my intention and I wish
In your good presence to unclothe myself,
And Father, you will here bear witness that
I strip myself of each paternal good
To gain the highest and eternal realm.   216

The bishop, once St. Francis's father has left, is moved with compassion for him, makes him reclothe himself, and says:
Arise, O Francis, my belovèd son,
For I will with my mantle cover you:
I pity you because you're just a boy.

And addressing his servants he speaks thus:
My servants, go and bring some clothing here.

And, addressing St. Francis, he says:
Hold fast, my son, for you are blest, and we

Shall yet be hearing wondrous things of you.
So follow closely your intended plan,
And with my benediction go from here.   224

After leaving the bishop, St. Francis speaks thus to himself:
No ship has with a better wind reached port
Nor with a surer pilot at the helm;
For that, how joyful I've become, how glad,
Since every worldly pomp I've left behind;
And such great joy I feel within my heart,
For all my intellect's aflame, indeed,
For with the cross's sign I'll arm myself
Once I've sloughed off the vain world's misery.   232

While St. Francis is walking along, one of his comrades discovers him and reclothes him, and says:
O my good fellow, you're the very man,
On what account are you undressed like this?

St. Francis answers:
Know that the true God wishes that, by me,
The foolish world should be disparaged so.

St. Francis's comrade says to him:
I greatly long to clothe you once again;
Pray, take this garment if it pleases you.

St. Francis answers:
Most happily do I receive it, and
I pray you, right now let me have a rope.   240

Reclothed and belted with the rope, St. Francis says to himself:
This will be my decorative garb,
This rope will be my belt, and penitence
My every celebration will become,
As long as in this world my life shall last.
O righteous God, what lofty grace this is,
Because your sweetness ravishes my heart.[2]

2. Compare Petrarch, *Rerum* 23.71–72.

And in parting he says to his comrade:
>O my belovèd brother, go with God,
>To God, through me, you do such charity.   248

After St. Francis returns to Assisi, a gentleman named Master Bernardo of Assisi, who had already had news of St. Francis's good life, invites him to come to stay at his house:
>Let me beseech you for a grace most singular:
>Into my home today, please come; repose
>With me because I would confer about
>A private matter of my own with you.

St. Francis answers Master Bernardo:
>I'd surely not refuse you such a grace
>Because some good may follow from it and
>Because the wellspring may my coming be
>Of some work worthy, honorable, and good.   256

Master Bernardo tells St. Francis how, inspired by God, he desires to become a religious and his companion:
>Know that the righteous God has touched my heart
>Through good examples and your holy life
>So much that I'm beside myself, indeed,
>And, therefore, I've resolved to take my leave
>From this blind world, so full of error false,
>And to your boundless love I only pray
>That as its servant low it will accept
>And honor me, and not this sinner scorn.   264

St. Francis accepts Master Bernardo and says:
>I cannot tell you how much happiness
>And joy your words have given me because
>You have revealed to me your inner wish
>To serve forever Jesus Christ, and if
>It's your desire to do this perfectly,
>Then be apprised that you must parcel out
>Among God's poor your every treasure if
>You want the peace of the eternal choir.   272

Master Bernardo tells St. Francis that together they should distribute his goods to the poor:
>Father, I pray you, let it please you to

Distribute with me to the poor of God
My every luxury and all my wealth,
For I have a compelling wish to serve
And go along in company with you
And sweetly end my life, O Father mine.
Do with this money what you will because
My only wish is searching for true peace.   280

St. Francis takes some of Master Bernardo's money and gives it to the poor of God, saying:
You poor, decrepit ones, this money take
So that you can sustain your lives with it.

One poor man says:
For this, Christ will reward you, Father,
And may he give you merit up in heaven.

Another poor man says to his comrades:
My friends, take note of what is going on;
I see much charity in progress here,
I want to go at once and leave my drink,[3]
Come on, my friend, and bring your little sack.   288

A poor man says to St. Francis:
O holy Father, do us some small good,
For we're abandoned, useless, and infirm,
And in great suffering our lives we'll end,
And be tormented by appalling woes,
In giving it to these, you've not done well,
Because, soon, they'll have gambled it away;
O, holy Father, please give it to us,
And we shall always pray to God for you.   296

St. Francis, having already gathered together twelve companions from various places, addresses them to teach them to follow the doctrine of the gospel and says this:
We have so many brought together, indeed,
That I see God wants us to multiply,
Oh my sweet sons belovèd, full of grace,

3. Ital. *barletto*—little barrel or cask.

Your intellects lift up unto our God,[4]
And do not let yourselves ungrateful be,
But praise him for such generosity.
With pure intentions and with perfect zeal,
His holy gospel see that you observe.   304

St. Francis continues:
His peace, my sons, you must go forth to preach,
And penitence for the remission of
One's sins, and constant you must be in your
Afflictions every one, and must be strong,
And ever in your praying, persevere;
In every work, be prudent and be wise,
And in your manner serious and chaste,
And all must clear and cleanse their consciences.   312

He next tells them how he wishes to go to the Pope to have the [Franciscan] order approved:
My cherished brothers, I've been inspired by God
That we must to our Holy Father go;
He only can approve all that which we
Do customarily among ourselves,
As in my sermon I've instructed you
About our diligent observance of
The gospels' lofty teachings, my sweet sons,
And you must come and keep me company.   320

One of the disciples answers for all the others:
We are content, O Father, to obey
Your will, and all you tell us to, we'll do,
Such sweetness it has given us to hear
With you the holy stories, and the precepts good;
And every place we wish to come with you
And ever be your subjects, for with love
Divine you have us so inflamed that we
Hold ourselves blessèd in obeying you.   328

They go to the Holy Father, and having arrived St. Francis speaks thus:
Most blessèd Father and my lord, I have

4. Compare Petrarch, *Rerum* 10.9, 264.8, and 360.89.

Into your presence come so that you may
Assent to my desire; I hope you're not
Put out by granting me this audience.

The Pope says:
You pitiable wretch, go you with God;
You have my leave to go back as you will.

St. Francis, addressing his companions, says:
My sons, we must not be upset by this.
It is not time to ask for such a grace. 336

St. Francis prays to God, asking that the Pope grant his request:
Just as Assuerus answered Esther's prayer,
And through her was the populace set free,
O just God, through your mercy infinite
Let the Holy Father hear my prayer,
It's certain, nothing's done without your help,
You must not look upon my heavy sin;
Make your pastor understand my wish
And me the victor in my enterprise. 344

The Pope, having thrown St. Francis out, repents of what he had done and to himself says this:
Too great an error, driving him away
I've made; he seems a man of holy life.

And turning to a servant says:
Have him called back, for in my heart I have
Resolved all his requests shall granted be.

The Pope's servant answers:
Most blessèd Father and good pastor, I
Shall instantly obey your will in this.

The servant, having reached St. Francis, says to him:
Poor fellow, to the Holy Father go,
And every grace from him you shall obtain. 352

When St. Francis reaches the Pope, the Pope speaks thus:
Ask fervently for that which pleases you.

Know that, since you can any grace request
Of me, my mind entirely is made up
To want to satisfy your every wish.

St. Francis again asks the Pope that he approve his order, showing him its rule written down:

O Holy Father, I pray again that you
Will give us your approval for this now,
For it is our desire to follow it,
Set forth in gospel with great mystery.   360

The Pope takes the written rule from St. Francis and shows it to the cardinals, to whom it seems too harsh, and one of them tells the Pope that he should not approve it:

We've never heard of such a rule before,
We're sure no one could ever follow it;
O Holy Father, it's too harsh a life,
Do not for anything consent to it.

The Pope speaks thus:

Let that be as it may, for, firmly and
Immovably, I don't wish to deny him this.

The cardinal answers:

You can do anything as pastor, but
Be careful that you don't too greatly err.   368

Another cardinal gives advice opposite to that of the first:

If we belittle, Holy Father, the
Request of this poor fellow, have a care
That we do not offend our God. To me
It seems that it would do a grace to God
Were we to contemplate the life of Christ,
It won't be wrong to grant him this request.

The Pope, addressing St. Francis, says:

Every desire of yours will be fulfilled;
Go hence in peace; the Lord lend you his aid.   376

The Pope continues speaking to St. Francis:

I also give you, Francis, license full
To preach throughout the world and sinners call
To penitence; through you God wishes to

Make manifest great wonders, and to such
Devotion has your presence stirred me that
It seems you can disseminate the faith
For me; I grant you this and every grace,
I'm only pleased to gratify your wish.   384

*St. Francis tells his companions to give God thanks and next declares that he wants to
go to preach to the sultan.*
My sons, to our God render thanks because
He's made us worthy of so great a gift,
And you must preach his holy gospel, and
Must clearly demonstrate for everyone
The way for rising to the highest realms—
And some of you are worthy this to do.
My wish is still to go to Babylon,
And one day I shall follow this desire.   392

One of his companions answers:
O Holy Father, we are always pleased
That we are able to fulfill your wish.
However, know that I am quite prepared
To keep you company in any place,
For I consider myself blest to be
With you. Now we can travel as you wish.

St. Francis says:
Our God so great will keep me company,
Belovèd sons, upon this sacred path.   400

Going before the sultan, St. Francis prays to God:
O righteous God, may you be pleased to grant
Your simple sinner's prayers: O may my prayer,
Redeemer in the highest, find its way
Into your presence, and may you be pleased
To open wide their intellectual eyes
So that these Saracens, who *will* persist
In such great error, O supernal God,
You'll worthy make of your eternal realm.   408

*St. Francis, having arrived in Babylon and seeing some enraged Saracens coming
toward him, says to his companion:*
Let us, my brother, in the Lord rejoice,

And let us render him unceasing thanks;
And willingly, for his love merciful,
In peace each torture we shall suffer, for
I see them coming toward us so enraged;
But we must not, indeed, have any fear
Of being beaten or abused by them,
For we shall be more blessèd up in heaven.   416

St. Francis continues:

Let's think about the way our God was scourged
For us ungrateful sinners miserable,
And of the cruel thorns they crowned him with,
His righteous blood that he poured forth for us
On that unyielding wood where he was nailed.
Their wicked hearts may good become if we
For love of him, O my belovèd son,
Can bear in silence every torment harsh.   424

A Saracen, coming up to St. Francis, says:

What are you doing in our midst, false Christians?
The interdiction you must not have heard,
For here we torture knavish curs like you.
You certainly have made a foolish choice
In having brought yourselves into our hands.

[To another Saracen, aside:]

(Look you how bold and ready this one is!)
You will be brought before our sultan now;
That you have ever come here, you'll regret.   432

A servant leads them before the sultan and says to his lord:

To you these evildoers I present,
These wicked, cursèd, ingrate Christians who
Are ridiculers of our faith, and who
Most certainly deserve to tortured be,
Perverse and cursed and deceitful men,
Who have ignored your interdiction, sir.
Let them be punished in your presence here,
So little deference to you they've shown.   440

The sultan says to St. Francis:
>   How is it that you have arrived, poor chap,
>   Within these parts? Explain to me the cause.

St. Francis answers:
>   Know that I have been sent a messenger,
>   Inspired divinely, just to you from God,
>   Because enlightened shall you, sultan, be
>   About the holy faith by me so you
>   Won't go to hell because you heed your sect,
>   Mohammed's false and wicked faith accursed.   448

St. Francis continues speaking to the sultan:
>   From nothing did the true God make the earth,
>   The heavens, and all the universe, and for
>   His charity and his zeal consummate,
>   He wished to live among us mortal folk,
>   Only so he could lift death's darksome veil
>   From us; for our first parents' heinous sin
>   Was each of us to the inferno damned,
>   Because they'd tasted the forbidden fruit.   456

St. Francis continues:
>   He chose, too, from a virgin to take flesh,
>   And free us wholly from such evil great
>   And with his word proclaim what each one of
>   The prophets had predicted; and he wished
>   To taste both death and suffering upon
>   The cross where he was crucified for us.
>   Then, after the third day, restored to life,
>   In his supernal glory rose to heaven.   464

St. Francis continues to the sultan, speaking thus:
>   For certain, sultan, credit what I've said;
>   For my God's faith is true and is assured,
>   And do not longer wish Mohammed's faith
>   To follow, for your faith is surely vain.
>   Let Jesus, a perfect Lord, reveal the way
>   Of his salvation open wide to all who wish
>   To follow it; will you [therefore] consent
>   That I may now baptize you [in his faith]?   472

St. Francis continues:

>If it seems hard for you to leave your faith
>And to believe that you should follow mine,
>I wish to clear away your every doubt,
>So I shall have a witness come to you:
>A priest of yours and I will enter fire,
>And if I chance to die, impute it to
>My sins, but if I should escape, then you
>Must in the Son of Mary put your faith.   480

The sultan says to St. Francis:

>For my Mohammed, no one could suggest
>That he would wish to suffer any pain,
>For what you ask to see could not be done,
>I don't think anyone would go in fire.
>Know, Father, that I should be pleased to believe
>In your God if I saw my people wished
>To follow me, for were I able to
>Obey you, it would gratify me so.   488

The sultan continues:

>I willingly would baptized be, except
>I am afraid of persecution by
>This crazy, wicked populace so that,
>For now, I don't intend to do it since
>The time that would be right for doing it
>Would not be now because it surely would
>Bring on your murder, mine as well
>By this accursèd, wicked populace.   496

The sultan continues:

>O Francis, long may you remain with me,
>For I've not filled my heart with seeing you,
>And with great pleasure do I see you, for
>Great is my desire to see you and
>To hear you speak. Take these my treasures and
>Pass them out among your poor of God.

St. Francis to the sultan:

>Your treasure, sultan, I do not esteem;
>I only seek that of the eternal choir.   504

Addressing his companion, St. Francis says:
>O my dear son, let us depart this place;
>Because his heart's so hard, my sermons don't
>Avail with him at all, and it may be
>That righteous God is saving him
>Until another time, and so I wish
>To go again amongst our baptized folk.
>I hope we may produce some worthy fruit
>With that one's help who governs everything.   512

A servant tells Master Orlando how St. Francis has arrived in that place, that is near
La Vernia, at one of his castles:
>Sir, know that here the holy man has come
>Who has so famous grown throughout the world
>That you have greatly yearned to look on him,
>And Francis is the name one calls him by.

Master Orlando says to the servant:
>Go, servant, tell him how he'd please me if
>He came to stay and rest awhile with me,
>For I shall gain great pleasure seeing him.

The servant answers Master Orlando:
>Good sir, your will at once shall be performed.   520

The servant, having come to St. Francis, speaks to him, requesting that he come to
Master Orlando's house:
>That true God whom the universe adores
>Save and preserve your Holiness; each work
>Of yours inspires us through your infinite
>And lofty goodness. Father, be advised:
>My master who dwells here requests that you,
>Because of your compassion, will be pleased
>To come pay him a visit at his home
>Because he greatly longs to look on you.   528

St. Francis answers the servant:
>I willingly shall go along with you
>To see your noble master; since he finds
>My presence pleases him, my every thought
>I shall address to doing what he asks.

Having come to Master Orlando, St. Francis says this:
    May he who wished from Mary to take flesh
    Preserve and save you, noble gentleman,
    And may he grant you long and tranquil life,
    And, at your parting, grant eternal rest.   536

Master Orlando answers St. Francis and says:
    That I might see you with my very eyes
    In person, Father excellent, indeed,
    I long have wished. You do me too much grace
    That through your clemency you deign to spend
    Some days with me. And I, since reverence
    So great I feel for you, account myself
    But blest, O matchless Father. Grant this grace:
    Stay here with me and so fulfill my wish.   544

Master Orlando continues to St. Francis:
    It has occurred to me if, Father, you
    Might in my region wish to stay, I own
    A mountain here quite suitable for prayer,
    That I wish fervently to give to you,
    And, Father, my opinion surely is
    That it's just right for contemplating God.

St. Francis to Master Orlando:
    Master Orlando, let's go see it for
    I feel a great desire to look at it.   552

Master Orlando speaks to St. Francis, and they go to Mount Vernia:
    Belovèd Father, willingly I'll go
    Along with you and show to you the way
    And I, with pure intent, pray righteous God
    That he'll be pleased to grant my wish and that
    You'll find the mountain town acceptable
    For being near you is my heart's sole wish.

St. Francis to Master Orlando:
    Good sir, this mountain's dedicated to
    And right for prayer because it's so remote.   560

On arriving at Mount Vernia, St. Francis says to his companions:
    Belovèd sons, I certainly believe

This place has been prepared for us by our
Redeemer, just and merciful. A mighty sign
Has been revealed to us by him. Observe
With what festivity these people all
Invite us to remain in this locale.

Addressing Master Orlando, St. Francis says:
　　I give you thanks, O noble gentleman;
　　This mountain, too, I gratefully accept.　　　　　　568

St. Francis addresses Brother Leo, saying:
　　I mean to isolate myself from you, my son,
　　Upon this mountain to restore myself;
　　Keep watch so no one may disturb me, then.

And [still] addressing Brother Leo, he says:
　　Take heed, O Brother Leo, of my wish:
　　Come far enough with me to sing a psalm,
　　And when at prayer you see me, then turn back,
　　And do not come into my presence there,
　　And do not, in my praying, hinder me.　　　　　　576

Standing upon the mountain in prayer, St. Francis asks God for the grace of the stigmata:
　　Two graces, righteous God, I ask of you
　　Before I leave this world: the first, let me
　　Feel in my body and within my heart
　　How great the boundless sorrow was that you
　　Endured with cruel torment on the cross
　　So you could give eternal life to us;
　　The other, that I see the boundless love
　　That could in silence suffer so much pain.　　　　　584

God, as a Seraphim, answers St. Francis, marking him with the stigmata:
　　Since you have been my cherished servant, I
　　Wish to renew in you my suffering,
　　Because with pure intent you have served me,
　　Therefore I want to show you, Francis, how
　　Acceptable you've always been to me.
　　I wish to decorate you with my wounds.
　　No deed like this was ever done before—

For such a great gift, prized throughout the world.   592

Having received the stigmata and seen God in the sign of the crucifix, St. Francis
thanks him saying this:
    I'm full of sorrow, and I'm filled with joy,
    My Lord, at having seen you bear upon
    The cross for me, ungrateful sinner vile
    And wicked, such affliction great. You have
    So with your sweetness kindled me, O God,
    Redeemer righteous, O Eternal One.
    Because you've made me worthy of such grace,
    My will can't get enough of praising you.   600

St. Francis continues thanking God:
    As much as I am able, Lord, with all
    My heart, I render to Your Majesty
    My thanks for such great charity, such love
    As you have shown me through your mercy, God,
    In changing yourself into me, sweet Lord.
    O everlasting Father, Good divine,
    My thirst for thanking you cannot be quenched
    O my Eternal Savior, Jesus mine.   608

St. Francis says to his brothers how he wishes to depart to go to St. Mary of the Angels
and commends to them Mount Vernia:
    O my sweet sons, pay heed a while to me:
    You know that I must go away from you,
    I wish with consummate desire that you'll
    Keep safe upon this holy mountain where
    You dwell, and where surpassing happiness
    I have received. Dear sons, I cannot tell
    You certainly what memory will call
    This place where God revealed his majesty.   616

St. Francis continues to his brothers:
    My sons, pray listen to my words a while
    And understand that I desire to go
    Unto St. Mary's place. I wish to go
    At once, and with no more delay. I pray
    You, nonetheless, that it will please you to
    Desire to satisfy my will in this.

One brother responds for all:
>Your every wish we'll quickly satisfy,
>Just to obey you is our highest grace.   624

The brothers, having prepared a donkey, set him on it to carry him to St. Mary of the Angels and they lead along with them the owner of the donkey—that is, a peasant.[5]
>Climb up, O Father, on this burro's back,
>And in the name of God let's take our way.
>We've borrowed him from this poor fellow here,
>And we'll take him along to give us aid.

St. Francis to his companions:
>Sweet sons, let us to that unbounded God
>Give thanks and let us bear in peace
>This cruel cold for love of him alone
>Who spilled his righteous blood on our account.   632

That peasant, unable to walk because of the cold, entrusts himself to St. Francis, saying:
>Alas I feel my life is weakening
>For this harsh cold, poor wretch unfortunate,
>I cannot travel on for anything,
>Alas, ah me, I feel the pangs of death.

St. Francis, having dismounted from the donkey and having touched the peasant with his hands and immediately warmed him, says this:
>Poor fellow, do not be afraid because,
>At present, by the love of God you're warmed.

The peasant to St. Francis:
>Beloved Father, you have warmed me up
>So that my every pain has gone away.   640

A woman, hearing that St. Francis was passing, brings a crippled son of hers whom St. Francis heals, and first the woman says to St. Francis:
>O righteous Father, since you're near to God,
>Be pleased to offer for your saintliness
>Upon my son's behalf a prayer, for you

---

5. The Italian literally says "il padre dello asino"—the father of the donkey. In this context a class joke at the expense of the peasantry seems strange.

Can see with what extreme infirmity he leads
His life in wicked pain and torment harsh.
For your compassion, this I ask of you.

St. Francis to that woman:
I shall be happy to implore my Lord
That he be pleased to liberate your son.   648

St. Francis prays to God:
Immeasurable Father, hear my prayer
Unworthy, and upon my heavy sins
Don't look; through your surpassing mercy show
A sign so this poor man may be set free.
Pray make me, Lord, deserving of such grace,
For you have never anything denied
To me; then let your pow'r descend on him
Through your surpassing mercy infinite.   656

The woman thanks St. Francis for having healed her son:
O just and Holy Father, what a gift
This is, for in a trice you've cured my son.
What sweetness great I feel within my heart!
My sorrow has been changed to feast and song!
O thou, Lord God, receive my thanks. As much,
Belovèd Father, as I can, for your
Unbounded goodness I give thanks, and I
Shall be your servant all throughout my life.   664

Having arrived at St. Mary of the Angels, St. Francis speaks to his brothers,
announcing to them that he must die:
The peace of God, eternal, measureless,
Be always with you, my belovèd sons
For surely my desire is now fulfilled;
Thou, Mother Mary, pray accept my thanks.
Ah, listen to my words, belovèd sons,
For in a short time now, my life must end.

A brother answers:
Alas! What are you saying, Father dear!
Without your presence, what are we to do?   672

By divine inspiration, a Roman woman comes to find St. Francis at his death and has brought with her many substances for burying him, and coming before St. Francis she speaks thus:

>May our Redeemer lofty comfort you,
>Belovèd Father, in your frailty.
>Please understand that I have been so filled
>With grief because I sensed your holiness
>Was nearing death—our rightful Lord
>By holy inspiration from afar
>Through his compassion has revealed this fact
>To me while I was praying through these nights.   680

That woman continues:

>Into your presence I have come because
>You must have solace, Father, and I have
>Brought to your reverence some needful things
>And those with which the rites may be performed.

St. Francis [says] to Lady Iacopa:

>My lady, may the Sapience Divine
>Award you grace because of the kind thoughts
>You had in paying me this visit and
>In comforting a wretched man like me.   688

Embracing St. Francis's feet and seeing there the holy stigmata, this woman says:

>O holy feet whereon the ancient wounds
>Appear again, O Father worthy and just,
>Alas that in an instant I must lose
>Each good, belovèd Father, that sustains
>My heart. And since you are so welcome in
>The highest kingdom, with your tranquil power,
>Please pray for me so that God will be pleased
>To grant that I may end my life with you.   696

The brothers console this woman and they raise her from St. Francis's feet, speaking thus:

>My lady, you must not lament like this.
>You must take consolation in our love.
>We too are suffering torment great, but since
>Our loftiest Redeemer wishes this,
>We must be satisfied that it's his will.

Cast out, therefore, each sorrow from yourself,
With fervent zeal, my lady, hope to see
In heaven our good Francis once again.   704

St. Francis, nearing death and teaching his brothers, says:
How deeply do I feel aggrieved, sweet sons,
That I feel my last hour pressing near;
I therefore leave in your good care the rule,
Which it will please you to administer
The way our high Redeemer will find right
And pleasing; and above all else hold dear,
Belovèd sons, that sacred poverty
That is so welcome in the sight of God.   712

Addressing God, St. Francis entrusts his family[6] *to his safe keeping.*
To you, belovèd Father, God so great,
My family I entrust; already I
Can care for them no more because of my
Infirmity—from you that's not concealed.
Therefore, my Lord, I pray that they will be
Forever welcome in your sight. To you
I now entrust them, governed by your rule,
For it will guide them to your timeless realm.   720

Grieving at St. Francis's coming death, the brothers say this:
O Holy Father, how shall we behave,
Your wretched sons, in this your passing on?
Who'll give us, any more, good counsel? help?
To Clemency divine now pray for us
That he will gather all your cherished sons
And to the Heavenly Being lead us up.

And, addressing St. Francis on their knees, they say:
Your benediction, Father, leave with us,
Remember us in heaven, too, we pray.   728

Blessing, comforting, and teaching them, St. Francis tells them this:
Do not distress yourselves, my cherished sons,
For each of us is born for such an end,

6. *family:* that is, his Franciscan brothers.

All wretches we and subject all to death,
And our last hour hovers always near,
Therefore with pure affection serve our God
In penitence and holy discipline,
And with my benediction carry on,
And dutifully attend your sacred prayers. 736

St. Francis says to the brothers who will undress him and place him in the earth:
Belovèd sons, because I mean to die
A certain way, please lay me in the earth,
And quickly strip away from me these clothes,
For naked I would come to my life's end.
Our boundless God, as you are well aware,
For us desired to bear great suffering,
Inflicted on that hard and crooked wood
To make us part of his celestial realm. 744

Stripped and on the ground, St. Francis prays to God:
From earth, my Lord, you fashioned me, and now
These wretched leavings earth will be again.
You brought me poor and naked to this earth,
And naked from this mortal verge I go.
Be yours my soul who sent it forth to me,
Its only joy to be unchained from sense;
It calls you, Lord, with humble voice; you were
For me, a thankless servant, crucified. 752

Having St. Francis reclothed, the sacristan says to him:
It is your sacred duty to put on
These clothes of yours before me here, let this
Your son clothe you again, and you must here
Be brought with stately reverence, and thus
We in this holy temple shall not be
Upset by your departure decorous.

St. Francis answers the sacristan and says:
Belovèd son, I want to do your will,
So put my clothes once more upon my back. 760

The angel comes and dismisses the audience:
Ah turn the eyes of your pure mind, O soul

That in the world is led astray, and with
Your diligent attention contemplate
The holy life of good St. Francis who,
While leaving here his worthy memory,
With wounds was likened unto God because
His boundless goodness had pleased God so much.
Today to highest glory he was raised.   768

THE END

THE PLAY OF
SAINT [FLAVIA] DOMITILLA

Here begins the play of Saint Domitilla, Virgin, made and written in verses by Lady Antonia, wife of Bernardo Pulci in the year 1483.[1]

[Someone speaks the prologue:]
 O Good Jesus, by your power great
 Grant to my lowly intellect such grace
 That through your clemency I can present
 The great renown and sacred history
 Of Domitilla, who with love most pure
 And filled with wisdom pledged herself to God.
 A Christian Virgin, having been betrothed,
 Was consecrated secretly to God.   8
  This virgin whom I spoke about was niece
 To great Domitian, the emperor;
 She, still a girl, fled from her plighted groom
 And to her worthy Maker pledged her soul,
 So she might find the true and perfect way
 That she could go on dwelling with her Lord,
 Seeking the crown of martyrdom at last
 She gave herself to perish in the fire.   16

---

1. *St. Domitilla* is the earliest of Pulci's plays whose date of composition (1483) is certain. The Florentine edition of Miscomini (1490) is the earliest surviving text. At least ten sixteenth-century editions and six seventeenth-century editions were printed: Florence, 1515, 1554, 1555, 1561, 1571, 1584, and 1594; 1602, 1624, and 1648; Orvieto, 1608; Siena, 1578, 1602, 1608, and 1621; Venice: 1588. St. Domitilla's story appears very much as Pulci dramatizes it in Jacobus de Voragine's *The Golden Legend,* under the entry for Saints Nereus and Achilleus. Pulci shifts the focus from the sanctimonious males to the more interesting female character.

The emperor speaks to one of his barons called Aurelianus and says how he has given him Domitilla as a wife:

Aurelian, since I have ever loved
You like a good and cherished son,
Because I've found you chaste and well brought up,
Entreated by your father secretly,
I've given you for your belovèd wife
A damsel of a noble mien and mild,
My niece, one greatly valued and renowned,
And she is Domitilla by her name.   24
    Accept her as a mark of my respect,
And I know you'll be pleased to love her more
Than anything; be glad on that account,
For she is very gracious and she's fair,
And with these barons you will quickly go
With great festivity and ask to see
Her at her home, and may these wedding rites
Generously propitiate our gods.   32

Aurelianus answers the emperor and says:

Although for such a highborn spouse am I
Unworthy, since your majesty is pleased
So graciously your loyal subject low
To match with your nobility, I thank
You with my humble intellect, my lord,
And may your will be done; these barons, have
Them get prepared that they may go
To pay a visit to my newfound bride.   40

Aurelianus with many barons goes to visit his spouse Domitilla, and on arriving says to her:

You are well met, my dear, beloved bride;
You only are the sweetness of my heart,
O Domitilla, more than anything
With perfect love by me beloved,
You know my every hope is placed in you,
For, past all others, you are the true prize.

Domitilla answers Aurelianus:

And you are welcome, husband mine,
With all this worthy company as well.   48

After some festivity of playing music and dancing, Aurelianus bids farewell, and says this to Domitilla:

> Remain, my bride, in your tranquillity;
> I cannot longer linger at your side,
> Since parting from you grieves and saddens me,
> A thousand years 'twill seem before we meet;
> If he can anyway delight or please,
> Aurelianus stands at your command.

Domitilla answers Aurelianus:

> What can I, husband, wish from you except
> That you come back to see me once again?   56

When Aurelianus has gone, a servant of Domitilla, one Nereus, says to the other servant, Archileus:

> Archileus, you know with what great love
> Her mother, nearing death, entrusted her
> To us by destiny because she was
> Her mother and to us, her servants, was
> A sister, since we were instructing her
> In Jesus Christ the Lord who in the court
> Eternal reigns; and she, a Christian girl,
> Is now united to the pagan law.   64

When Aurelianus has left, these two servants go to Domitilla to convert her to preserve her virginity, and they speak between themselves, and the aforesaid Archileus says:

> O God immense, pray give us such great strength
> That we may turn her to you, by your grace,
> For your law does not value leaving her
> To go to perdition with her mortal spouse
> Who her virginity at once desires
> To steal, Redeemer kind, as well you know;
> And you can work it out so that you show
> Your servants how they may [convert her now].   72

Archileus turns to Nereus and says this:

> Nereus, with God's help now let us go
> To see our lady Domitilla, for
> He, most clement, just, and pitying,
> Will, to convert her, give us holy strength;
> And he will want to satisfy our wish—

Within her heart will kindle such a spark
Of gentle love that her we shall convert,
And thus become the cause of much great good.   80

Having come before Domitilla, one of the aforementioned servants says:
My lady, though it seems presumptuous
To have a servant educate his lord,
Because I feel affection great for you
It is improper for me to conceal
The truth that, once you believe it, will become
The happy cause of setting you in heaven
In company with virgins chosen,[2] if
You choose to take the straight and narrow way.   88
   O, Domitilla, with what garments you
Array your body to make glad your spouse,
But if with other ornaments your soul
You would adorn, then could you Jesus have
To be your spouse, who to his servants grants
That they may dwell in heaven by his grace.
He is the true God, an eternal spouse;
A mortal man is your Aurelianus.   96

Domitilla answers the servants and says:
What greater sweetness could be, I don't know,
Than having a husband worthy to be yours
And sharing with him the flower of his youth,
Young and rich and with a courteous wit,
Thereafter children, who in your old age
Will be your life's support, its staff; and who
Can cease to value certainties? Who would
Exchange them for uncertainties to come?   104

One of the servants answers:
You, Domitilla, have placed your every trust
In the pomp of this false world, which will,
Just like a flower, pass and not endure,
And where you seek, peace never can be found,
You think not on that one who quickly steals

---

2. *virgins chosen:* These are the elect of God—the 100,000 virgins who go singing before
the lamb in the vision of St. John on Patmos.

When life delights us most, and every hope
Most pleases, but no man's so strong that he
Will not be conquered by the one named Death.   112

The same servant continues:
Therefore it is in Fortune's hands, you see;
Against her, no defenses can avail
If someone worthy should with mishap meet.
And thus no one who lives beneath the moon
Can be called happy, but a person who
Will set his face against the world and turn
To him who is the source of every good.
Any opinion else is false and blind.   120

Domitilla answers her servants:
What is more difficult than to despise
The riches of this present life and not
Desire to taste the pleasures manifold
Of human splendor, great nobility,
So one can want, at last, another life
That one gains for oneself with torment and
With harshness, fasting, and with discipline?
These your doctrines—who can understand?   128

One of the mentioned servants answers and says to Domitilla:
When you have been united with your spouse,
The title of virginity you'll lose,
And whether he will kindly be to you
Is hidden from you, for one's often blithe,
But knows not why; always, to know about
The future is unsure, and so one weighs
These outcomes: you today a maiden's gown
Wear, then you'll be a woman and a wife,   136
    And you, who could not even entertain
The very notion that your virginal
Nobility might be defiled, would to
A pagan base submit and bend yourself
To every pleasure of his, transform your life,
Your habits, and your manners, and your style,
His every vile commandment would perform
So that his appetite might sated be.   144

All these husbands put their best foot forward:
When their lady is engaged to them
How humble, then, they wish to seem, and mild—
At least until they've led her to their home.
However, secrets like those you can't know—
If you have not first spent some time with him
You will be filled with fear and full of doubt.
Be sure you think about such outcomes well.   152

Domitilla answers and says:
My mother suffered, as I well recall,
So many torments throughout all her life;
Because of her husband's jealousy alone
Bore very great distress; and if I were
To think that I would follow such a path,
The garments of the world I'd never don,
Though I don't think my spouse Aurelian
Would act like this because he is so kind.   160

One of the servants mentioned says to Domitilla:
That which I tell you often comes to pass,
Lo, some keep mistresses or concubines,
And some their ladies batter painfully,
Torment them with harsh discipline so cruel;
Many scornful outbursts, too, they bear;
One needs to think through all things to their end—
About the pangs of childbirth and the woes
So grievous when the children are brought forth.   168
    Sometimes, as well, when coming forth, a child
Will be born dumb, deformed, or senseless, whence
The mother will experience great grief,
For one who's born blind by the world is scorned;
Consider now if you'd have great regret
For ever having borne a child like these.
Sometimes the children, too, when they are born,
May be the causes of their mothers' deaths.   176

The other servant arrives and says:
O sacred maidenhood, what worthy joy
You bring to God, and to the angels dear
Who for eternity in heaven live

And with their bright and shining Maker reign!
How blest whoever may, beneath your sign,
That journey undertake, whoever scorns
This bitter life so trouble-filled to find
Another life more tranquil and serene.   184
       With penitence can one atone for sins,
But once virginity is lost, no more
Can it return to its first state again;
Who doesn't understand this, woe to her!
Though every other virtue conquers and
With joy is welcomed midst the saints in heav'n,
Just as the queen is greater than the rest,
So is virginity the glory true.   192
       It wafts a sweet aroma up to God.
If you preserve this, for a spouse you'll have
A noble youth both pious and benign,
Who will not ever go away from you,
That is Christ Jesus, who with yearning for
His brides rejoices greatly in high heav'n.
Here certain joy, here true repose—she's blest
Who is devoted to so great a spouse.   200
       Whichever of these two most pleases you,
Choose now: take either this Aurelian
Who must die, leave his riches in default,
A fleeting hope for such long suffering;
Or, if you Jesus wish for your true spouse,
And him alone to serve is your desire,
Untroubled sweetness infinite to you
He'll give, and after death will give you life.   208

Domitilla answers her two servants and says:
       Truly I seem to feel my heart unfold,
Such power have your words, and what within
I feel I can't tell you, but I'm much grieved
I took a spouse because I wish
To serve Christ Jesus and his holy law—
Be one who wants to flee the world and each
Vain thought—yet I desire to go away
From my intended spouse, Aurelian.   216
       But how may I flee from his hands?
Yet I trust in my God, for with his aid

Such strength and courage great he'll give to me
That my just purposes will be fulfilled
Because he will not let his servants perish,
And, since he has me as his bride again,
Virginity in me he'll want to shield
Through his great goodness infinite and high.   224
    Arrange for me to take the veil at once
And to be consecrated to my Spouse
Eternal who entirely has inflamed
Me with his love, for his delights and peace
Most high, behold me present here, prepared
To serve my lord, compassionate and just,
Thou who has opened me and seized my heart
Oh, make me constant in thy tender love.   232

One of the servants mentioned gives thanks to God and says this:
I render thanks to you, supernal God,
Who mercifully have let us do such deeds,
So pleasing, too, and it is our good wish
That we beneath your banners setting forth
Shall see her who was bound for wicked loss.
Now you for your supernal realms have veiled her.
How much your goodness you've revealed to us
Since to perform our wish she is resolved.   240

These two servants go to Pope Clement and tell him how they have converted
Domitilla and that he must come to see her and comfort her:
O Reverend Sir, good shepherd of the Christ,
Pray understand why we have come to you;
It is because the emperor's niece, your kin,
We have converted—though she was to wed
Aurelianus, noble knight, quite soon
With honor great. She does not care to leave
That spouse who wants to keep her maidenhood
Inviolate [forever as it is].   248

Pope Clement answers the aforesaid servants and says:
I thank you on behalf of Jesus, for
You have performed a feat of such great good
That his sweet flame has quite enkindled me;
Behold me present and all ready here;
Good Jesus, if I've rightly understood,

You have revealed how just and loving you
To your devoted are, and pleasing to
Supernal God for doing such good work
Since to yourself you have this virgin called.   256

[Pope] Clement comes to Domitilla's house, and on arriving he says:
That true God who in Mary took on flesh
And who for us was crucified and dead,
My daughter, save and keep you; his sweet peace
And comfort may he give to you as well.
I see you on that straight course setting forth,
Which leads you to a harbor safe at last.[3]
I consecrate you, give to you this veil
That will conduct you to your heavenly spouse.   264

Many poor persons come to the house of Domitilla for alms and they say:
Good lady, a paltry pittance for this old,
Infirm one who cannot see, a little bread,
A little of your wine for Jesus Christ,
In whom we all believe [and put our faith].

Domitilla says to one of her house servants:
Arrange to have that needy wretch attired,
Those others too, since they are of our faith,
For God has granted us much good, and if
For him we use it not, we may be lost.   272

The one who is giving alms says to one of the poor:
Take this, see that you pray to God for us,
For her, as well, that she in chastity
May live, and all of you share out these gifts,
And don't behave like fools about these things.

One of the mentioned poor answers:
We'll pray to God together with his saints,
For heaven will reward such charity.

Another of the poor persons mentioned answers and says:
Let's go from here, why need we parley more?
Promise him to do what she desires.   280

3. *harbor safe:* See Petrarch, *Rerum* 80.31–39 and 264.120–21.

A servant, having heard of Domitilla's conversion, comes to Aurelianus and says:
> Too hesitant you've been, Aurelian,
> In marrying this cherished bride of yours,
> For someone has reported to my men
> That she's made Christian, is secluded now.

Aurelianus says to himself:
> Ah woe is me that such a thing is said
> To me, that such a thing she'd ever try!
> I want to go to see if it's the truth,
> Since this I cannot hope or believe of her.   288

Aurelianus goes to the house of Domitilla and says to her servants:
> Report at once that I have come to see
> Just what, today, my Domitilla does.
> Tell her I've arrived, because my heart
> Alone desires that I may look on her.

One of Domitilla's servants answers Aurelianus:
> Immediately shall we perform your will
> So that your coming will not be in vain;
> We shall at once your errand undertake
> And say to her exactly what you've said.   296

A servant goes to Domitilla and says:
> Know that Aurelianus here has come
> And says that you should come to him at once.
> About what you have done, perhaps, he knows;
> Beside himself with grief he seems to me.

Domitilla answers:
> Tell him he's wasted both his steps and time
> And that I do not wish to speak to him
> At all, for I another spouse in heav'n
> Have taken whose sweet love inflames my heart.   304

The servant says to Aurelianus:
> To you this message Domitilla sends,
> Aurelian, that she won't come to you—
> That to obey you she can't be induced;

Vainly you tire yourself awaiting her,
For she has taken another spouse to serve.
This we report to you on her behalf.

Aurelianus says to himself:
I see that everything I've heard is true;
Alas that I'm deprived of this fine match!   312

Aurelianus goes to the emperor and says:
Great Emperor, Your Highness most serene,
This sect of Christians, you should know,
Against your honor and your majesty
Have with their hollow counsels managed it
So Clement with his hands my Domitilla
Has veiled, dear lord, and consecrated her
A virgin to their god, unless this case
So wicked you can manage to set right.   320
    I went to see her at her house, but I
Could not say anything to her because
She stays within, no more will speak to me,
But says that she's become the bride of Christ.
Be pleased, on that account, to send for her
Whom I adore beyond all else and see
That those responsible are punished and
That, as is proper, she becomes my wife.   328

The emperor answers Aurelianus:
I promise you and swear, Aurelian,
That by our gods I'll have revenge for this.
I shall destroy this Christian populace,
These people wicked, cursèd, and perverse,
And I'll make her, perhaps, with her false sect,
Repent of this preposterous idea.

And facing his servants the emperor says:
Go, my servants, go for her at once,
Tell her to come, for I would look on her.   336

The servants go for Domitilla and say:
On our exalted emperor's behalf,

You must now come with us to him because
In giving him offense you've greatly erred,
But instantly you will repent of it.

Domitilla says to the servant mentioned:
Let's go, for I do not esteem your lord,
And threats you make against me have no force.

And she turns to heaven and says:
O Jesus good, in whom my heart believes,
O, make me constant; guide and escort me.   344

When Domitilla arrives before him, the emperor says:
O woe is me! what's this I hear, my niece?
For this is sorrowful news that's reached my ears
About you. Woe, because you give such grief
To me, and have thus scorned our gods and me.
This is the way that you repay me for
The celebration I made at your birth,
For well you know how much I honored you
In giving you the name that is my own.   352
        Poor wretch, for through the fatuous advice
Of Christians false you've been thus veiled;
Your actions are no longer rational,
You know I've loved you, not as uncles do,
But as a father loves his dearest child,
Now you have renounced my sacred trust;
If I can catch that ancient sorcerer
Who veiled you, I shall pay him back for that.   360
        The indignation of our gods have you
Not feared, for they, for motives of their own,
Have granted us such wealth abundant and
Support us happy in such eminence.
O foolish girl with your opinion false,
Because you will go seeking hardships great
In following the teachings of these Christians,
A life with torments filled and discipline.   368

Domitilla answers the emperor:
What I have done, O highest Emperor,
Would I on no account again undo;

So far from error blind and false I've fled
That now I clearly know the way of things.
My Lord has shown me now the proper path
On which I am resolved to travel forth,
Ever prepared to serve my Jesus, who
Agreed to die to expiate our sin.　　　　　　　　376
　　　This present life in which we find ourselves,
Which seems to you so brimming with delights,
You do not think how briefly we enjoy
Because we all are subject unto death
And to reach this end we all are born—
The One of whom I speak well understands
These outcomes; at the final trumpet we
Shall rise and to our bodies all return.　　　　　384
　　　The tongue does not exist that could recount
The grandeur of the maidenhood that I've
Resolved to hold in reverence, and you,
O Emperor, whatever you may do
With all severity, if you could taste
The sweetness of that glory measureless,
You would abandon all these idols vain
To follow these my laws of Christendom.　　　　392

The emperor answers Domitilla:
　　　Why I have such forbearance, I don't know,
That I don't kill you in my fury now;
But since our gods have borne with patience thus
This grievous injury, perhaps they have
For you good confidence that you will yet
Return unto their worthy creed once more,
I also shall endure your madness so
That you may tread again the proper path.　　　　400
　　　But let's suppose that what you've said were true,
How easily can one prove the reverse:
We don't find marriage banned in any book
Of ours; that's simply strange, and false to all
Received opinion—[this false lore] that you
Are pleased to follow and to contradict
The natural blessing that is spoken of
In every writing on it, as you see.　　　　　　408
　　　How very much I am surprised at you

Who have perused and studied well our books
That praise begetting a worthy family
Whence many monarchs are raised up: O wretch,
O fool!—more those who counsel you,
Vile fishermen by everyone disdained!—
Believe him who loves you, he does not speak
In vain, and yield to your Aurelian!   416

Domitilla answers the emperor:
The words that you have spoken have in them
A mystery—profound, great, wonderful!
If you desire with reason true to grasp
Aright the consequences of such things,
Far more than all your empire can effect,
A simple fisherman with his good works,
And with the cross's sign has raised the dead,
And set at liberty the deaf and blind.   424
      More can the crucifix accomplish in
The hearts of men than Mercury or Mars—
No matter how revered you make them be
Among your people everywhere, they can
Themselves do nothing, nonetheless; for by
Man's hand they're counterfeited and by craft;
They're all false images, and full of tricks
To lead you to your everlasting harm.   432
      O Emperor, you say your poets much condemn
Virginity; you do not fully grasp
These secret matters; you cannot, indeed,
Comprehend the truth nor know how both
The ignorant and the afflicted say
You speak words falsely, though your poets set
Them in the very highest place above
All other virtue worthy of esteem.   440
      How greatly was this virtue valued by
Your scholars, whom you wrongfully insult?
Divine Diana at her temple was
Adored by Rome; why reprehend me then
And wish that of such good I'd be deprived;
The more you say, the more my heart's alight
With the sweet love of my eternal spouse
Who's pledged to give immortal life to me.   448

Appealing to your poets I can prove
The dignity of every Sybil who
Earned the reward of prophesying Christ;
And how much it pleased Turnus to exalt
That virgin Camilla;[4] one writes about
That Calidonia, and Postilla
The vestal virgin whom Rome loved, indeed,
And Claudia, one whom we often name.   456

The emperor says to Domitilla:
Do you not know I have the power, wretch,
To either set you free or cause your death?
Did I not choose to show my clemency?
I could make you unsay what you have said;
For that you'll have a long time to repent
Before again so boldly you will speak.

And he turns to his servants and says:
Confine her on a Pontine Island, for
She has become so cursèd and so strange.   464

Domitilla prays to God, saying:
Illimitable God, spouse of my soul,
Upon my heart and my contrition, look,
For what's inside me is not hid from you;
Keep your handmaiden ever in your care;
I know you're merciful, and you will cause
Her by the straight and narrow path to go
Just as this tyrant most inhuman is,
Most faithful, Lord, and constant fashion me.   472

Turning to her servants, Domitilla says:
O my belovèd servants, you have seen
How much we're harmed by others' cruelty;
With me entreat, therefore, our Jesus, that
He will defend us from harsh tyranny.
Now we shall see, if you will follow me,
How far your charity extends, for soon
Shall we acquire the crown of martyrs that
The highest realm of heaven has promised us.   480

4. *Turnus . . . Camilla:* See Dante, *Inferno* 1.106–08.

A servant of Aurelianus comes and says how he has left Domitilla on the Island of Pontus:

> In bitterness surpassing have I left
> Your lady on an island, O my lord,
> Where she remains confined in solitude;
> Alone, her every hope is fixed on Christ,
> Expecting only with great eagerness
> To worship day and night that God of theirs.

Aurelianus says to himself:

> This matter to my lord I must make known,
> For not another hope remains to me.   488

Aurelianus goes to the emperor and says this:

> Great Emperor, O Prince, be pleased to know
> How obstinate, and even more than she
> Was ever, is our Domitilla still
> In her mistake, so much that many folk
> She has converted; therefore, dear lord, grant
> Me license plenary to punish those
> False knaves with every harsh asperity
> Who are the cause of such great wickedness.   496

The emperor answers Aurelianus:

> Aurelianus, license plenary
> I give you, do your will with them and her;
> Had I not chosen to be merciful,
> The utmost pain she would have undergone.
> To you and to your prudence it is left,
> For I don't know what more to do with her.

And turning to the servants he says:

> And, servants, you obey Aurelian,
> And don't neglect whatever he commands.   504

Aurelianus says to the servants:

> O faithful servants, go among those knaves
> That are around my Domitilla, and
> Explain how my lord's freely given them
> Into my power and that I desire
> To look upon them, for they must with you
> Immediately come in company.

The servants say to Aurelianus:
    What you command, Aurelian, we'll do.
    Before you we shall lead them presently.   512

A servant comes to Domitilla and says to her menservants:
    Come before Aurelian at once,
    Perfidious Christians, for into his hands
    Our lord has freely given each of you;
    See that you quickly get yourselves prepared
    And for your unavailing thoughts, perhaps,
    Will you at this time be repaid in full.

The servants answer:
    His every wish we shall at once fulfill,
    If he will grant us just a little time.   520

The one servant says to the other:
    Behold the time has come, sweet brother mine,
    To leave behind this life, but as it is
    So pleasing to our God, let us give thanks
    To him for goodness infinite; for me,
    My highest aspiration will be death;
    But only for this wretched one whom we
    Leave here in cruel Aurelianus' hands
    Does this harsh circumstance make me lament.   528

Domitilla to her menservants:
    Say what needs saying, O sweet brothers mine,
    There never should be need to make such harsh
    And loud lament because I have to die,
    From me do not conceal what you within
    You feel, for I'm content to end my life
    And any torment for my spouse endure.

The servants answer Domitilla:
    One has to praise what's pleasing to the Lord,
    But having to leave you fills us full of woe.   536

A servant says to Domitilla:
    Know that Aurelian has sent for us,
    For he has license from the emperor

Who's given each of us into his hands,
And we are only loathe to die because
Of your love, Domitilla; arm your heart
With our Lord's highest grace; take care to think
About the one you're wedded to so that
Aurelianus may not you deceive.   544

Another servant arrives and says:
Dear sister, with great diligence, you know
How you must your virginity protect
And bear each bitter pang, on its account.
Of any torture do not be afraid,
For every thing that Holy Essence in
The highest heaven can restore to you,
As much as you are tortured here below,
So much more there above will you be blest.   552

The other servant says to Domitilla:
My dearest one, since God is pleased to part
Us from you, keep your cherished spouse within
Your heart, and he will give you peace; nor must
You grieve about our love; with you will stay
Your lawful spouse, and he will always be
Your help and your defender, for to his
Good servants he is merciful and kind,
Sweet sister mine, thrive in the grace of God.   560

Domitilla says to them:
Belovèd brothers, who can take your place?
For so well you've instructed me and you've
Explained the darkling places and the strait,
And have made crystal clear the holy faith
With your good precepts and your words; and this
Unfortunate woman now you leave alone,
Afflicted, of all company bereft,
For if she stands or walks, she knows no more.   568
    So harsh is this departure cruel for me!
Alas, for in an instant every hope
I lose; I stand here like a woman lost
Because it is not granted me to lose
My life together with you, brothers dear;

That strongly, with vast sorrow, my heart fears!
Pray God that he'll be pleased to let me die
With you, if that might be his will for me.   576

One of the servants mentioned says to Domitilla:
Forgive me if ever, through my ignorance,
I have done any injury to you;
Your business, with a heart sincere, I've done,
And in your spouse I have a steady hope,   .
For he will be your help and your defense.
And on your constancy you now must call,
Pursue your worthy resolution and
To each of us your benediction give.   584

Aurelianus, having sent for the two menservants of Domitilla, says to them:
So that you'll understand the reason why
I've made you come before me, be aware
How great a love, with consummate desire,
I feel for Domitilla. If you know
How, with your preaching, to arrange it so
That she'll choose to consent to me, you shall
Be kept by me as brothers, and with great
Emoluments and many offices.   592

The servants of Domitilla answer Aurelianus:
Would it not seem despicable to you,
Aurelian, should someone wish to steal
Our emperor's dear and plighted, cherished wife?
This dreadful error don't commit! Now think
How much more odious it would be to tear
Domitilla from a much greater lord
Whom she's resolved to serve eternally.
Thus foolish your proposal is, and vain.   600

Aurelianus says to Domitilla's servants:
This cursed, nasty, wicked Christian sect
Has not been broken yet because
You take delight in your own death, and all
My prayers have been addressed to you in vain.
A cruel vengeance I shall take on you:
I'll have you ripped to shreds, you pack of dogs.

And he turns to two of his servants and says:
> See that they're soundly beaten, tortured too,
> Since wicked they remain, and obstinate.   608

Aurelianus commands his servants:
> Conduct them then before our gods, and if
> They do not wish to worship them, cut off
> The head of each of them if they insist
> On persevering in this error great.

The servants of Aurelianus say:
> What you in your beneficence command,
> That shall be done at once without delay.

The executioner says:
> Make haste, for I have waited long enough;
> I've halfway spent the fee that I have earned.   616

The knight, having led them before the idols, says:
> Pay homage to our gods if you expect
> To be released from our hands; if you don't
> I shall inflict the punishment on you
> If you will not repudiate your Christ.

The two servants of Domitilla answer the knight:
> That power neither you nor these gods have,
> These bodies' cravings only can you sate.

And turning to heaven they say to God:
> The soul is for you who created it,
> O Lord, who spilled your holy blood for us.   624

Aurelianus says to Domitilla's two female companions:[5]
> O my dear sisters, cherished in my heart,
> I think you've seen into what anguish now
> My life has fallen, and what bitter pain
> Because my spouse will not perform my will,

5. In the Miscomini edition (1490) in an early sixteenth century hand are penned the names either of the two servants or of the two women playing the parts, Eufrosina and Theodora.

Whence I appeal to each of you to grant
My wish and go to her, and with good words
Find out if that one will for you consent
To acquiesce in what I'd have her do.   632
     I have cut off her servants' heads, and I
Can see that nothing will avail because
Her mind's made up, and she is obstinate,
And therefore I desire to try once more.
I know she has been reared with you, and it
Would be an easy thing for her to be
Persuaded by your words and good advice
That it would please our gods to have her take.   640
     And since I see the time already near
For you to wed, together with you I
Intend to celebrate my marriage with
My darling bride, my dear and cherished hope,
If you know how to win her sympathy
And tell her how her leaving crushes me.

The two maidens answer Aurelianus:
We willingly will do what you have asked,
Because some good result might come of it.   648

These two maidens go to the Pontine Island to Domitilla, and on arriving say:
Belovèd sister, more than dear to us,
By the unbounded love we feel for you,
We are distressed to find you suffering,
Afflicted in this place, and obstinate—
All on account of vain advice from folk
Who do not love you, and because you've left
Your young Aurelianus, comely, rich,
And very noble; you'll not find his like.   656
     If you will heed our words, the happiest bride
Who ever was within our city, you
Can even now become. How blest you'd be
If you'd give your consent to do this thing.
For would you wish to end your life in woes
Surpassing and in troubles harsh, but not
Submit by yielding to your worthy spouse
When so much good can still proceed from that?   664
     In Christ's own law is marriage said to be

Both just and holy, and no Christian this
Will contradict; and Peter, it is true,
Who so much loved your God, indeed, and who
Enjoyed great happiness—he wed a wife,
And then in such great grace remained that Christ
Selected him as his disciple and
He's very pleasing in the sight of God.   672

Domitilla answers the virgins:
The truth cannot be fully understood
By those who have the veil of ignorance
Before their eyes. You've said a foolish thing
Indeed, because your every hope, I see,
You've placed in this world, which with falsity
Is filled. With what great arrogance you speak
To say that my eternal spouse I ought
To leave and find a mortal spouse instead.   680

Domitilla continues:
If by example you would understand,
Suppose that from your promised grooms you each
Were torn away; that parting would seem hard
To you, and it is very proper that it should,
For I know how, past measure, each of you
Loves them; your every thought's concerned for them.
How much more grievous would it be for me
To leave my spouse who will forever live!   688
        You do not in this fashion show the love
You bear me when you give me such advice
And say that I must leave my spouse and Lord,
And take a mortal man, Aurelian,
By losing him who is our Savior high,
Who has created us, whose children all
We are, him whom to know would make you blest,
If you will pay heed also to my words.   696

One of the virgins mentioned says to Domitilla:
If so great is the power of this God
Of yours, reveal it to us with your prayers:
My brother Herod, give him back his sight,
And likewise to this servant girl of ours

The power of speech restore, and our desire
Will be resolved your law to follow and
In your God, too, will both of us believe,
And we our mortal bridegrooms shall forsake.   704

Domitilla prays to God saying this:
O God benign, if worthy my prayers be,
Let this your servant be acceptable
To you; let my prayer in the highest realms,
O my Spouse infinite, before you come;
Of your mighty power display the signs:
Be pleased the eyes of this one to unseal,
And to this servant give the power of speech,
So that your great might may in that appear.   712

*Her speech recovered through Domitilla's prayers, the mute maidservant turns to heaven
and says:*
O vast, eternal God, by the just prayers
Of Domitilla have you deigned to show,
My Lord, your power surpassing; you were pleased
To give me back my speech. As much as I
Am able, I give thanks to you, and in
Your name I wish to be baptized; O let
My soul be turned to you, for by your grace
You have my tongue unfettered and set free.   720

The blind one, his sight restored by Domitilla, says:
O Son of God, O highest Sapience,
Who died for us and felt our suffering
Through your great mercy and your charity,
So we might be redeemed, you came down here,
Your mighty power is surely manifest
Since this unworthy servant's eyes you have
Unsealed, so with the true light he might see;
In your name I desire to be baptized.   728

Having seen these miracles, the two virgins say to Domitilla.
O sister sweet, such signs miraculous
Of your eternal God we have observed
That in the highest realms already do
We seem, and that you will baptize us we

Entreat, and that to welcome us you will
Not scorn, for with you we would live and die.
O highest God, who understands our hearts,
Inflame them with your mercy, kindle them.   736

Aurelianus, having sent for the grooms of the two virgins, says to them that they should go to find out what has been accomplished with Domitilla [by the brides]:
I have ordained the weddings right away;
Therefore I pray you that in joy you'll go
To Domitilla and that you'll inquire
If she is yet prepared to do my will.

The bridegrooms answer Aurelianus:
Our minds are ever ready just to do
Whatever gives you pleasure; we at once
Shall do whatever pleases you in this
Since she will also wish to do your will.   744

The two bridegrooms, having come before their ladies, say:
Belovèd brides, whatever does this mean
That your heads in this fashion are thus veiled?
Explain this circumstance to us at once,
For to us it seems we've dreamed this thing.
Aurelianus, in his troubled case,
Is awaiting news of what you've done
With Domitilla, what success you've had,
Because in great confusion he's remained.   752

The virgins answer their bridegrooms:
The fruit, O chosen spouses, of our coming
So marvelous and such a mystery
Has been, from you it won't be hid
So you can see and think upon the works
Of God, just, infinite, and merciful,
Who to his subjects shows his worthy works
Observe how Herod has received his sight,
And this mute servant girl has spoken, too.   760
     And through such miracles are we baptized
Into the Law of Christ by mysteries
Immense that we have seen; this is the cause
Of our now being veiled, but, nonetheless,

Belovèd bridegrooms, in such error great
We pray you will no longer persevere;
Unseal the eyes of your intelligence
And be content to place your faith in him.   768

Converted, the two bridegrooms answer:
O boundless Father, O love infinite,
Who has through this your handmaid shown to us
Such worthy matters that however much
I think about your grace my heart grows bright;
With your sweet fire you've set me all alight;
O Domitilla, bride most sanctified,
Baptize us in the name of your God, for
Our every wish is bent on serving him.   774

A servant goes to Aurelianus and tells him how the two bridegrooms have converted to the faith of Christ:
I'd bring you better news, Aurelian,
Of Domitilla, whom you love the best,
Know, then, that she has managed things so well
That those you sent to see her now have been
Baptized by her—their plighted grooms as well
Has she converted [to the Christian faith].

Aurelianus turns to his servants:
Go quickly, and make every effort so
That you somehow may bring her here to me.   782

The servants, having come before Domitilla, say:
Domitilla, by force, or else for love
Set out upon your way with us at once,
For thus commands your husband and your lord
Who waits for you with his great barony.

Domitilla prays and says:
O Jesus mine, Redeemer tender, kind,
Be pleased to shelter my virginity,
And you, belovèd friends, come on with me;
Of torments do not be afraid, or threats.   790

Upon Domitilla's arrival, Aurelianus says to her:
O Domitilla, my supreme desire,

You whom I value, prize above all else,
Graciously be pleased to acquiesce;
You're noble, why are you not merciful?
Why does it please you so to end my life
In such great torment and without surcease?
Command what you desire; it will be done.

Domitilla turns to God and says:
Now, Lord, how much you love me we shall see.   798

[Aurelianus dances himself to death.] A servant goes to Lussurius and tells him how Aurelianus, dancing, has fallen dead:
Know you that Domitilla with her spells
Has made your brother fall down dead while he
Was dancing thus to instruments and songs.
Therefore come quickly if you want to see him.

Lussurius, Aurelianus' brother, says:
That death, if all our gods are not astray,
Will not go unavenged. That sorceress
Accursèd apprehend, for I intend
A cruel vengeance to exact from her.   806

Lussurius, having come to Domitilla, says:
Perverse enchantress, if it's you who have
Deprived me of my elder brother; now
At once for him the most unhappy paths
You'll tread. So on the emperor's behalf
You his subjects are detained; he says
That all must with great violence be stripped;
You shall the utmost torment undergo
And in the fire be burned without delay.   814

Domitilla, having turned toward her companions, says:
Now shall our steady constancy be seen,
And, however hot the vast flame burns,
In God repose your hope, for very soon
We all shall at his holy table be.
O risen Jesus good, within whose care
Our life from such great suffering shall be free,
You very clearly see what we intend,
Don't let sensation vanquish reason, Lord.   822

The knight, having led Domitilla before the idols, and before he kills her and her companions, says:

> Though I have license for it, I don't wish
> To sentence such a worthy one to death,
> Therefore if to our gods you promise me
> To offer sacrifice, I'll set you free.

Domitilla answers the knight:

> Do you imagine that for idols false
> And wicked I'd forswear a spouse so great?
> For his love, be aware, I'm pleased to die.

The executioner says:

> Come on, that trial at once you'll undergo.   830

Domitilla prays:

> These your handmaids, O my Lord, forgive;
> Have mercy Lord for all their foolish thoughts.
> Forgive these childlike and unworldly lambs
> Who've fallen into the power of wolves today.
> *In manus tuas*, O Lord, receive them now,
> And others who were Christians made by us.

The executioner, wishing to burn them, says:

> Let's go along, you've made me waste my time;
> Submit to me, you whom I have to burn.   838

The angel dismisses the audience:

> O, everyone who has considered well
> The sacred story of St. Domitilla,
> Thank Eternal Goodness for his grace,
> That he may teach you to find victory
> In this blind world where you are all involved
> Like her, who to eternal glory pledged
> Her lovely spirit and her sole desire,
> Not heeding any torments of the world.   846

THE END

THE PLAY OF
SAINT GUGLIELMA

Here begins the play of Saint Guglielma, written by Mona Antonia, lady of Bernardo Pulci. [1]

And first comes the angel to announce the play:
    O Highest Savior, O Eternal Right,
    You, for us sinners, came amongst us here,
    Though you of heaven the father are, and Lord—
    For that you clothed yourself in human flesh,
    And like a shepherd good to save your flock
    You died upon the cross and felt its pangs;
    Let me just for your glory here show forth
    The lovely history of Saint Guglielma.   8
        Having been in the faith of Jesus Christ

---

1. The earliest known edition of this play, Miscomini, vol. 2. There is another fif-teenth-century Florentine edition.
    Thirteen sixteenth-century editions are known to exist: Florence, 1538, 1557, 1568, 1572, 1580, 1588, 1590, 1594, 1597, and two undated; Siena, 1579 and one un-dated. Seventeenth-century editions appeared in Venice, 1604, 1607, and 1630; in Siena, 1617; in Viterbo, 1667; and in Macerata, Perugia, and Pistoia (simultaneously), undated. The story of Saint Guglielma belongs to a kind of medieval story told by many about patient wives. The archetype of the story appears in the *Confessions* of St. Augustine, where Augustine recounts the spiritual benefits for his father of his mother's unflagging patience. It reappears in the story of Griselda as told by Boccaccio (*Decameron, 10th tale of the 10th day*) translated by Petrarch into Latin, and retold as *The Clerk's Tale* by Chaucer, whose story of Constance (*The Man of Law's Tale*) is also an example of the type. The version most familiar to Antonia Pulci was perhaps the story of Crescenza, the daughter of the king of Africa, though there existed a lively tradition in the Italian town of Brunate about a woman named Guglielma who had come from a foreign place and dwelt there with nuns, healing and doing good works, until her royal husband ultimately came to fetch her. This story, Antonia Pulci may have known (D'Ancona 3.199–208).   *103*

Baptized of late, the King of Hungary
Decided that he wished to take a wife,
And sought by means of every embassy
To be allied with England's mighty king;
A daughter of his was chosen, one devout,
And she was named Guglielma and was graced
With habits chaste and manners beautiful.   16
    This Guglielma many miseries
Long bore, and was a wanderer in the world
And to the fire with fraudulent deceits
She was condemned, whence Majesty divine
Freed her from every faithless one, from harms,
Because he succors all who call on him.
Though she had been tormented in the world
Like Job, at last like him she was restored.   22

The King of Hungary, addressing his brother and his barons says:
Attend me well, belovèd brother mine,
And all you barons, listen to my will:
For my desire is fixed to take a spouse.
In England, therefore, make your inquiries
For one who may reveal our Lord to us,
One graced with chastity and habits good,
The great king's child, Guglielma is her name.

The king's brother answers:
All your instructions, sir, shall be obeyed.

The brother of the king and the barons, having come before the King of England, speak to him—first the brother of the king:
O Highness most serene, the high renown
That of your daughter sounds throughout the world
Induces us, sent here by Hungary's king,
Your lordship to beseech with heart sincere
That you'll permit your daughter dear to go
With us in person; if you will consent
To this—confer that gift—I shall indeed
Be joyful and content on that account.   38

The King of England answers:
With utmost gratitude I thank your lord,

That he should deign to want my daughter's hand,
And I greatly long to gladden him,
But first I wish to seek the queen's advice;
Let Guglielma and her before us come
So we can well consider this affair.

And, having turned to the ambassadors, he says:
With your proposal we are very pleased,
And soon a welcome answer we'll return.   46

Guglielma and the queen having come into the court, the king speaks first to the queen:
My most belovèd one, my consort dear,
These worthy messengers into our court
By Hungary's lord were sent, and every one
Beseeches us that we will not object
To giving him Guglielma with great joy.
For love through many realms he's searched, indeed,
Urged on by good repute and zeal, and seeks
Alone our Guglielma, longs for her.   54

The king, facing Guglielma, speaks thus:
And you, belovèd daughter dear to me,
If that one who rules everything is pleased
That you've been chosen by so great a lord,
One recently converted to our law,
It waits on nothing but your word to give
This answer to that one who's chosen you.
To your belovèd Father give consent,
And likewise give it to your mother sweet.   62

Guglielma answers her father:
O most belovèd Father and my lord:
Take pity on my chastity; does it
Suffice not that I'm promised to our God?
A spouse eternal of such dignity,
My every desire's intent on serving him.
Have mercy, Jesus, on my virginity,
For I had thought to tread your path; now I
No longer know what's to become of me.   70

The king speaks with Guglielma and says:
A worthy condition is virginity,

Of course, this no one will deny; but you,
When in the world you are a wife, can like
A modest woman well behave toward God.
The more you strive in the faith of Jesus Christ,
That much more pleasing to the king you'll be.

The queen says to Guglielma:
If many, many prayers deserve your thanks,
Be sure that you discharge our will in this.   78

Guglielma consents to her father and mother, saying:
To not be disobedient to you,
I wish to yield to prayers so pressing, yet
My mind had been resolved to be a maid,
A virgin chaste to live and chaste to die.
My kindly Father, merciful and just,
For that I can't refuse you, and should not,
If it's so pleasing to your majesty,
My lord, then let your will be done.   86

The king has the ambassadors called:
Hear, O gentlemen, the words I speak,
Which give our answer in the best of faith:
Although Guglielma, sole delight to us,
Had been resolved on serving Jesus Christ,
Because an obedient daughter she would be,
She kindly has acceded to our prayers
At last. Write our pronouncement to your king,
And take Guglielma now to be your own.   94

*The ambassadors answer the king, thanking him, and first the King of Hungary's
brother says:*
For this agreement, our unending thanks
We render to you on our lord's behalf
For such a fine gift of so great a spouse
And so magnificent with joyful hearts.

And facing Guglielma, they give her certain gifts, saying:
Guglielma, whom none equals in the world,
For our devotion, please accept this gift.

The king says to his servants:
> Make sure that she's attired in rich array,
> And many feasts and dances organize.   102

The ambassadors tell the king that they have letters from the King of Hungary, and first a courier with the said letters enters:
> We've letters from the king that make these points:
> To your grace, first, does he commend himself.
> With joyful heart he longs but for his wife,
> And therefore we're obliged to take our leave.

The King of England answers:
> Guglielma must obey her lord. We give
> You license to depart as soon as all
> Seems ready for her; meanwhile, to your care
> I give her as your sister and your child.   110

Guglielma, having to depart, on her knees says to her father and mother:
> How am I able to depart from you,
> My Father sweet, O cherished Mother mine?
> If my life's never caused you any grief,
> I pray you, give me blessing. Let that one
> Who is surpassing, boundless charity
> Show me his way so perfect and so true.
> O my heart's fortitude and faithful guide,
> Escort me, light my way, abide with me.   118

The queen, blessing Guglielma says:
> O, my daughter, may you blessèd be,
> Be sure that you're respectful to your spouse;
> Be wise in speech, in actions chaste, devout,
> To all your subjects, merciful and kind.

The king joins in and says:
> Remember us wherever you may be,
> In charity be zealous, and be sure
> That in the fear of God you live your life.

Guglielma answers:
> So shall I do, my father and my lord.   126

Having arrived before the King of Hungary with his bride, the king approaches Guglielma and takes her hand and says:
> O my sweetheart, my belovèd spouse,
> More than a thousand times you're welcome here,
> Every desire of mine is fixed on you,
> O you surpassing refuge of my life.
> If anything should please you, ask for it;
> At your command is everything of mine.

Guglielma answers her husband:
> I wish naught else—unless I ask for grace
> That I, my lord, may here perform your will.   134

At this point, celebrations are held and the nuptials completed. The king addresses Guglielma and the barons and says that alms should be distributed, and that they should go to the churches to give thanks to God:
> Now since our wedding festivals are done,
> Our joyous nuptial rites, it's fitting that,
> With worthy offerings and observances
> Divine, we visit holy temples, and,
> So that these days may prove propitious, give
> Donations to God's servants. Certainly
> These riches come from fortune to those who
> Can in the world amass the most of them.   142

Many poor persons go for alms to the one who distributes them. They crowd around him. After he has distributed the alms, the seneschal says:
> You lazy louts get out of here and work;
> Whatever one gives to you is thrown away.

A poor man says:
> You should not with reproach give charity;
> You do not yet know what's in store for you.

The seneschal says:
> You ugly loafer, didn't I see you gambling?
> Of that folly do you want a cure from me?

Another poor man says:
> Hey, you're the mad one, giving us these gifts.

The seneschal says:
> If you'd like me to thrash you, just you wait. 150

The king and Guglielma, having risen from their seats, go to the temple to pray. Guglielma, on seeing a crucifix, turns to her husband and says many things about the life and suffering of Christ, and finally persuades him to go to the sepulchre at Jerusalem:

> Look here, my spouse, upon that worthy Lord
> By whom the universe was saved, that one who
> Has condemned to hell our primal father
> For having overstepped the mark[2] when that
> Forbidden tree he tasted—that one which
> In Paradise was set: But he has come
> To make atonement for another's crime
> As each prophet wrote that he would do.   158
>
>   Though King of Heaven, he came down to the earth
> And by a virgin chose to take on flesh,
> Take on himself our miseries; our thirst,
> Our hunger and our sorrow wished to taste,
> So greatly did he burn with love of us;
> To bring us rest in heaven, through the world
> And through the desert he went wandering, poor,
> For three-and-thirty years with many trials.   166
>
>   The Shepherd by his flock, though, was betrayed,
> And given to those scribes and pharisees;
> By Herod was he scorned, and Pilate, too—
> Was beaten by perfidious Jews and nailed
> Upon the cross, whence to his Father he
> Was heard to pray for those false, wicked ones.
> Once buried, on the third day he arose,
> And, decked in glory, he returned to heaven.   174
>
>   Now think, my lord, how it would be to see
> These things that you have just been hearing of
> With your own eyes. What sweetness would your heart
> Experience to kiss the spot on which
> The cross was raised, where Mary held him, dead,
> Upon her lap, the sepulchre where they
> Laid Jesus—all these marvelous things and more

---

2. See Dante, *Purgatory* 14.33 and *Paradise* 26.115–17. Pulci's passage not only employs the concept and image but echoes the language as well.

That, from us Christians, ingrates have concealed.   182

Moved by Guglielma's words, the king agrees to go to see the sepulchre.
You have my heart so kindled with sweet flame
That what you've spoken of seems present here;
My mind's unsure what it should contemplate,
Yet my mind seeks and yearns for nothing else.
Because to see the place his body hung
Upon the cross to save the human race,
I'm firmly resolute, Guglielma, I
Desire to go to see the holy place.   190

Continuing, Guglielma asks the king that he allow her to go with him:
Our worthy Lord will grant you grace for this;
And so I may accompany you I pray
With every faculty at my command
That you'll agree to grant this grace to me.

The king answers:
I know it is not lawful to desert
The realm; so you must in my place remain;
With justice and with prudence will you rule;
And you must not feel grief when I depart.   198

The king needs to go tell his brother how he will leave him and Guglielma to govern the realm together.
Pray listen, prudent brother mine, and wise,
You barons, too, take note of what I speak:
By inspiration sacred have I been
Impelled to journey to the holy land;
In this my sacred pilgrimage, I leave
Guglielma my dominion; in exchange
For me receive her as your queen,
And be to her, as queen, obedient.   206

The king's brother, seeing him resolved to go, says:
Since you are resolved that you must go,
What you find pleasing must please us as well;
Guglielma we shall always honor, though
Your departure much will sadden us.

Embracing the king at his departure, Guglielma says:
> May he who with the good Tobias went
> Be your true escort; may he be your guide.

The king turns again to his barons and says in parting:
> To God I leave you, and, above all else,
> In your safe keeping I leave my darling spouse.   214

After the king's departure, his brother pretends to have to speak with Guglielma in her
chamber so he can tempt her as a lover with dissembling speeches:
> My glorious lady, secret things must I
> Say to your reverence; I should like to speak
> About them with you, if you don't object
> To giving me an audience with you.

Guglielma, not being aware of the deception, consents to hear him:
> We'll go, for I am pleased to listen to
> What in your prudence you would say to me,
> Nothing's more dear to me, except the king,
> Than having a conversation with yourself.   222

The brother of the king declares his love for Guglielma, saying:
> My sweet love, what I must confess to you
> Is that on earth I love you for my star,
> Let love report to you what my heart feels,
> And be as wise as you are beautiful.

Guglielma, made aware of his unchaste thoughts and enraged, addresses him and
commands that he leave her, saying:
> Alas, where is my love? Where is my hope?
> May Jesus and may justice me defend!
> You want to ravish Guglielma from your brother!
> Make sure you're wise, and speak to me no more.   230

The brother of the king having exited, Guglielma, alone in the room, speaks to herself:
> I will keep still, woe, now how great a wrong
> That he's attempted to seduce the queen!
> The king's great majesty has been disgraced.
> My court will be in turmoil if I speak—
> O God, you're my defender, you my guide;

Susanna was, I know, preserved by you;
I don't know what I ought to do or say;
I shall keep silent till the king returns.   238

The king's brother, after leaving Guglielma's chamber, enraged and making threats within himself, says:

I know for sure that only on account
Of fear does she appear so brusque and pure
To one who'd tempt her, put her to the test,
For being false is nothing new to her.
Let's see how much that heaven of hers will care,
For I shall find a way to be avenged;
I'll pay you back for that, know what you may,
And I am sure that you'll regret it soon.   246

A messenger comes to an inn and says that the king is near at hand, returning from the sepulchre, and wants something to eat:

Find something quick to make our breakfasts—
From us more than one florin you will have—
Have you some partridge for us? pullets? squab?

The host answers:

What pleases you is here, sir, good wine too.

The messenger, continuing to speak, says to the host:

On foot he's coming here for piety,
For as a pilgrim does our lord approach;
A man discrete you seem; so humor me
And close the door to those who later come.   254

A messenger comes to the court and says that the lord is nearby:

Know, all of you, our lord is near at hand,
I've left him merely two days' journey off,
On foot and as a pilgrim clothed he comes.
Announce these tidings to his royal queen.

The brother of the king says to the barons:

Let us all go to meet him on the road.

The same messenger says:

Who will do my duty if you go?

The brother of the king says to the barons:
>What he wishes, give him; it's his own;
>Consider that the lord must be at hand.   262

They go to meet the king, and having arrived at the inn, the king's brother speaks for everyone and says:
>King most serene, my brother and my lord,
>How happy I am made by your return.

The king doesn't answer with relevance, but asks only about Guglielma:
>Of Guglielma, my perfect love, what news?
>I yearn for nothing but her lovely face.   266

The brother of the king says to his brother:
>Guglielma has your honor much abused,
>To tell about it one day won't suffice.

The angry king says to his brother:
>Alas my brother, what may this thing be
>That you desire to tell me of my queen?

The king's brother answers and speaks thus:
>I fear to tell you what will trouble you:
>The life of your corrupted Guglielma,
>Since you departed, has in balls and feasts
>And singing clearly been reprovable,
>So greatly that it is indecent just
>To speak of it; your whole court is stirred up;
>If in your prudence you don't deal with this,
>Our entire lineage will be disgraced.   274

The king answers his brother:
>O woe, is this the prize, the honor great
>Of that Guglielma to whom, over all
>My realm, my power and dominion I
>Entrusted, left her in a worthy place?
>So great a wrong will not unpunished go,
>Go make example of such great offense;
>Unless convinced that justice has been done
>For her ill deeds, I know I won't return.   282

*The brother of the king comes to court and commands the sheriff to have Guglielma
executed.*

Upon our lord's behalf, behold his charge
That orders you thus prudently to act:
As secretly as possible have the queen
At once brought to you; without asking her
About her other faults, let her be killed—
And do it secretly—by means of fire,
And with no token of respect for her.

The sheriff answers:

That which he wishes I shall have performed.   290

*The sheriff goes to Guglielma and tells her she must die, asks her pardon and comforts
her:*

May highest God grant peace to you, O queen.
I'm grieved to have to bring you such hard news,
But since my lord, your husband, thus is pleased,
Consider that I'm bound to heed his law;
He who sees all things knows how sorrowful
I am, for know that I must make you die;
Your mind with prudence govern, and address
Your intellect to your Creator now.   298

The sheriff continues:

And you, my lady, pray you, pardon me,
For your death is for me too great a grief,
But, as you know, no one can flee from death,
For in the end fate brings it to each one.
Your soul, therefore, address to God, for soon
Within his court you'll be, and you shall have
That happiness which always will endure.
Therefore, Guglielma, take your leave of me.   306

Weeping, Guglielma says within herself:

O me unfortunate! And for what sin
Must I endure this torture without cause?
O Father sweet, why have you sent your dear
Guglielma to perdition here?
Ah, cruel spouse, why have you sentenced her
Who never once has disappointed you?

Like Isaac at the holy sacrifice shall I
Be given to such torment as a prize!   314

Guglielma continues:
    O Father mine, at your request alone!
    I took a spouse against my every wish.
    For always pure and chaste I meant to live
    And wearisome to me those worldly spoils
    For which I now must bear such heavy grief;
    My life I end in weeping and in woes;
    Ah, woe is me because you wanted to
    Appease the world, ah, filled with every pain.   322

Guglielma continues:
    Are these the solemn celebrations and
    Delights my spouse has kept in store for me?

And addressing the serving maids she says:
    Those garments rich return to him, my maids,
    And let me be arrayed in one of black.

The servant of Guglielma, that is the chambermaid, having heard her great lament, says:
    What things are these, dear lady, that we hear?
    Because of your lament we're all upset!

Guglielma answers her maid:
    From you I must be separated, for
    My spouse my execution has ordained.   330

Her maid answers Guglielma and says:
    My lady, tell us what the reason is
    That of your life you thus must be deprived.
    Does Your Highness really merit this
    For having so well overseen the court?
    If you do not disdain our company,
    To die with you would welcome be for us.

Guglielma, taking her leave from her servants, says:
    My maids belovèd, rest you here in peace;
    For I'm required to die to please my lord.   338

Going to her execution, Guglielma says to herself along the way:
O Love unbounded, Father consummate,
Who shed your blood for me upon the cross,
Help me, and guide me to the final pass
As you, indeed, set Daniel free, because
Without you I am terrified, afraid;
Have mercy, Lord, on all my spotless thoughts,
For which I, wrongly thus, have been condemned;
My soul, at least, to you commended be.   346

Guglielma, having come to the place of execution and fallen to her knees, says:
And you, O Virgin Mother, Daughter, Bride,
If by you I am worthy to be heard,
Let not your pity hidden from me be;
To all who ask for aid with all their hearts,[3]
I know, kind Mother, you are merciful.
Let my soul be united with your own;
My every secret you know perfectly,
And know I'm wrongly sentenced to the fire.   354

Guglielma continues:
My innocence, my Lord, may you defend,
Don't let me die in such great infamy;
O, by your mighty power let my prayers,
Your servant's, granted be, O worthy Lord.
Since never have I wronged your clemency,
Forgive me and do not give your consent
That I be put into this blazing fire,
Benign Redeemer, merciful and just.   362

The gentleman, having heard that she was innocent, asks her why she is condemned:
Tell me, if my questioning is right,
My lady, what the cause is for such prayer?

Guglielma answers the gentleman:
That one who took on flesh from Mary, he
Can properly give judgment in my case.

The gentleman considers setting her free, and says to his companions:
I think it's certain that she's innocent,

3. Compare Petrarch, *Rerum* 366, especially lines 47–50.

Let's not, then, offer such a sacrifice.
I have determined that we'll let her go,
And burn her clothing in the fire instead. 370

The gentleman says to Guglielma:
Because I know and since I clearly see
That for resentment you have been condemned,
We all here present, therefore, are resolved
That from such punishment you should be freed.
But in this case you must be circumspect,
For in this realm you never must be found
Because, for having set you free from death,
We'd not lose our own lives on your account. 378

Guglielma thanks God for having escaped and says:
I thank you, Lord, devoutly as I can,
With all my heart and with my intellect;
I am entirely kindled with your love,
You have from such a wicked sentence set
Me free. I mean, my Spouse, to serve you all
My life. Be with me, Mary, mother mine,
And let me not, unfortunate, alone,
Be eaten by the wild and savage beasts. 386

*Guglielma comes into a wasteland, and when she is about to fall asleep, Our Lady,
dressed as a woman, appears to her, and not revealing who she is, says:*
Belovèd daughter, place your hand in mine,
And rest secure; of nothing be afraid
Because you're isolated in this wood.
You know that I am with you steadfastly;
To me forever have you pleasing been,
And ever firmly in the service of
My Son; for doing good, you will not bad
Receive; I rather wish to comfort you. 394

Our Lady continues, saying:
Whoever will confess his sins to you,
With penitence and with contrition true,
By you may from each evil be set free—[4]

---

4. *evil:* Ital. *mal.* As in English, the Italian word for "ill" can allude to ills of the flesh

This is the promise that my Son has made:
With the sign of the cross they will be healed.
He'd be revealed through your unceasing works
Because the time has come that every one
Of your desires should be achieved in full.   402

Awakening, Guglielma says to Our Lady:
Pray, who are you that in this gloomy place
Thus visits me who suffers such great woe?
So much your countenance assures me that
My every sorrow now has fled from me.
Your name, O tell me openly and clear,
And may it be that you will grant my wish.
You must be queen or else a baron's wife,
Such consolation do you give to me.   410

Our Lady reveals herself to Guglielma by speaking, but she doesn't recognize her until she departs.
My cherished and belovèd daughter, know
That I am she who saved you from the fire;
In this harsh wasteland you are not alone,
For I shall come with you in every place.
Guglielma, clearly understand my words:
Your every torment into joy and game
Will be converted for your constancy
So great, for you have trusted in my name.   418

Guglielma regrets that this lady has departed from her:
Alas, delight of mine, where have you gone
While in this wandering wood I linger still?
So quickly, why have you abandoned me?
For you before revealed yourself so kind.
O who will now bring comfort to my life?
O gentle Jesus, let me constant be,
There's nothing here to eat, and no place more
For rescue: Oh, I don't know what to think!   426

---

or ills of the spirit. In the ambiguity of this word reposes the possibility that Guglielma receives not only the power to heal the physical sickness of sinners, but to absolve them of their sins as well. This power was the exclusive prerogative of priests. If Pulci means what she says in both senses, this is an early instance of the suggestion that in the view of Christ and his mother, if not the church, women can serve as priests.

After she says this, two angels come to comfort Guglielma, and putting her between them, they say to her:

>My sister, tell me, for what reason do
>You seem so greatly troubled and distressed?
>Do you not believe that promise, then,
>Made by the queen who tarried here with you?

Not recognizing them, Guglielma says:

>I am so totally bewildered that
>There's nothing I would welcome more than death.

The angels say to Guglielma:

>If you would like us as companions we
>Will go along with you upon your way.   434

When they come to a certain place, they find a ship's captain sitting with certain companions, and one of those two angels calls out to the said captain and says:

>My brother dear, pay heed a moment, please:
>On our lord Jesus Christ's behalf, please see
>That you conduct this lady, who is God's
>Exalted servant, and with great respect
>Please treat her; take her where she most desires
>To go, for she's a lady of great worth,
>And she will compensate you very well.

Not recognizing the angels, the ship's captain answers them:

>If I am paid, I'll go along with her.   442

Guglielma thanks the angels and says:

>O belovèd, cherished brothers mine,
>I thank you in the name of God, but how,
>When I've no money, shall I pay my fare?
>This man won't like that, if I judge aright.

One of the angels gives a ring to Guglielma, saying:

>Receive this gift, a marvel in the world.

And the angel turns to the captain and says:

>With this be paid; to your safekeeping I
>Entrust her, captain; for my love receive
>And prize her, for which wondrous signs you'll see.   450

Turning to Guglielma, an angel says:
>And you, my sister, you shall journey on
>Escorted thus, and in good company,
>Until you in this woodland find
>A dwelling chaste, the one your heart desires,
>Your husband there you very soon will see;
>His brother, who displayed his false deceits
>To you, shall you bring back to health.
>Requited for your suffering then you'll be.   458

Guglielma laments that those two angels must leave her, and she says this:
>O wretched me, for I had thought to lead
>My life in chastity and ever serve
>My God with dedication absolute, but now
>Another life I must expect to have.
>I pray you, if you find my righteous prayers
>Acceptable, do not disdain to show
>Me who you are; acquaint me with your names,
>And I forever shall remember you.   466

The angels answer Guglielma:
>The time has not yet come for us to tell
>Our names to you. But you will know them soon,
>And you will come to dwell in those parts where
>Our home is, for that country you will see.
>Be pleased to be accompanied by these
>Alone, for you will safely come to port[5]
>At last, and aid divine will be with you;
>We are obliged to take another path.   474

The two angels having departed unseen, Guglielma asks the captain and his companions if they have seen them:
>Ah wretched me, have any of you seen
>My brothers, cherished and belovèd? For
>Behold, I've lost them for no cause; alas,
>Where can I once again recover them?
>If they should chance to come among you, I
>Would be content to only look on them.

---

5. An instance of Pulci's frequent use of the Petrarchan image of the boat coming safely to port.

The captain answers:
>We've not seen anyone except yourself;
>Our word you may most certainly believe. 482

Once the angels have left, Guglielma realizes who they were, and, sorrowing within herself, she says:
>O heavenly Goodness, now I recognize
>Who these are that have my companions been.
>With all my heart, O kindly Mother, I
>Give thanks to you, O my sweet advocate,
>The holy angels of your Godly choir,
>Have in this forest kept me company;
>Ah, blessed be thou, Queen of Heaven, who
>Escorts this pilgrim and directs her way. 490

The captain prays Guglielma to condescend to heal one of his sick crewmen:
>Since you're so greatly favored with God's grace,
>Petition, please, his great Benignity,
>That, through your holy prayer he will relieve
>This wretched, ailing man, and if so great
>A gift your heart can claim, then I desire
>To vow your faithful servant to become.

Guglielma answers:
>So great a grace I'd like to gain for you;
>You must believe that what you ask will be. 498

Guglielma prays to God and heals the sick man:
>O Monarch great, O just and worthy Lord,
>Who saved your servant formerly in life,
>Sweet Advocate, Defender of my heart,
>By your surpassing mercy infinite,
>Be pleased to listen to my humble prayer:
>For just as my own prayer was granted, Lord
>Benign and kindly, grant this boon to me:
>That this sick man by me may be made well. 506

Healed by Guglielma, the sick man says:
>What a gift this is, eternal, boundless God,
>To this poor sinner you've revealed today.
>As greatly as I can, with all my heart,

I render thanks, O righteous Lord, to you,
And each desire of mine is only fixed
Upon abandoning the world that's filled
With error; to obey you, worthy Lord
And just—you've shown me such a wondrous sign.   514

The captain says to Guglielma that he wants to lead her to a nunnery where she can dwell:
O reverend lady, if you will be pleased
To come along with me into my land,
I've found a very fitting place for you
Since you desire to always serve your Lord;
For holy women it is much renowned;
There you will be allowed to end your life.

Guglielma answers the captain, and they go to the nunnery mentioned:
To serve God is my firm intent, but not
Confined in the religious way of life.   522

On arriving at the nunnery, the captain says to the abbess:
Reverend Mother belovèd, in Jesus' name,
Because I bear you great affection, this
Servant elect I shall present, for she
A source of your felicity will be
Because her prayer is so acceptable
To God; for she has many persons cured
Who've felt contrition for their sins—by her
From every illness have they been released.   530

The abbess accepts Guglielma and says:
May you, Lord Jesus, be forever praised!
For such a worthy gift we give you thanks.
If being our companion pleases you,
We now accept you as our sister here.
My sister sweet, consider well what task
You would prefer that we assign to you.

Guglielma answers the abbess:
I'd like to pray to God for sinners and
Do every humble task there is to do.   538

The abbess says to Guglielma:
> I'm very pleased, belovèd sister, that
> You've been so well instructed, but what do
> You want to tell? and what's the reason that
> You've turned up in these parts? And by what name,
> Dear lady, are you known, that you should be
> So greatly satisfying to our God?

Guglielma answers the abbess:
> Know, then, that I am called "the one who sins."[6]
> Know nothing else of my unhappy life.   546

Guglielma continues and speaks thus to the abbess:
> My discourse would be far too long if I
> Should wish to tell the story of my life,
> Or the occasion for my coming here;
> My homeland's name do not desire to know.
> For God has promised it will not be long
> Till every deed of mine will be made clear;
> Jesus, the Son of God who sees all things,
> To every deed of mine will witness bear.   554

Many poor and sick people come to the nunnery to Guglielma, for she was the gatekeeper, and a poor man asks Guglielma to give him alms; she prays, and there she cures many withered and blind and lame, who, made whole, rejoice and throw their crutches away, and a poor man says:
> O holy lady, for the love of God,
> Let this blind person here implore your grace.

Guglielma answers the poor man:
> No coin have I to give you, brother mine;
> I shall pray God that you may be restored.
> Be sure your every wish is fixed on that,
> And for each sin of yours contrition feel.

And facing the poor man she says:
> O kindly God, let my unworthy prayer
> Through me your servant manifest some sign.   562

---

6. *one who sins:* Ital. *peccatrice:* a verbal icon regularly applied to Mary Magdalene, the prostitute whom Christ reformed.

The brother of the King of Hungary, fallen ill with leprosy by the judgment of God,
leprous goes before his brother, and begging the king to have him cured, says:
> My lord take pity on me, for you see
> The wrath of God, the unrelenting scourge,
> And all parts of my flesh tormented thus;
> Your brother in the flesh, do not despise.

The king says to his servants:
> My servants go, convene the College of
> Physicians and make clear to them this case
> With diligence, and let whatever they
> Can do be done, and that immediately.   570

A servant goes to call many doctors and says:
> I am directed to command that all
> You doctors and physicians come to see
> A case with all your learning, for to you
> It soon will be explained how, all at once,
> The king's own brother finds himself beset
> With leprosy all over; you must come
> And offer your opinions in this case.

One doctor answers for all the others:
> And we shall offer them; that do not doubt.   578

When the doctors are assembled before the king, having seen the symptoms and
examined the sick man, one of them says to the stricken one:
> This is indeed a very serious case,
> And cautiously we must proceed, as in
> His second volume Avicenna notes,
> And on this problem Galen much remarks—[7]
> But have no fear, you will at last be cleansed,
> And will be treated very skillfully.

Another doctor says to the sick man:
> It's black bile in the blood that causes this;
> It can't be cured except at great expense.[8]   586

---

7. Avicenna and Galen were medieval Arab medical authorities and much ancient Greek medical knowledge had been transmitted to Europe through their work.
8. Pre-modern Western medicine was founded on the four elements of Greek physics.

A servant tells the king that he should send away the physicians and take his brother to
a woman who performs miracles at a nunnery. (This was Guglielma):

>Forgive me, sir, if I am over bold.
>None of these men have understood the case.
>Their science seems entirely false to me,
>For all these doctors have no consciences,
>And who falls in their hands—him woe betide!
>His purse at last will be the penitent,
>For long or fatal they'll his illness make.
>O lord, believe me; send them all away.   594

The servant continues:

>For I am certain I've heard wondrous things
>About a woman, servant of our God,
>Who dwells beside a wasteland; she with her
>Works marvelous has opened up the eyes
>Of many who were blind from birth; her works
>Have been so full of grace, and persons deaf
>And mute she has released, and she would be,
>If you'll believe me, very good for him.   602

The king's brother asks the king to lead him to that woman.

>If I am worthy, lord, I pray that you'll
>Be pleased to lead me to that holy place,
>Unworthy, wretched sinner though I be,
>You see how, bit by bit, I rot away.

The king says to his brother:

>I'm happy to, and I shall leave the realm
>Because this wish of yours must be fulfilled.

And turning to a baron he says:

>You govern and command till I return—
>It will be but a few days, as I think.   610

Disease was attributed to an imbalance of "humors,"—bodily fluids thought to be the
counterparts of earth (black bile), air (yellow bile), fire (blood), and water (phlegm).
An excess of black bile produced a melancholic disposition and associated problems. By
mocking the physicians' pedantry, ineptitude, and greed, Pulci is having utterly
conventional fun at their expense.

Having arrived at the nunnery where Guglielma was, the king, not recognizing her,
begs her to heal his leprous brother, and says:
>The fame of your surpassing holiness
>Has made us, lofty lady, come to you;
>For this my brother, who is leprous, have
>Compassion, for he lives in fearful pain;
>If you will give him back his health once more,
>His every desire will be to serve that One
>Who died and was derided on the cross,
>And I shall never from you parted be.   618

Guglielma answers the king, pretending not to recognize him, and speaks thus:
>I cannot such a grace alone perform,
>But rich my Lord is, and his power can,
>When it may please him, be made manifest.
>And to his clemency, I'm glad to pray
>That he'll be pleased to wish to cure this man,
>But in your presence he must first confess
>If ever in his life he's done you wrong,
>And, for my love, you then must pardon him.   626

The king says to Guglielma:
>I freely, lady, promise this to you,
>That I shall pardon him to earn your love.

And turning to his brother he says:
>Speak up, my brother, don't fear anything,
>And openly confess your every fault;
>For God is always ready to forgive,
>Like a good lord, a person who repents;
>If you want Jesus to fulfill your wish,
>You will speak clearly so you may be heard.   634

The brother of the king reveals how he had accused Guglielma, and asks forgiveness:
>I do not know well how I should begin
>To make my sin here manifest, or how
>You, brother, will be able to forgive
>My having done you such great injury.
>You know you left me to advise the queen,
>And counsel with your principality
>When you went visiting the Holy Land,
>And much you trusted me to keep her safe.   642

The said leper continues:

    I feigned to want to speak with her about
    State matters in her chamber privately;
    Once there, with wicked and dissembling words,
    My heart's great love I opened up to her.
    She, who understood my every thought
    And the unbridled love that burned my breast,
    And fearing lest I might attempt much more,
    Then ordered me no more to speak to her.   650

The leper brother continues:

    When soon thereafter I before you came,
    About your consort you inquired of me;
    Of infamy I falsely her accused,
    And that she had disgraced your court, I said;
    And you were so infuriated by
    My speech that finally you charged me with
    Her death, whence I, who wished to give my thoughts
    Free rein, consigned her, guiltless, to the fire.   658

The said man continues:

    You've never heard of such great treachery!
    God's justice, when it came, came late
    Because she bore the greater torment when
    That fire burned her; it's right that you burn me—
    Indeed, too late and hapless, penitent—
    It's right that you esteem me pitiful.

And turning to God, the king's brother says:

    And you who see each thought within my heart,
    Have mercy, Jesus, mercy for such great wrong.   666

Dumbfounded and enraged against his brother, the king says:

    O woe is me, for what I've listened to!
    I've never heard about so great a crime!
    Then, wicked ingrate, tell your brother how
    You could be bold enough to blame her so;
    It wasn't enough that you had tempted her,
    Left in your care—betrayed your brother, too!
    You even had to seek her death, too cruel,
    Though faithful she had always been to me.   674

Thinking Guglielma dead, the king addresses his next words to her, and says:
Ah me, Guglielma, my belovèd wife,
Unwittingly I've done you such great wrong
Without inquiring anything from you,
So greatly kindled by disdain and wrath.
Though you had treated me so graciously,
I lowered myself to this man's false requests.

And addressing Guglielma, he says:
But since, for your love, I have promised it,
Let every sin of his forgiven be.   682

Guglielma prays to God for the leper, and heals the leper:
My Jesus, O, if any prayer of mine
Was ever welcome in your presence, may
Your pity and your clemency appear;
Upon this wretched leper may your power
Be manifest before this company.
O Jesus sweet; O my belovèd spouse,
In the name of the blessèd trinity,
Restore his true well-being to this man.   690

The leprous man having been healed, kneeling to God and thanking him, says:
O Pity great, unbounded Charity,
O show me how I can perform thy praise:
This weary soul and all its wayward course,
Sweet Lord, I want to consecrate to you!
O lady, as you're so at one with God,
Please, on your servant's part, beseech him that,
Released by such a prayer, I won't become
Ungrateful for a gift so generous.   698

Guglielma raises the veils from her head and reveals herself to the king her husband, and speaks thus:
O hope so sweet, O my belovèd spouse,
Your Guglielma you have so forgot
That you no longer know her, and grow grave;
She whom you had sentenced to the fire
Would not have such a felony concealed;
That one who finally preserved me here,
He who observed me wandering in the world,
Wished merely to assay my constancy.   706

Guglielma continues:
> Already to that gruesome torture led,
> And while to heaven I prayed devotedly
> That I from mortal justice might be freed,
> My Lord abruptly touched the mind of him
> Who had to do an evil deed like that,
> And so he said to me that, secretly,
> I must go thence, and he'd burn just my clothes,
> Pretending thus to satisfy your will.   714

Guglielma continues:
> I went from thence, though I knew not the way,
> And many days I travelled through the woods,
> Where Mary called upon me and where I
> Two angels met with her, and they became
> My chaste and daily company until
> I came within the walls of this place where
> We've healed so many people, as our prayers
> Have proved so gratifying to our God.   722

The king, having recognized his wife Guglielma and having understood how she escaped, says to himself and his servants:
> I don't know if I dream or know aright,
> Or if I am deluded by my woes.
> O what a gift this is, high, mighty God;
> You in a blink can many years restore.
> Let us report this case to everyone,
> So the celestial choir will more rejoice
> For one blest spirit midst the chosen ones,
> Than for the ninety-nine already saved.   730

And addressing Guglielma, he says:
> Forgive me that I was deceived like this
> By this the cruel brother of my flesh
> Whom you have cured although you had no cause,
> Since he'd made me so want to murder you.
> Please make a supplication for my sin
> With your "Our Father" that so much avails.

Guglielma answers the king, her husband, and says:
> Let God forgive you every sin of yours,
> For I forgive you, O my husband sweet.   738

Guglielma, joyful at having found her husband again, says to the king and to God:
> I felt as sad at my departure as
> A soul that feels the final punishment;
> How happy is my life, how joyful that
> My every good at once has been restored.
> And for such sweetness, which is infinite,
> Unto your tranquil power I give thanks,
> O high and boundless, uncreated God!
> How just you are, how holy and benign!   746

The leprous brother of the king recognizes Guglielma, and, apologizing to her, says:
> O you most holy lady, worthy, chaste,
> How can I ever make amends with God?
> For she, so worthy, whom I had betrayed
> Has by her prayer today restored my health
> Though my voice too unworthy was to speak
> With her; forgive this ingrate sinner vile.

And addressing his brother he says:
> And brother, you in Jesus' name forgive
> This one who treated you so heartlessly.   754

Addressing his brother, the king says:
> Because to you the Lord's been merciful,
> I too desire to treat you courteously,
> The queen benignly has forgiven you,
> As well, for such abominable offence.

The king, addressing Guglielma, says:
> And you, my ever dutiful Guglielma,
> So you can go with us into our realm
> Again, bid your farewells to those kind nuns,
> From mother and from sisters, take your leave.   762

Guglielma, having to depart, bids farewell to the nuns, and first says to the abbess:
> Belovèd sisters mine, since God is pleased
> That this my husband I accompany,
> My mother and my sisters, dwell in peace,
> With you I'd thought to live, had planned to die;
> I know my going much will sadden you,
> But his requests I am obliged to heed;

Though I must leave you, yet with ardent zeal
To see you again in heaven I expect.   770

The abbess, sorrowful at Guglielma's departure, speaks thus:
I had not thought that anything but death
Could separate us from so great a love;
With you, you bear our love for you away;
Be sure, your leaving's difficult and hard
For us, but, as it's pleasing to your lord,
That one who governs in the court most high
Will give to us his perfect patience good,
O sister sweet, in this your going forth.   778

The king, having returned to Hungary, shows Guglielma to his barons, and recounts the case as it happened:
Look carefully if you would recognize
Guglielma, who was once your queen, indeed,
And who, as you all know, unjustly was
Condemned, poor woman, in the fire to burn.
Things marvelous shall you hear: in order that,
Through her, God's grace could stand revealed, that man
Who was supposed to burn her body was
Inspired by God to free her from the fire.   786

The king continues:
When this my leprous brother I had led
Before that lady at the convent blest,
Her prayer so just was and so merciful
That he was healed by sacred mystery;
Then hearing her call me husband and his whole
Narration of each circumstance, as I
Was looking at her, suddenly her face
I recognized and knew her voice as well.   794

The barons rejoice for Guglielma, and they say to her:
O gracious lady, most beloved and chaste,
O Godly goodness, what a joy is this!
O blest be he who has preserved you so!
How great a trouble for us was your case!
O Guglielma, much belovèd queen,

Who does all this; if it is clear to us,
For such a great gift, such great benefit,
At our shrines shall we offer sacrifice.   802

Guglielma reveals herself to her servants and says:
Most faithful and belovèd servants mine,
Right here before you in your presence now,
Behold Guglielma, to whom you were so dear,
And for whom you, at her departure, wept.

The servants, embracing Guglielma with great celebration, say:
O heavenly God, we never thought again
To cast our eyes upon your clemency.
That you live in the world great happiness
Gives us; our empress once again is found.   810

*The king, addressing the barons, says that, mainly because his leprous brother was
healed, he wants to leave his realm to them, distribute his treasure, and go away with
Guglielma and his formerly leprous brother to a solitary place that he has seen God
reveal through Guglielma.*
And you my friends so dear, give thanks with me
Together to our good and gracious Lord
And these my treasures, please share out among
His servants poor for love of him. As you
Will see I have determined to divest
Myself of regal honors, since my Lord
So worthy has revealed to me how I
May grow much richer in a greater realm.   818

The king continues:
And all the days remaining of my life
I wish to spend in serving God with this
My dear Guglielma in my company,
And every human joy I shall despise.

And addressing the barons he says:
For you, O barons, shall the kingdom be
To govern in the manner that you please,
For you'll do honor to my royal stock,
And this will be the pleasure of your lord.   826

Passing through the wasteland, he speaks with Guglielma and with his brother:
>This hermitage my royal palace will
>Become, these hair shirts my rich clothes,
>These caverns will our solace be, our feasts
>So sumptuous will be stern discipline.[9]
>O false, O foolish world, O blind and mad,
>That just for your delights provide yourself!
>To God I leave you, human glory, pomp,
>And, Lord, may you show me the victory!   834

After they have entered a hermitage, the angel comes and dismisses the audience:
>O you who wander in this erring wood,[10]
>This mortal life where nothing is secure,
>Toward God, who is unswerving, turn your gaze,
>Where one finds certain every hope at last.
>How worthy and obedient was Guglielma
>With her humility that overcame
>All else; they're happy whom the world torments,
>For then they'll live in heaven, ever blest.   842

THE END

9. *discipline:* Ital. *disciplina:* Also alludes to the whip and the ritual of flagellation.
10. *erring wood:* recalls Dante, *Inferno* 1.1–6.

THE PLAY OF
THE PRODIGAL SON

The Angel heralds the play:
O just Redeemer, full of clemency,
Who spilled for us your blood upon the cross,
O thou surpassing wisdom, infinite,
Through you alone has boundless God called us,
By your divine authority, to heav'n,
Summoned us with your pity's suffering,
Kindling our hearts with utmost zeal so we
Can here perform your gospel's sacred word.   8

The prodigal son finds a person named Randellino, and says:
O Randellino, let's play a game of cards.

Randellino answers:
Ah yes, because I feel obsessed with them.

Randellino says to another of his companions:
Have you the cards there, Riccio del Beretta?[1]

---

1. Riccio del Berretta. A recondite and multiple pun. *Riccio* means "hedgehog" or
"curly"; *berretta* alludes to the cap worn by priests and also figures in a saying, *val più una
berretta che cento cuffie* [one man is worth more than a hundred women] (Reynolds 93). No
fifteenth-century editions of *The Prodigal Son* are known to survive. The earliest surviving edition is that of Florence, 1550. Cioni remarks that the epigraph *nuovamente stam-
pato* (newly published) on the title page suggests a first printed edition. But he doubts
that this edition is in fact the first one (138). If it is the first, however, it means that
a manuscript version, perhaps an autograph, survived the author by half a century. At
least nine sixteenth-century and nine seventeenth-century editions survive: Florence:
1572, 1583, 1584, 1585, 1591, 1614, and 1620; Bologna: 1611, and an early eighteenth-
century edition; Lucca, undated; Siena: 1573, 1590, 1606, 1610, and 1624; Treviso and
Venice, 1627. The story of the prodigal son appears in Luke 15.

Riccio answers Randellino:
>I have them, or I couldn't get along;
>Whoever wins must pay me half a jug.

Randellino answers:
>Let that be as you wish at any rate,
>Let's get a move on; come on, now, let's play;
>I'll cut because I have the cards in hand.   16

The prodigal son to Randellino:
>I want to be the first to draw a card;
>All this says it's an ace, good buddy boy.

Randellino answers:
>Whoa, not so fast, this is no time for jokes
>Indeed—the stakes you wager are too high!
>You don't see that I can't pay or that I
>Don't wish, I swear, to profit in that way.

The prodigal son to Randellino:
>You're blind drunk, Randellino, don't say no.

Randellino answers:
>The worse for you if you lose, then; I'll cut.   24

Randellino says:
>An ace, a second, I advised you well,
>One doesn't want to set the stakes so high.

The prodigal son answers:
>It often happens that I lose like this,
>It seems that I can't ever change my luck.

The prodigal son tears up the cards, and says:
>O ace, accursed with all the pains of hell,
>You always were the reason that I played.

Randellino turns to the company:
>Since I've been lucky, let's go out and drink,
>For I want everyone to have some fun.   32

The grieving prodigal son says:

    O cursèd cards, O fate malevolent,
    Adverse, perverse, and sorrowful event,
    I don't think that beneath the moon before
    Was ever found with luck like mine a man
    Who of a thousand bets could not win one.
    "Unfortunate" I surely can be called—
    I am not paid up yet—I want to go
    And ask my father for my inheritance.   40
        It's sure if nothing's ventured, nothing's gained;
    I want to go away and try my luck,
    Go seeking in every land throughout the world
    And reveling in each joy without restraint;
    I know that my inheritance is great,
    And one with money travels without fear;
    For those who can enjoy it this world's made,
    I want to banish this unpleasantness.   48

The prodigal son goes to his father and says:

    O venerable, beloved Father mine
    I pray you to bestow a grace on me;
    That which I ask, with happy outcome, please,
    Do not deny, but now fulfill my wish.
    You know how firm my fancy's always been,
    Just wishing through the world to fare and play.
    In this way is my fantasy inclined;
    For this reason, let me have my share.   56

His father answers:

    Alas, dear son, what you have said to me,
    How from your father you desire to part,
    You've set a grievous sorrow in my heart.
    Don't let me hear you say such things again.
    Without a thought you wish to rise in flight,
    For nothing will I give you my consent.
    Consider staying here with me, sweet son,
    Because near you I wish to end my life.   64

The son replies to his father:

    O Father dear, you have been wasting time,
    You shouldn't overtax your strength so much;

You'd sooner touch the heavens with your hand
Or, surely, dry the sea than change my mind;
However much you waste your time in vain,
No longer think to argue with me now,
Give me, my Father, what belongs to me,
For I'm determined to bid you farewell.   72

The father says to the son:
    O my dear son, you are too obstinate;
    Consider well the course on which you're set.
    You know how comfortably I've brought you up,
    You've never tasted any hardship, and
    You're used to being well provided for.
    Now through the world you'll go in great distress;
    Poor wretch, don't think to err in such a way,
    Ah, don't let anger overcome you so.   80

The son responds:
    You're wasting time, and vainly tire yourself.
    I am resolved to go to foreign climes.
    You've no need to repeat yourself so much,
    Or exercise your wit or art, for sure,
    Or think, indeed, that you'll refuse me now.
    Through a thousand pages you could hold this course—
    A man decided doesn't want advice,
    So please oblige me, let me have my share.   88

The father to the son:
    In former times, beloved son of mine,
    Always you were humble and reverent—
    Alas, by God, do not insist upon
    Departing from me thus on such a whim.
    You know with what great love I hold you dear;
    My heart for you, it's certain, feels great pain,
    Sweet son, do not desire to go away,
    Ah, bend your will to yield to such great prayers.   96

The son to the father:
    My Father, I don't want to argue more,
    Give what is mine, and rest in peace
    Because I am resolved to do this thing,

And this delights and pleases me, I know,
And your incessant pleading is a bore—
Don't hold me longer so persistently;
Ah, Father, don't put up such great resistance,
Because I am resolved to take my leave.   104

The father to the son:

Oh, don't make me so sorrowful, my son,
Take pity on me who has brought you up;
You know that I have loved you even more
Than my own self—forever loved you thus,
Beloved son, the comfort of my heart.
Oh do not think to leave me in such woe,
Son; overcome such great hard-heartedness,
For my old age show some compassion, please.   112

The son to the father:

I do not hold your preaching worth a bean,
You must, my Father, understand me well,
Because my mind is all made up in this.
My will and kindled heart are set to leave;
In this I shall be disobedient.
No longer do I need to be reproved,
As has been done for others; give me mine,
And don't keep pouring forth such long excuse.   120

The father says to the son:

I see, son, that I tire myself in vain,
Since you are quite resolved to take your leave.
You are, it's certain, to yourself a foe,
Who wants to disobey me—wretched boy!
By my faith, I again admonish you:
I know that you'll repent this enterprise,
But for your portion I consent to have
Ten thousand florins given to you now.   128

The father turns to his bookkeeper and says:

Ten thousand ducats from the bank arrange
To have deposited to his account.
Be sure to count them out with diligence;
Unhappy boy, for my ill were you born,

These sorts of joys have you reserved for me,
You that in such comforts I've brought up.

The bookkeeper answers:
I shall go, by your leave, to count them out;
Take comfort, sir, be patient if you can.   136

The prodigal son says to the cashier:
I want Venetian ducats—all full weight,
And slowly count, be careful not to err.

The cashier answers:
Ah, let me work, for I have understood
You well; you want to teach my job to me.
I don't want to be stopped by you, for sure.
We're losing time, so start to draw your cash;
The worse for you, it won't do you much good,
For it will buy you double pain, at last.   144

The prodigal son says to the cashier:
It seems as if you give me your own goods
For you to need to grumble such a lot,
You have too greatly tangled up my brain
With haste, I won't recount these, but
I'm very certain you have cheated me,
And I don't mean to pay heed to your words.[2]   150

Becoming upset, the cashier says:
I can prove I'm better than you at this;
I caution you, I'm starting to get mad;
I am efficient, just, correct, and good—
But I excuse you owing to your youth,
And I forgive you for your father's sake,
Whom I have always loved in simple faith.
Recount them, for my duty I have done
For you; you're wrong to whine about my work.   158

The father resumes [addressing] the son, and says:
You're always seeking to provoke a quarrel—
One should not want to run amok like that.

---

2. Here, amidst ottava rima stanzas, a sestette uniquely occurs.

Beyond all reason, son, you are indeed
To wrongly injure my associate.
I know your bad condition, the worse for me;
What have you done in taking leave this way
Has struck me as a sign of things to come;
In you reigns neither prudence nor good sense.   166

The father continues speaking:
You have not even parted yet from here,
And yet I see you start to pick a quarrel;
How sad and full of sorrow is my life.
My son, alas you'll come to no good end,
For you my mind's completely gone astray.
Since you desire to go to other lands,
You'd better learn to be more temperate—
There none will care for you for love of me.   164

The son, taking leave of his father, comforts him, saying:
Beloved Father mine, O be at peace,
I know that many comrades I shall find,
Ah, from each suspicion free your heart.
I don't want you to complain about my love
So much; I'm filled with joy I promise you,
Because I'm hopeful still to earn a lot.
This proverb often one is wont to say:
"Who has cash in this world has what he wants."   172

The brother, seeing him depart, follows him saying;
Do you desire, sweet brother, thus to part,
And leave your father greatly stricken so?
It's certain you will be the death of him;
See how for sorrow he can't stand erect.
Ah wretched boy, do not give your consent
To leave your father vanquished by such woe.

The prodigal son says to his brother:
I have but lately argued this with you;
Mind your own business and let me depart.   180

The brother follows him saying:
Alas, beloved and dear brother mine,

At least shake hands with me as you depart;
I don't think that I'll ever see you more,
And so can it be you've grown so distant, strange?
You would be kind to answer me, by God,
Ah, do not let me vainly beg for this,
Master yourself! Be like a prudent man.

The prodigal son answers him:
Do not confuse me; let me go my way.   188

Departing, the prodigal son says to himself:
I can forever triumph, by my faith,
And certainly I have no lack of cash;
I want to head toward the piazza now;
I know that many comrades will be there,
And I shall lead a troop of them with me,
And though there may be some who wish for toil,
I want to think of always having fun,
And don't desire my thoughts to trouble me.   196

The prodigal son arrives at the square, where he meets seven boon companions, and the leader of them says:
We seven boon companions, by my faith,
Will all go with you if you so desire,
And never move an inch away from you;
If you are pleased to have us for your own,[3]
Then we shall love you more than anyone,
Your every pleasure will you always have.

The prodigal son answers to the leader of them all:
The circumstances of each one I'd know.

The leader answers:
That which you ask is rational and just.   204

The same continues:
I'm captain of these seven fellows and
My name is Pride, this other Avarice;

3. The Italian phrase *ci possederai* implies both the feudal relationship between overlord and servant, and the relationship between one possessed and a familiar spirit or demon.

We go together, comrade dear, and if
You want to know the names of all of these,
Each one in turn, I'll tell you; many folk,
Indeed, they've conquered: Envy, Wrath, and Sloth
They're named, and Gluttony and Lust.
Now I have made their natures clear to you.   212

Pride continues speaking:
I want to tell you of my nature now,
And to reveal, in part, my faults to you;
Far to surpass each creature is my wish.
Ambitious folk delight me most it seems,
And I want everyone to pay me heed;
Each one in word and deed I would outdo,
And wish to win in every enterprise.
My nature have you just now understood.   220

Avarice turns to the prodigal son and says:
My name is Avarice, and I can think
Of nothing but increasing what I own;
I value neither friendship nor my kin,
As long as I can gather many goods.
This is my goodness, this my every joy;
To prosper more, I'd even hurt myself;
I never have enough for future need;
In gathering goods, I disregard my life.   228

Envy says:
O boon companion, Envy I am called
And I take great delight in others' ills,
With poison always bitter is my heart,
And only vexing others pleases me,
And this agrees with me beyond all else;
Now I have told you what my concept is
Of seeing ill; what's worst most pleases me—
I take no joy in seeing someone's good.   236

Gluttony says:
Since here these others have informed you well,
My name I would acquaint you with;
I'm Gluttony, filled with iniquity,

Who thinks of nothing else but to consume.
I know how to make famine out of wealth,
Know how to turn great riches into nought,
And of great poverty I am the cause—
Now my condition have you understood.   244

Wrath says:
I'm sure that you'll be pleased to know my name;
You know that in me patience does not reign.
Woe to whoever seeks to trouble me,
For violent and with no tolerance
Am I, by my faith, you can see it's so.
Try the experience of it as you please:
Wrath is my name, pledged boon companion mine,
And I can pick a quarrel,[4] I promise you.   252

Lust says:
So I shall not be scolded by this one
My own name [now] shall I report to you;
And I know surely when you hear it you
Will scruple not a bit to love me well,
To grant my every wish; the kindled heart
Without restraint I have enraptured all
At once; and by my name one calls me Lust;
To this in frenzy, lecherous I rush.   260

Sloth says:
Since we in friendship are united now,
I want to tell you something of my state.
I am Sloth, one filled with wickedness,
And oftentimes I have no purposes,
For tedium delights me, laziness;
A hundred times an hour I change my mind,
And often I don't know just what I want;
With torment I am always plagued, and woe.   268

The prodigal son, having understood the circumstances of each of them says:
Your circumstances I have understood,
And fortunate it surely seems to me,

4. pick a quarrel: Literally "I know how to chase flies away."

O boon companions, to have found you here,
Each one prepared to come along with me,
Above all each intending to have fun;
Look here at all the cash I have with me.
I want us to prohibit all hard work,
And let the last one out lock tight the door. 276

The prodigal son leaves with these companions, and the father calls his elder son and says:

Your brother, son, as you perceive, has left
Us thus afflicted and disconsolate,
I have no hope of seeing him again;
Because my years weigh heavily on me,
My son, it's necessary that you be the one
Who'll manage and maintain our property,
And you must be the staff of my old age—
My every hope is surely fixed on you. 284

The son answers his father:

Beloved Father, I pray to God the just
That he will give you patience, comfort you.
Together with you I bear this sorrow great
My brother's caused in leaving us like this;
Good Father mine, command me as you wish;
I'll always stay obedient to your will,
And I shall ready be, good Father mine,
For every directive you may give. 292

The father says to the son:

O my sweet son, it's my desire to go
To look on our possessions once again;
I'm old, and I must do the right thing now,
For there is nothing one can do for me.
This still will be for me a sorrow great,
And much, much shorter will it make my life;
You will learn to do your work yourself,
For you are young and hardy and can do it. 300

The son answers:

What you command, that willingly I'll do;
From your heart, Father, banish every woe,

From all cares free I hope that you will live,
So in good spirits stay beside me still.
I shall attend to what needs doing, so
Set free your mind from all anxiety,
And exile from you such great suffering
So it will not precipitate your death.   308

The prodigal son returns home entirely bedraggled, and says:
Ah, how has fortune carried me away!
The worse for me, how I have passed my time.
Exhausted, naked, quite abandoned, poor,
I surely am brought low as I've deserved,
And were it not for acorns, I'd have starved;
Unclothed, all wrapped in rags, in broken health,
While servants flourish whom my father keeps—
Alas for me! Were I but one myself!   316
     Of tasty dishes I once had excess,
How many servants once all round I had!
Now what a price I pay for such great pomp.
In faith, poor me, if Father I had believed,
On acorns I would not be forced to feed.
Poor me, would I had taken his advice;
I want right now to go again to him,
And plead for mercy for my foolishness.   324
     "Just Father," I shall say to him, "I am
Not worthy, surely, to be called your son;
Make me your servant, hold me not in scorn
Because I have been disobedient
And gone beyond the bounds of your good will;[5]
Pray, as a servant please accept me now,
Give me some bread your servants leave behind
To ease my hunger, Father, if you will."   332

The prodigal son comes before his father and says:
Take pity on me, Father compassionate,
Have mercy, mercy, for my former sins.
Since I was disobedient to you,
Employ me as your servant at this time;
I know that God is ready to forgive,

5. Literally "overshot the mark," as in archery.

Like a good Lord, one who repents; for love
Of him, good Father, pardon me; not as
Your son but as your servant keep me on.   340

The father answers his son:
Ah, you are welcome back, beloved son;
You have enflamed my heart entirely with
Great joy, you know, for in suspicion, woe
And fear I've always been, son, since you left;
Let God be thanked with simple gratitude,
Since to safe harbor you've again returned.
I wish to host a solemn, worthy feast,
And clothe you in rich vestments once again.   348

The father calls one of his servants:
Come hither, Badgrass,[6] my dear servant, bring
To me a decorated, handsome robe, for this
Is my belovèd younger son who has
Returned in so impoverished a state.
In my heart never has there been such joy;
With diligence, please, strip him [of those rags].

The servant answers:
Good sir, it will be done as you command,
In full, without delay, please rest assured.   356

The father answers the son.
O my beloved son, I pardon you
The injury you've done me in the past.
Your being pardoned is a blessed state,
Be sure; see that no more into such sin
You fall. You see I have been merciful to you,
And I, since I have freely pardoned you,
Wish to make it manifest to God,
Because I cherish you so tenderly.   364

---

6. The servant's name—Mal'erba, "Badgrass"—literally means "weed." The term, however, has both popular and theological undercurrents. Popularly, it might be read as "ill-favored" or "ugly"; theologically, as "vice" or "sin." At one level the choice of name is a class-based jest, giving a buffoon's name to a servant. At another, the choice of name underscores the lesson of the parable.

And he continues:

> O Lord most pious, merciful, and good,
> Who in a blink can give back many years,
> You surely seem to me to be my son,
> Now that you've shed your rags; thanks be to thee
> Eternal God who lives and reigns above
> In Mercy's Highest throne: tell me, sweet son,
> Where you have been and all about those whom
> You have encountered all along the road.   372

The son answers:

> I am afraid, sweet Father, to begin
> To tell you of my life so villainous.
> I've not had any purpose but to play,
> And to surround myself with a brigade
> Of ruffians, who led me into grief.
> And I have wasted all my substance, too,
> On women, taverns, banquets, games of chance,
> On horses, falcons, and on garments rich.   380
>   And seven boon companions have I led
> Along with me filled with sad vices and
> With villainy. Used to bad, ribald deeds,
> Those ruffians—they were endowed, I'm sure
> With every wickedness of the worst sort,
> And every evil state; the whole world calls
> Them wicked. These stayed by me, never left
> My side while, Father, I had coin enough.   388
>   My time in ill employment have I spent;
> I have committed every sin and would
> Prefer not, Father, to remember them;
> Distinguished by infamy my life I led
> Until my money started running low.
> Then in such misery I found myself
> That as a servant I thought to be employed,
> Consider how low, Father, I had sunk.[7]   396
>   There was great famine in that country, then,
> And on a cruel master I had chanced,
> Who forced me to eat acorns with the swine—

---

7. Literally "how like a deer I seemed." In this context "deer" symbolizes the fallen state of the prodigal son both materially and spiritually. The usage is proverbial.

Toward me, he never felt compassionate.
My diet was those acorns, certainly.
Now think, sweet Father, if I had deserved
To be afflicted, and, transfigured thus,
With nought but acorns to be satisfied.   404

    Seeing myself reduced to such a plight,
I started to consider coming home—
When I recall it I entirely quake—
And to myself I said: "I want to go
Back to my father merciful, and I
Don't fear, indeed, that he will not accept
Me as a servant if I'm pleased to ask
His pardon and beg mercy for my sin."   412

    I don't deserve to find such grace in you,
Having done you, Father, such great wrong;
For pity have you wished to pardon me,
And wrap me in so rich a cloak again;
Enough I cannot thank you, Father kind,
So greatly merciful to me; Resolved
Am I henceforth to serve you always, and
In this the purpose of my heart is firmly fixed.   420

The father answers:
How greatly do I wonder at the words,
Alas, you speak to me, beloved son;
If at your parting I was sorrowful,
From all you've said, I had good cause to be!
Now I can say that you're alive again,
Sweet son, and that my blessing you enjoy;
Never wish to part from me again,
Nor yield again to your vain appetites.   428

The father says to a servant:
To my instructions listen, bursar dear,
And what I tell you, in full measure do
With diligence, O faithful servant mine:
Arrange a splendid banquet, and do me
Above all else great honor, and invite
Our relatives and friends to it, and let
The fatted calf be slaughtered for the feast;
Rich let the banquet be, and opulent.   436

The servant answers:
> As you direct me, sir, it shall be done;
> How to arrange an entertaining feast,
> A banquet greatly pleasing, I know well.
> That I shall do you certain honor, sir,
> Doubt not; don't worry, leave it all to me.
> I'd like to go prepare the banquet now.

The master says:
> Have players there of every instrument.

The servant answers:
> Dear master I shall see you're satisfied.   444

The banquet having been prepared, and those who were invited having arrived, the father says:
> You are all most welcome, everyone!

One of the guests answers:
> A thousand times over are you fortunate!
> Let God with all his saints as well be thanked
> Because returned is your belovèd son;
> Long weeping has been altered into joy;
> Each one of us is heartened much by this.
> Called by your servants, we have come to you,
> And graciously you have received us still.   452

While the playing and feasting go on, the elder son, coming home, hears the music and says to the servant:
> I hear playing many instruments
> At home; now tell me, servant, what may be
> The cause of this, for I can't fathom it.
> It's certain that I wonder much at this,
> Just thinking of it leaves me thunderstruck.
> A thing like this beyond all reason seems
> To me because my father, when I left,
> Seemed utterly beside himself with grief.   460

The servant answers:
> Know that your brother has returned to him,
> And that, to celebrate, your father has

Arranged a splendid banquet and has slain
A fatted calf. Now come inside the house
If you desire to see it. Never will
One see such a magnificent display;
By what I know, and see and hear of it,
Your father has not ever been so glad.   468

The elder son says to the servant:
How can it be that for this wicked wretch,
My father has prepared a feast like this?
For he has gambled all his worldly goods!
He surely should not take him back again;
It seems that he's returned with profit great!
So many instruments resound for him,
"One who does ill gets good in recompense,"
I can say this; it's happening to me.   476

He continues:
Wretched me, if only a measly lamb
Had ever been butchered for the love of me!
For this scapegrace, my brother, him who is
The very pinnacle of vice and every sin,
To make a greater feast and kill the calf—
With sorrow for myself my heart will break;
To such a party I don't wish to go,
Nor do I mean to come back home again.   484

The servant goes to report to the father and says:
Be advised, sir, that your elder son,
Won't come into the house for anything.
This celebration's tone he has perceived,
And, as it seems to him, unjustly have
You thus his brother honored splendidly,
Since that one ever disobeyed you, sir.
He's all upset and filled with suffering,
And will not join us in such revelry.   492

The father goes to the elder son and says:
Come now, sweet son, do not be so upset,
Because I have regaled your brother so;
Don't think that I don't love you, certainly.

Ah, do not be offended by this thing!
Come on into the house; rejoice with me!
Do not be troubled for your brother's sake
Who's recently returned to us again,
And one could say has risen from the dead.   500

The [elder] son answers the father:
I don't intend (and I've made up my mind)
To ever enter where you are again;
Nor will entreaties move me any more.
Thus is my fantasy resolved in this,
Since for this sorry fraud so great a feast,
And such great revelry there seems to be
That all the universe resounds with it,
So many instruments ring out for him.   508

The father says:
Belovèd son, obedient, reverent,
Do not desire to say again such things,
And from your mind all envy strip away;
For love of me, oh, do come home again,
For you obeyed me ever, in the past,
And in the future still so shall you do;
The hope I cherished for your brother, ah,
Be happy to rejoice in it with me.   516

The son to the father:
By these sweet words of yours am I induced
To want to do your bidding, Father dear—
Your every wish in full to satisfy.
Pray, grant me your consent to pardon me,
The worse for me that I've distressed you so!
No more do I wish from your will to part;
Do with me, Father, what you want to do,
Me you are able freely to command.   524

The elder son, returning home, embraces his brother, and says:
Dear brother you are welcome back again.
I surely never thought to see you more,
And to the son of Mary I give thanks
When I recall to mind, sweet brother, how

You had departed without company;
By night and day I used to sigh for you,
But now may highest God by all be praised
Because to this safe harbor you've returned.   532

His brother answers him:

Sweet brother mine, I never believed that I
Would look on you again in all my life;
If you but knew in what great griefs and woes
I've been since I departed, certainly,
For me much more compassion you would feel.
My father, through his goodness infinite,
Has wished with joy to have me back again,
However, and forgive my heavy sin.   540

The angel says:

We render thanks with upright hearts to God
Who always is prepared to pardon us.
There is no sinner who's so wicked, lost,
That Jesus mild will exile from himself.
Whatever errors great he has committed,
Since he desires to be set free from bonds
Deceitful and return with heart contrite
To him, Christ will exalt him in his reign.   548

The angel speaks and gives license to depart:

O each of you, who has considered well
The sacred gospel's history devout,
Give thanks with pure affection to the true
God, who reigns in lofty glory [there above],
So how to gain the victory he may
Teach you though you are covered with this flesh,
So that, when this brief life comes to its end,
You will be granted glory infinite.   556

THE END

THE PLAY OF
SAINT ANTHONY THE ABBOT

The play of St. Anthony the abbot, who converted one of his sisters and made her a nun of the convent of the Murate of Florence. And how three thieves, not wishing to accept his counsel, killed each other and were carried off to the dwelling of Satan. And he was horribly beaten by the devils. Newly reprinted.[1]
    Let the play of St. Anthony of the beard, a hermit, begin.

The angel speaks the prologue:
  O, may the ardent fire of love divine
  Cleanse all your passions and illuminate
  Your intellects and set your hearts aflame
  So you'll be servants waiting upon God—
  To honor whom and in whose blessèd name
  I pray you be attentive and desire
  To look upon this noble history
  So you may keep it in your memories.   8
      We wish to represent some of the life
  Of that most holy abbot, Anthony
  Of Egypt, famous hermit glorious,
  So you'll be able, having looked on it,
  To follow Jesus, who will always aid

1. Two fifteenth-century editions are known: that of the Miscomini collection, volume 2, and a quarto edition in italics of the late fifteenth century. Eight editions are known from the sixteenth century: Florence, 1517, 1547, 1555, 1589, and 1592; Siena: two undated editions and one in 1592.
The story up until Anthony's dispute with the philosophers is taken from *The Lives of the Holy Fathers*. The source for the story of the three thieves is taken from a collection of short stories called *Il Novellino*, from which Chaucer also got the plot for *The Pardoner's Tale* (D'Ancona 2:33–34).   **155**

Those who in purity of heart serve him,
And make them live in joy and give them then
The crown eternal after they have died.   16
    You'll see how quickly he replied to God,
Feeling himself called, and faithfully
Gave all of his possessions to the poor,
And left the world behind, and how that old
And envious serpent set out many snares—2
From all of which he happily escaped;
How, tested by two wise pagans, he prevailed
Against them, showed how they were wrong.   24
    You'll see how he gave excellent advice
To three fell robbers to flee avarice
So they from mortal peril might escape;
They, persevering in their evil ways,
Were seized by the cruel talons of dark death
For their iniquity. If you'll be still,
And think about it carefully, you can
Derive much pleasure from it and much fruit.   32

Now Anthony is in prayer, and, kneeling, within himself alone he says:
Our Father who art in heaven, you who hear
From earth whoever calls on you in faith,
You never deny your light to anyone
That loves you with his mind and all his might;
You know so well who all the sinners are,
Even though to serve you my will yearns,
I pray, however, that you'll grant me grace
That into your disgrace I'll never fall.   40
    And as, my Lord, you have created me
I am made very noble by your love,
And you have given me free will and wished
That in your very image I be formed,
And you have bought me with your blood again,
Arrayed yourself in lowly form for me—
Thus you were pleased to show to me the path
By which I may be safely led to you.   48

2. *serpent . . . snares:* Compare Petrarch, *Rerum* 99.6–8.

Anthony goes and finds a hermit, and speaks thus:
    O holy Father, servant to great God,
    The Lord's peace be with you eternally.
    I hope that I can have a talk with you,
    And I desire your counsel, if you please.

The hermit answers Anthony:
    You're welcome, O my son; may Jesus make
    You worthy of his love. Sit here by me,
    And speak of what you wish; then I shall say
    Whatever it is that God inspires me to.   56

Anthony sits with him and then speaks thus:
    This morning at the service in the church
    I heard a passage from the gospel which
    Has quite filled up my mind with thought because,
    Though I've a fervent zeal for serving God
    I feel I lack those holy virtues that
    Are means to gain us heav'n: "Leave behind
    All things if you would perfect be"—That's what
    This verse was saying, don't you, [Father], see.   64

The hermit answers:
    Our God eternal who created us,
    Wishing to save us, gave to us his law
    And his commandments holy, which he means
    By all his human flock to be obeyed;
    Whoever breaks his law falls into sin—
    Will die condemned if he does not reform;
    Beyond the law, he gives us then advice
    That it were well for you, my son, to take.   72
        Concerning his advice, when he tells you
    "Leave everything and you shall perfect be,"
    For one who cuts off every worldly root,
    And gives all his allegiance just to God,
    His soul will be made happy when he dies,
    For everything, without him, hold but vile;
    What's pleasing to the world displeases him
    Who bears in peace all pain for his Lord's [sake].   80
        If your Lord calls you, son, however, you

Must answer to his call obediently.
He yearned so much to give us paradise
That he died on the cross us to redeem.
Flee honor's trappings and all fame
For our salvation's damaged by each one,
And think how brief is this our [earthly] life
Compared to that which infinitely lasts.

Anthony answers the hermit:

To our Redeemer, Father, I shall pray
That he reward your charity because
My heart that strayed in utter darkness you
Have given light to, and I understand
This point by means of his love; I shall choose
The way of holy poverty, I know,
And in your prayers, O Father mine, I pray
That you will say a prayer to God for me.   88

Then he departs, and along the way he says to himself:

O Lord of heaven, maker of the world,
O Mary's Son, Christ Jesus, pray be pleased
To be my father and my governor;
I know you are my guide and light and hope,
That you will keep me from the pangs of hell
And make me travel on your holy path.
Into your wisdom, I commit me, Lord;
Now make me do what you consider best.   96

Anthony says to his companions:

My brothers dear, if we think well about
How much we're obligated to our God—
How he created us and only he
Sustains us, and to save us who were damned
Chose death with utmost suffering and shame,
And all this for our sins he did—then we
Must always penitent remain so that
We may be saved on the last judgment day.   104

One of his companions answers Anthony and says:

One should leave doing penitence to monks
And friars and hermits. Badly they must sleep,

And practice abstinence, bare-footed walk,
And wear ill clothing on their backs while we
Can luxuries enjoy and festivals.
And pomp and banquets often can we have—
While we are in our youth and happy thus,
We're not forbidden to enjoy the world.   112

Anthony answers his companion and says:
Although the world seems lovely to behold,
It is entirely filled with snares and pains;
With little sweet, much bitterness one gets—
A little joy and troubles infinite.
The cheerless soul, unfortunate and blind,
Is often taken in by its deceits
And doesn't see time quickly fly away;
Repentance after death will do no good.   120

The second companion answers Anthony:
Brother if, as you say, time flies away,
And if death always closes in on you
So every pleasure's snatched out of your hand
And never ceases to betray us, does
Not this cause alone make clear to you
What must for me seem doubly clear: that when
We can, we flee unhappiness and seek
To live in bliss forever more.   128

Anthony answers his companion and says:
The ones who have this world forsaken—they've
Been very wise as it has seemed to me;
That is, both rich and strong, and those in stations high
Are almost in an instant seen to fall.
Therefore, my brothers, have I made the choice
To altogether leave the world and leave
Vain pleasure, and desire to serve my Lord
Who died for love of me upon the cross.   136

The third of his companions answers:
If I have understood your words aright,
As your good friend I'm deeply sorrowful
That some friar has deluded you and that

You've turned, it seems, into a wondrous fish,
For, brainless, you put on the monkish hood.
For often one will take it off with shame,
And even then that madness travels blind
And leads a hard life in vile bickering.   144
    I think that those, Anthony, who remain
In the world in many fashions can be saved;
Just two sins could send me to the abyss:
If I stole goods, or if I murdered men.
And those who become friars—I answer you—
Most do it so they will not have to work;
If with your thought you still wish to proceed,
Don't be a friar unless one of All Saints.[3]   152

Anthony turns to his sister and speaks thus:
My sister, all the world is filled with tricks,
Nor is there any thing that is secure,
And all is vain indeed to one who his
Way follows, although all may cheerful seem.
But one who knows the world with spirit pure
Desires alone always to please our God;
Therefore I'd wish that, since we are alone,
We might seek his true children to become.   160

The sister answers Anthony:
When you say, Brother, that the world is full
Of tricks, all filled with vanity, and that
So many are deceived by it, that seems
To me to be a major truth to one
Who thinks about it well, yet nonetheless
In this same darkness everyone is found;
But when you speak of being God's own child
In no way can I fathom that at all.   168
    For all of us God's children are, and his
Commandments must we all obey so we

---

3. Konrad Eisenbichler has suggested that this anachronism is probably a pun: Don't be a friar unless you're a brother to every saint, and don't be a friar except at the convent and church of Ogni Santi—an Observant Franciscan church, i.e. one that strictly observes the Franciscan rule.

Can be then numbered with the saints above
When we must from this place at last depart.

Anthony answers his sister and speaks thus:
    My sister, we're like travellers on the road;
    Also, at any moment we could die,
    I therefore wish that, while we're able to,
    For God we might abandon all the world.   176

His sister answers Anthony:
    Now have I understood and think you tease,
    And think that these are words obscure, therefore
    I pray you that you mock me not, for I
    Won't believe you then when you speak true.

Anthony answers his sister:
    Lest you believe that I make fun of you
    When I am telling you the truth sincere,
    Rather this same thing I affirm to you,
    And I don't vacillate like one unsure.   184

His sister answers Anthony:
    Then, brother, you desire me to give up
    This great magnificence and luxury,
    My lovely house, possessions numerous,
    And, though I'm used to living joyfully,
    Poor to become, and to religion give
    Myself with every harsh austerity?
    To tell the truth, in this there surely seems
    But little wisdom—less experience.   192

Anthony answers his sister:
    So, sister mine, it seems to you I speak
    Of matters foolish, silly as it's thought?
    Because you have been formed the senses' friend,
    The virtue of reason has been stripped from you;
    You surely know what pains our father spent
    In storing these possessions up, and now
    As you can see, he's been discovered by
    The worms for food; what good to him these things?   200

The sister answers Anthony:
> Come now, can one not otherwise do well—
> Not living as a religious in the world?

Anthony answers his sister:
> The obstacles are numerous and great,
> And, without doubt, it's very dangerous.
> Believe what I say, and to it give assent,
> And don't desire to stay here in repose;
> Instead, by means of this brief suffering,
> Seek to secure eternal happiness.   208

The sister answers Anthony:
> O my dear brother, I am happy to.
> Forgive me if I was impertinent.
> For foolish was my speech and wicked too,
> So do with me whatever pleases you.

Anthony answers his sister:
> Well have you answered, and may our sweet God
> In his peace keep you, O my sister. Now,
> Mona Piera will keep you company
> Till at the Murate's convent you arrive.   216

Then Anthony sends for several paupers and when they have come he says to them:
> Dear brothers you are very welcome here—
> A hundred thousand times each one of you.
> I want to have my goods distributed
> Among your fathers, children, mendicants,
> Because for God's high sacrifice and for
> The marvelous and sacred gifts of God
> We must be grateful ever, share them out;
> For love of him thus I share them with you.   224

Having given them alms, he goes thence to the hermit and says:
> Behold me, Father, for I have returned
> And done at once what you have told me to,
> And all my patrimony to the poor
> I've given out; reclothe me now, I pray.

The hermit answers Anthony and says:
> Forever be the name of Jesus praised,

And give you grace to persevere; our God
Will inwardly create you a new man,
As I at present robe you outwardly.[4]   232

Satan converses with his companions, and speaks thus:
Companions mine, since without cause we are
Quite banished by that reign celestial where
We so noble were brought into being,
When I see that God's made another plan,
That our place he has given to mankind,
I am consumed with envy and disdain;
My every catch is needful to us so
That, though we're injured, we won't suffer shame.   240
    We therefore must perform great wickedness,
For it's most just that very few of them
Can go from you to him who's banished us.
And those that sin will not be saved
If they die in their wickedness;
With us in darkness they'll be made to stay.
Therefore let us some sins now fabricate
So with us all of them will be condemned.   248
    I here create all seven of you chiefs
Above the others, captains, guides. Now go
Fill up the world with evils infinite:
Let them deceive each other, kill themselves.
Pride, envy, carnal sins; let some become
Extravagant, and let some lie;
Above all, make men miserly so that
For money they'll do many evil things.   256

Alone, Anthony falls upon his knees and says this:
O Jesus, Lord benign and sweet, how can
I ever from the many snares of this
World false and traitorous escape—so full
Of troubles, tricks and infidelities?
Take pity upon every sinner, Lord,
And, teach men how you want them to behave;

---

4. I have chosen to translate Italian *vestire*, literally "to clothe" or "dress," and here used
to mean being inducted into the religious life, as "ordain," "create," and "robe" to
catch the nuances associated with Antonio's conversion to the religious life.

Without your aid and lacking your advice,
No one so many dangers can escape.   264
An Angel appears and speaks thus to Anthony:
    God's servant, Anthony, O do not doubt
The world is full of tricks, as well you see,
And full of snares that wicked demons set
To lead all men to the profound abyss.
But our Redeemer is so pitying
And is so joyous made by charity
That whosoever does good deeds in him
Escapes the shackles of eternal pain.   272
    But one especially who clothes his soul
With true humility will by the devil be
In vain assaulted; Pay no attention to
His falsehood, for from Jesus good will you
Be parted never; rather he will make
Defense from each adversity, for who
Demeans himself for him, sets self at naught,
Is shielded most, and great heights will ascend.   280

Anthony speaks to the spirit of fornication:
    You cursèd spirit who's appeared in such
An ugly form, you I command, for by
The pow'r of blessèd Jesus must you tell
Me what your nature is and say whence comes
Your fright, for you display such wrath and fear.

The spirit answers Anthony:
    Alas, no more, no more, no more such words,
For you'll destroy me as sun melts the snow.   288
    The spirit I am of fornication; for
A long time I have persecuted you
With every strong temptation and grotesque,
And ever, day and night, I've set myself
To making new fantasies for you, and I
Have placed new snares and ambush new,
Have simulated women's faces oft
That would have conquered Nessus and Hercules.[5]   296

---

5. In Greek mythology, Nessus was a centaur who fought twice with Hercules. The second time Nessus had tried to rape Hercules's wife, Deianira. Dying from poisoned

And yet, however much I've honed my wits
To light a hotter and a brighter fire
To weaken you like dry wood, make you grow
Lascivious, you did not even show
A little sign except as a man who's
Deprived of life, so I'm devoured with ire
And envy since 'gainst you I vainly work.   304
　　Ah me, alas, how many aged men
Have I today led into my sweet net?
For mirages how many lonely saints
Have suffered not this raging thirst? Just you
Have passed among so many thorns without
A scratch and still your quietude enjoy,
Because of which I'm overcome and shamed,
And wish to exit from this labyrinth.   312

Anthony answers the spirit and says:
Let that omnipotent God be praised who let
Me look upon your swarthy face, whence it
Is certain, should my mind grow fearful of
Deceits that you perform, since you're so foul
And ugly, one's diminished—wicked too—
Who has embraced you, certainly. And now,
Be gone from me, infernal beast! for I
Know seeing evil fills you with delight.   320

The spirit returns to Satan and says:
Unhappy, lord, more than I've ever been
Do I return because of what's transpired.
Considering the case, I'm terrified,
Seeing that I have nothing earned at all;
More than a hundred I'd already have
Won over in the same time that I tried
That youthful monk of Egypt, Anthony,
By whom I was defeated in the end.   328

---

arrows, Nessus gave her a potion concocted of his blood and semen, advising her to dip Hercules' garment in it if she ever wanted to regain his love. She did, Hercules's flesh burned and peeled off, and he committed suicide to escape his pain. Here both are symbols of lust and its outcomes.

The spirit of sloth answers Satan and says:

My lord, no medal he deserves when all
The world seems blooms and battles and
Both day and night one works eternally—
Except chaffinches, nothing catches he;[6]
He's but a fire of straw, as one might say,
Though many things he may know how to do.
Let me, however, work my artistry;
His fantasy shall I entangle quite.   336

The spirit of fornication answers and speaks thus:

So you say that I'm not worth much and vile,
That any evil I can't use at all,
Nor work deceits except for childish ones,
But you know I'm the foe of laziness
And so accomplished and so very sly
That from his justice I've brought to ruin
More men in one day with my tricks than you
Could in a thousand years undo, indeed.   344
     But go ahead, if you're so vigorous,
And spread your nets, and you'll find out
That you're not cutting down some coward who's
Of small worth who neglects what he should do.

The spirit of sloth answers and says:

A leopard he must seem to you to be,
But I shall conquer him, as you shall see,
To spite you, merely, I'll heap shame on you;
In early morning there he'll dream the truth.   352

In the guise of a hermit, the spirit of sloth goes and finds Anthony and says:

O noble youth, where are you travelling?
You seem so burdened with a load of cares.
If some misgiving troubles you, tell me,
For I shall give you counsel willingly.

Anthony answers the spirit of sloth:

To tell the truth, O my dear father, I
Am unaccustomed to these paths, and I

---

6. That is, the spirit of fornication catches only persons with exaggerated sexual appetites, like chaffinches.

Am almost like one who has lost his way
In seeking to discover some hermit here.   360

The spirit of sloth to Anthony:

And you've had the good fortune to have found
Exactly that which you were wishing for;
This shows, therefore, your purity of will
So that the soul infirm finds some relief,
And have you taken, above all, good care
To tell me all the weighty things and light?
Because whoever his temptations hides
Makes them grow greater, different, and more deep.   368

Anthony answers the spirit:

I'm pleased to open all my heart to you
So it can gain some measure of relief:
I once felt a great fervor in myself,[7]
But now with boredom great I start to live
In such a way that always I'm afraid
Like persons who have been besieged and all
Atremble like a leaf blown by the wind,
Though nonetheless I still am of good will.   376

The spirit answers Anthony:

Now you can see, my son, it was inspired
For you to come to be found in this place
So that you could be soon restored in this
Quite dangerous but little fire, because
If it had longer been delayed, it would
Have flared up greatly, bit by bit, in such
A way that you'd have been conducted where
You would have been quite shattered by despair.   384
        Attentively, then, listen to me now,
And understand well what I say to you:
We're in this world as in a forest dense,
Where that old serpent hides who does not sleep;
And with great malice often he pretends
To be our friend but, feigning to wish us well,
He tightly binds us with his chains instead.   392

---

7. This line is partly illegible in the text. The translation is partly informed guesswork.

So, seeing someone like you well prepared
For living virtuously though in the world,
He makes it seem the world is very far
From that supernal, joyous state; he spurs
Folk ever—says, "Go, rather strive to be
The first, and not the second"; this he does
So those who run may trip, experiencing
That this way is a savage one and harsh.   400
    That one who's used from childhood not to touch
Iced water—scarcely—and to be well off
And live in luxury and more than twenty years'
Accustomed liberty, when entering on
A life that's strict will always struggle with
Unhappiness, and, sighing, look askance
At penitence and do it in another way—
He dwells with boredom, but can't live with it.   408
    Now tell me, son, when you were secular,
What were you, and what urged you to come in
With us who live so sternly and so strict
And who continual tribulations bear?

Anthony answers the spirit:
Willingly I left the layman's life
Because God's love so strongly called to me,
And I was rich and twenty years of age
And both my parents had already died.   416

The spirit answers Anthony:
Then, per adventure, you were all alone,
If I have understood well what you said.

Anthony answers:
To speak the truth, O Father, with no woe,
There is a sister who remained with me.

The spirit answers:
Now, my dear son, this answer me as well,
What did you do with her when you came in?

Anthony answers:
I left her in a women's convent and
The girl I comforted with reasons good.   424

The spirit answers:

I promise you that when I hear you speak
You make me anxious and make me afraid,
And I've entirely made my mind up that
Your coming in was not well done; instead
You've played a strange and foolish part to wish
To serve God in this manner, for you ought
First to have seen your sister married well,
And then you could have left the world behind.   432
     Do you not think that she felt deep regret
At being shut away to her disgrace?
And, should she go back to the secular life
To live unchastely and in filthiness
You'd be the reason that she lost her soul
With sorry reputation and obscure.
So speaking with you I've perceived the truth,
And I encourage you to leave these robes.   440

Anthony responds:

Your inference has made me understand
That you're the cursèd devil, certainly,
And you have come intending to take me in
With holy garb and with an aspect sweet.
There is no need to waste more words, ill-timed
And vain, because I've put my finger on
Your subtle flaw. Now trouble me no more;
You see how I've destroyed your every snare.   448

The spirit of sloth leaves and encounters the spirit of gluttony and the spirit of gluttony says to that of sloth:

O dear companion mine, whence do you come?
You seem so disconcerted, full of woe.

The spirit of sloth answers:

Don't wonder at it if I'm grumbling so,
For what I've done, of honor am I stripped.
Thinking that I would earn a great reward,
I went with a good will to lay siege to
That hermit, Anthony, and when I judged
That I'd won him, he banished me with woe.   456

The spirit of gluttony answers:
>   I have decided to put it to the test
>   If this Anthony can overcome us all,
>   And if the justice that delights my mind
>   Can make him give his austere fasting up.

The spirit of sloth answers:
>   Unless you trick him with some ingenious ploy,
>   I'll say that he is wiser than anyone,
>   Though nonetheless I think that what you'll do
>   Will not be worth more than a line of straw.   464

In the guise of a hermit, the spirit of gluttony goes and finds Anthony and says:
>   Ah, my dear son, you are well met. Now tell
>   Me briefly how you think you're getting on.
>   To come to speak with you I've journeyed far,
>   And with love do I come to visit you.

Anthony answers the spirit of gluttony:
>   Now may the Son of Mary lauded be,
>   For he his servants never will forsake;
>   As if you were our son, sit here with me
>   And, if you please, give me some good advice.   472

The spirit of gluttony answers Anthony:
>   You know for certain that the virtue of
>   Prudence surpasses every virtue else,
>   And those who of the world have taken leave
>   Must have it—those in hermitage the most.
>   Oft times excessive patience is required
>   For the soul to make a sickly body yield,
>   For desperation can well come of that;
>   Discretion for this reason is a must.   480
>   Too thin, by far, you've grown it seems to me,
>   For you are just dry skin about the bone.
>   Raw grass with drinking water makes a meal
>   Most bitter; I don't think you can endure
>   With no bread. Nor, this way, can one who seeks
>   The grave before his time the holy realm
>   Attain; this bread for love I bring you, and
>   With me I'd have you eat in charity.   488

Anthony answers the spirit:
    I had believed that as a hermit good
    You came to me with comfort and good will;
    I now see that you surely have appeared
    As a demonic tempter of my will.
    Have you not heard God in his gospel say
    That man cannot be fed on bread alone
    But rather by the word of blessed God?
    Therefore, you cursèd spirit, get you gone!   496

Anthony asks permission to go to the desert and says:
    I have been thinking, Reverend Father, that
    The crowd distracts me very much, so I
    Ask of you the great privilege that I
    May go to dwell in solitude, and I
    Encourage you as strongly as I can
    To pray with diligence to Jesus good
    For me, for he will always guide me so
    I shall not ever be cut off from him.   504

The hermit answers Anthony:
    My son most dear, I give you comfort, for
    Whoever with a pure mind dwells alone
    Is very near to the angelic state,
    Because he is from every other care
    Set free. But rarely is this granted to
    A monk because this other way is more
    Secure, though nonetheless I don't deny
    You this; but ever live in dread, I pray.   512

*Having been granted permission, Anthony goes to the desert, and two pagans and an
interpreter say to Anthony:*
    O Father reverend and shepherd good,
    These two wise men have just arrived,
    Come running straight to your aroma sweet
    Because upon your teachings they have fed,
    For which they have a passion great revealed.
    And they have been most fervent, certainly,
    In having made thus long a journey so
    That they could meet a man so wise and great.   520
        For this they've come from Ethiopia

Despite great hardship and much danger and
Their being unacquainted with your tongue.
But they're equipped to be great counselors
And with great knowledge amply are endowed,
Whence I implore you as a son beloved
That you may show compassion for them since
You understand their good intentions now.   528

Anthony answers the interpreter:
To these wise men respond on my behalf
That certainly I wonder greatly that,
As they are holding in their hands the keys
Of that philosophy that hones men's wits,
And that makes humans wise, that they have come
More than a hundred miles with such travail
As you've recounted merely so they can
Look in upon a foolish man like me.   536

*And the pagans speak two stanzas in Greek to the interpreter, and the interpreter says to
Anthony:*
O Father, these tell me to say to you
That they were moved to leave their countries as
They surely knew what high intelligence
You have—one into which no error falls
And still less foolishness; they're rather sent
Here where all this ability resides.
Speak, therefore; do this grace to them,
And it will satisfy and please their souls.   544

Anthony answers the interpreter:
Not seeing them inside a palace great
But in this narrow little hermit's cell—
Though I'm reputed little wise or mad—
The greater madness must be theirs,
And surely a great solace that must be,
But as they think in me is such a store
Of wisdom as you've told me of, they must
Pursue this perfect state of mine.   552

For if to them I'd travelled such a way
With so much trouble and such danger grave,
How great a villainy it then would seem

If I were not to follow their advice;
So in the same way they're undoubtedly
Obliged my teachings to embrace as well,
And should with love receive baptism and
They should renounce their paganism false.   560

The interpreter answers, first speaking to them in Greek; he then says to Anthony.
They say that, being reared up in their faith
Since infancy, O Father, they don't think
That they are damned by any means, for they
Have always lived with justice in the world
So that they do not wish to be baptized,
But to remain friends with you they desire
Because of your sweet, efficacious speech.
They wish to leave, whence may you dwell in peace.   568

They depart. Then the spirit of avarice places a little plate of silver where Anthony must pass and says this:
Since my companions have not harmed your soul
With all their cunning, and if by your strength
Of virtue you're protected, to this hope
Must you submit yourself because by such
A snare can every wise man be beguiled,
And this means will be good to lead you from
Your way which greatly vexes me; now I
Shall see if you're as perfect as you seem.   574

Anthony goes through the desert and finds the basin and says this:
O, driven out from heaven, I know you well—
Some of your tricks these are, some of your snares;
You wanted to make me leave the wilderness,
For when men dwell alone, you think that's bad;
Your food seems sweet although it's poisonous,
And your delights are sorrow and distress;
This was not dropped by any mortal man,
But it has fallen from the infernal realm.   582

The spirit, seeing that he does not take it, places a mountain of gold there and says this:
As you have not consented to this, you
Perhaps have left it since it seems too small,
But I have set before you such a lot

That surely you will modify your game.
But if I'm still ignored in spite of that,
I'll never more return to this locale
Because the clink of gold wins everyone—
It doesn't matter if he's good or bad.   590

Anthony goes through the desert and finds the mountain of gold and says:
O evil beast, have you still not left off
Trying even in this old way to make
Me faithless? Yes, for a long time I've not
Gone one step ever that you haven't dogged,
But henceforth you can just go take a walk,
Because you've spent your labors all in vain.
Though you're of little worth, you think you're smart;
Though you thought you were gaining, you have lost.   598

Two scoundrels meet each other, and the one is called Scaramouche, and the other Pegleg,
and Scaramouche says:[8]
What are you up to, Pegleg? And where are
You coming from, do you have some good news?

Pegleg responds:
I'll tell you the truth, I don't get what you mean,
But that there's neither news that's good or bad
I know indeed, and I have reached the point
I'm nearly dead, and for some cash would come
Back from the stars, but I can find no peace,
For not a groat remains within my purse.[9]   606

Scaramouche answers him and says:
Now I tell you, I am not partnered well,
And we can say that I've caught the worst share—
Though at the fair at Reggio I was robbed
Of lots of cash—in all a thousand ducats.[10]
On this account, one grace I ask of you,

---

8. Italian: Scaramuccia and Tagliagambe. Scaramuccia is the swaggering soldier of the *Commedia dell' Arte.* He is descended from the *miles gloriosus* of the old Roman, Plautine comedy, familiar to English readers in the character of Shakespeare's Falstaff.
9. *groat:* Italian, *grosso,* a coin weighing about an eighth of an ounce.
10. The fair at Reggio Emilia—across the Appenines from Florence. Another anachronism that establishes a Tuscan setting for the play.

That both of us become now highwaymen
If to recoup our florins we desire.   614

Pegleg answers and says:
You've spoken well; with that I'm well content,
And from this time I'm pledged to you, and swear
If ever I did good, I shall repent
Of that, and I've a heart that's made so hard
That should I see the life destroyed of her
Who gave me life, I would not even care;
There isn't any evil I'd not do,
As long as I could have the cash and goods.   622

Scaramouche answers and says:
We do not need to argue over that,
Let that one of us who first dies repent;
Let's first discuss that which we have to do,
For time is passing and we've nothing done.
But, look, here comes a chum of mine who will
Upon that point do us some good if you
Agree that we include him in our gang,
For he is brave and full of recklessness.   630
          You're welcome, my old buddy Carapello,
Just look how fortune has escorted you
Into our laps; if you had brains to plan,
You couldn't have just bumped into me here.

Carapello answers, and says:
If with a knife I had been stabbed, for sure
I would have welcomed it just now, and this
Would be for me a nice gratuity;
All other matters seem just idle talk.   638

Scaramouche answers and says:
To tell the truth, old boy, we have arranged
That someone shall refund our damages,
So I entreat you, come draw near to us
So we can make you leave your woes behind.

Carapello answers and says:
Chums, seeing you is timely, that's for sure,

I've really not been worse in these ten years,
And so for this it seems great news to me
That every woe and sorrow will be eased.   646

Pegleg answers and says:
It's very good that we've agreed to do
The worst we possibly can to everyone,
But first a good reminder I would give
You both if we would be together long:
To this speech neither of you should be deaf:
Our plunder we must share out evenly,
For if one of us bilks the other two,
We instantly shall beat him thoroughly.   654

Carapello answers:
O Scaramouche, my friend, why do we wait?
Today is good for travelling on the road;
The fair of Alexandria has begun,[11]
And we'll find someone in the countryside.
To get both clothes and money is our need;
You bring your lance, you bring along your sword,
And let us all three go in company,
And what we gain we'll share among ourselves.   662
   Today my heart tells me, companions mine,
That we shall do what greatly profits us;
We shall find pilgrims, merchants we shall find
That to Damiata from Alexandria go.
Yet cursèd be the dice game, four and six,
Because it has my purse quite emptied out.
I don't know how to make a blind man sing,
But the first I find will have to pay.   670

All three go to the highway, and then Satan says to the devils:
By this abyssal fire I order you
To seek that lonely abbot Anthony
Who to increase the crucifix's faith
Has made so many of these folk convert.
As soon as he is deepest in his prayer,

---

11. This could simultaneously allude to both Alexandria in Egypt and to a town by that name in Piedmont.

His entire body you must beat with clubs,
Because deception's not done any good,
Let's see if tortures will affect him some.   678

The demons go to club Anthony, and, when they have beaten him, they leave, and Anthony, seeing Jesus appear, says:
O Jesus good, where have you been in this
My time of suffering? The demons, see
How they've torn me to pieces. How can you
Give your consent that this could come to pass?

Jesus answers Anthony:
Have no doubt, Anthony; in every state
My grace is always with you. But to test
Your constancy is what I have desired.
Go, your good works with every hope pursue.   686
    My trusty servant, Anthony, have faith,
For I am ever with you and shall be;
I shall forsake none of my faithful ones,
And by my power you will see how through
The world I'll give you such a gift that you
By everyone will come to be known as
My own good chevalier. Fight strongly for
After you die you'll claim the eternal prize.   694

Anthony is healed and goes through the desert and he meets the highwaymen and says to them:
My brothers, flee! Flee very fast away!
For your own good return the way you've come!
Do not go to that slope where death awaits,
Where he will murder you with sorrow great!
Your limbs and skillful arms will not avail,
Nor will your recklessness and valor great,
And if my counsel you do not accept,
Going further will soon cause you to die.   702

Pegleg answers and says:
He must be out of his mind, and come forth from
His cell because of hunger. They endure—
These hermits—tribulation great, and they
Have little fit to eat and awful clothes;

To mind him is to natter with the wind.
Therefore let's our departure make at once
And let us go to seek this fellow, Death,
For he will be a man that wants to live.   712

They go farther along and find the mountain of gold, and Pegleg says:
Behold, my brothers, what great madness reigns
In that old hermit, crazy as a loon,
Saying that here that wicked Death abides,
And calling "death" what always brings us life.
If we had not come here along this road,
Our fortune would have faltered for us. Much
Better this than debtors' jail would be,
And no more battles do we have to fight.   718
    Companions, I have thought, if you agree,
That one of us should to Damascus go
And bring back something fit for us to eat,
And bring us also some good flasks of wine.
Whoever goes should strive to come back quick,
Because I'm faint with hunger and with thirst.
Some sweetmeats bring, and bread and meat and wine,
And, if you must indeed, a florin spend.   726
    Let us cast lots to see who has to go,
And he that goes may take a piece of gold
With him to some bank that can assay it
And have them give him money for the gold.

Carapello answers, and says:
This pleases me, and so must we proceed,
For we don't want to stay here very long;
Have Scaramouche here start the straws around;
Let him who gets the shortest run at once.   734

Pegleg answers and says:
Go quickly, Scaramouche, and don't forget
To bring the grub, or find some cook, and buy
A capon, nestling pigeons, thrushes too;
Bring two wine flasks, for one won't be enough.
If someone calls you, make your ears be deaf,
And take care not to stop to play some game,

And bring a pair of weighing balances
So we can share this gold out in three parts.   742

Scaramouche departs and on the way he says:
A thousand times I've heard it said that when
Dame Fortune turns your way you can't be slow,
And you must know how you can follow those
Rare times when she revolves—they don't last long.
And when she comes, someone who lets her leave
Will reap the punishment of his own shame;
Who believes ought else on error great is fed.
Each has his fortune from his hour of birth.   750
        When could I have a better fate except
That I have lost my brains entirely, for
A great mistake I've made in leaving them
Before I had that gold. To get such goods
A traitor everyone will be, no force
That both of them would cheat a brother. I
Was crazy to set out along this way,
Thinking that all my portion I would get.   758
        They have the ladle in their hands and they
Can share the soup out any way they please,
But that need not concern me very much,
For my good wits instruct me on this point:
To have it all myself can be arranged,
With no threat to myself and damage none.
Thus if it can be done, that must I do
Because the profit will outweigh the shame.   766
        A druggist do I need to find who will
Some poison sell me of the strongest sort,
Then one of the wine flasks I can poison, for
There is no shorter way to bring them death.
Those villains thought that I would be deceived
By fixing it so the lot would fall to me,
But I'll outfox them in return for that,
And all the gold with no more work is mine.   774

He comes to a bank and says:
What will you give, O master, O cashier,
To buy this gold that I desire to sell?

The cashier answers and says:
>   My friend, first let us have a look at it,
>   Then we shall see what you desire from us.

Scaramouche answers and says:
>   I want to get exactly what it's worth,
>   But money I can spend is what I need.

The master of the bank answers him and says this [to the cashier]:
>   Look here, assay if this gold's alloyed, and
>   Your duty do to him and to the shop.   782

The cashier answers and says:
>   Twenty-one ducats is what this gold is worth,
>   But I'm content to give you twenty-two.

Scaramouche answers him:
>   Take care that you've not erred in weighing it,
>   For God can do whatever more he wants.

The cashier answers and says:
>   It's worth no more; I've weighed it carefully,
>   Our practice is always to speak the truth.

Scaramouche answers him and says:
>   To me who will remember you, cashier,
>   Your duty do, for I've no penny yet.   790

Then he goes to the druggist and says:
>   My master, you are well met for I've come
>   To you for help and for your good advice.

The druggist answers:
>   You are most welcome, and I am prepared
>   To treat you just as if you were my son.

Scaramouche answers:
>   Not long ago into my house have come
>   A number huge of mice, and I can't catch
>   Them all, because they are so many and
>   So old they're even gnawing at my ears.   798

So, master, for this reason give me, please,
A bit of poison I can kill them with;
And at your price I want you to be paid,
Because if it works well it will be good.

The druggist answers and says:
I'll give the perfect thing to you in truth,
But take care that no scandal comes from it;
Jump up, O Dominic, make haste and bring
To me that little box of arsenic.   806
      Here take what I am giving you; pay me
Two groats; for many reasons it will work,
For if they take it they'll be stricken with
Convulsions—in great agony they'll die.

Scaramouche answers:
I shall not ever spend, it seems to me,
My money; may you do the will of God.   812

Then he goes to the innkeeper and says:
My host, I want two bottles of good wine,
One white, one red, but let them both be sweet.

The innkeeper answers:
I have some chianti and wine of San Lorino,
Trebbiano sweet, vernaccia, and malvagia.

Scaramouche answers:
I'll have two flasks, and you this florin take,
And keep the change till I come back again
Right now I wish to go to and find the cook
To see if he has anything to eat.   820

Then he goes from there to the cook and says:
Have you got something, cook, that we'd enjoy?
I want enough to feed my comrades four.

The cook answers:
That which I have, my friend, is to your taste;
I have young capons here and nestling birds,
Fat sausages that go with drinking well,

        And macaroni, a whole kettle full,
        Blood-pudding and pig's liver too, today.
        Now see if there is anything you like.   828

Pegleg says to Carapello:
        I want to tell you, brother, what I think;
        But only on the understanding that
        You'll swear in faith that if you don't agree
        You'll forget it, and tell not a soul

Carapello answers:
        Say first what's on your mind, and then I'll tell
        A thought that into mine has lately come;
        And tell me boldly what you're thinking of
        For what we say is just between us two.   836

Pegleg answers:
        This treasure Fortune's made us find, I've thought
        About and think that all this gold should be
        For only you and me, and that we should
        Not have to split it up with someone else.
        Envy's tormenting me, to tell the truth;
        Answer me then, how does it seem to you?
        That others should have to have some seems unfair,
        And parting it three ways makes it grow less.   844

Carapello answers:
        Yes, surely, brother, you are right in this.
        No longer keeping truth hidden from you,
        I felt a passion strong in me that came
        From this same thought; it makes me sick to think
        That Fortune's made a friend of that dense lout
        Whose life's not worth a single loaf of bread
        And that he profits from our labors too.   852
            We'll both take part in what we have to do,
        For when he comes again and he sits down
        Then in a flash by us he'll be done in,
        And our intentions he cannot suspect.
        With but few blows we shall have finished him,
        But we'll say nothing at his coming here.

A hundred lives already have we snatched,
Why should one more or less mean much this time?   860

Scaramouche returns and Pegleg says:
Have you exchanged that piece of gold? And what
Did you then squander on this stuff you've brought?

Scaramouche answers:
Why should you ask me that, you clumsy ox,
When bit by bit in a trice you soon will know?

Pegleg answers:
Take that, you callow thief; you shall not have
The treasure that you thought you'd share with us.
You oafish lout! Cry out if you know how!
There's no one here who will stick up for you.   868

After they have killed him, Pegleg says to Carapello:
I'd say we can, belovèd brother mine,
Now eat and drink in peace and we don't have
To feel at all uneasy since this oaf
Is lying dead. So start to tear a piece
Of sweetmeat off, and sample first the wine
That pleases you. Then we can judge indeed
If it's as good and perfect as it seems.   876

Carapello tastes the wine and says:
It is superior; you taste a bit.
He was a gourmand and a connoisseur.

Pegleg tastes it and says:
This is a fiery wine indeed, it seems.
It is so robust, delicate, and strong.
Let's see now how the cook has treated us,
Let's sink our teeth in something good to eat
That's better than what we're accustomed to
So that each with his jaw bone helps himself.   884

When they have eaten, Pegleg says:
Now that we have satisfied our thirst

And filled our bodies so we nothing fear,
And have the leisure to consider this,
We need to talk together thoughtfully,
For we both want to live the quiet life
And every thought the soul yearns for we flee.

Carapello answers and says:
You're right, but I have less experience,
So you who well know grammar must speak first.   892

Pegleg answers:
My Carapello, now that Fortune has
Made both of us grow rich, we must be wise,
And we as well must be concerned that fast,
Indeed, the wheel's stuck and the nail
Is firmly driven in so that we won't
Fear ever that the wheel might come unstuck.

Carapello answers and says:
Your recollection is infallible,
Let's do what seems agreeable to you.   900

Pegleg answers:
I feel inside, my brother, a great heat;
It seems that I'm entirely filled with fire
Above my heart; I feel a constant pain
That makes me grow all weak. This villain
May, I fear, have mixed some poison in
This wine! Alas, alas, that it should be
That such a puny sluggard as this rogue
Has made us swallow such a bitter pill.   908

Carapello answers and says:
O brother, in my breast great heat I feel;
But do you think from drinking it could spring?
That these wines I've consumed cause me to be
Unable to hold my eyes open? I
Don't think that he's deceived us, for as yet
We had not held him in despite.
If it is true, we'll see our gooses cooked;
We shall have found the gold at our expense.   916

Pegleg answers:
>What devil do I have within my gut
>That seems to be a dog that's gnawing me?
>And little benefit to me the good news now
>That so much pleased me when I found the gold.

Carapello answers:
>Don't talk to me, my body's hurting so,
>Look how already I'm all swollen up;
>This was for certain not just opium;
>The devil very few bursts in this way.   924

Pegleg answers:
>If, brother, you would go for Bisticci,[12]
>I would give all my share to you; if not
>Go to the Ricci's barber—him who has
>The antidote for every malady.

Carapello answers and says:
>You want me to go although I hear, indeed,
>The shrieks of wicked, cruel, bitter death;
>Because of the poison of hypocrisy
>I haven't even strength to take a step.   932

When he sees that they are dead, the spirit of avarice departs and says:
>Now it is clear to me that all the pains
>I've lavished here have not been spent in vain;
>I can return with celebration great,
>And no one can speak villainy to me.
>Into our leader's power have I led
>With my primeval art not one but three,
>So that into his presence I shall go
>Contented and with courage filled as well.   940

Then he goes to Satan and he says:
>Behold my lord your faithful servant here
>Who has returned victorious to you,

12. Perhaps a contemporary Florentine physician who would have been recognized by the audience, but also a joking reference to the founder of the Medici line—Averardo di Bicci.

For with my falsehood and my bitter snares
Three comrades I've contaminated so
That with deceptions and with methods cruel
They have deprived each other of their lives.

Satan answers and says:
Since this good work you have accomplished you
Are worthy without question of a crown.   948

When the play is ended, an angel dismisses the audience, and speaks in this fashion:
O wretched mortals, open up your eyes
And see just what terrestrial treasure does.
The world that feeds you worthless trifles can
Not bring you any consolation more,
And do not wait until death's on the scene.
Do not continue longer in your sins.
Lift up your eyes to heaven whence life comes
So you can hope for glory infinite.   956
    Good people, see how many evils come
From this accursèd wolf who has been born[13]
In realms infernal and who satisfies
His hunger ceaselessly; this poison is
What steals life from these mortals blind
And breaks the health of foolish men.
Now think about these men; how useful was
The gold to them that they had just now found?   964
    Consider Anthony who in his youth,
Preferring poverty, left all his goods
To win his way to those supernal heights
Where there is neither wrangling nor dispute.
Seek God, who is true wealth; like wise men, learn
At the expense of others, and bear death
In mind above all else. Now in the name
Of God, you have permission to depart.   972

THE END

13. *wolf:* as a symbol of avarice the *lupa* (she-wolf) echoes Dante, *Inferno* 1, lines 49–51.

THE PLAY OF
SAINT THEODORA
Attributed to Antonia Pulci

Here begins the comedy or rather tragedy of Saint Theodora, virgin and martyr, but first, two nuns enter: Sister Angela and Sister Hippolyta.[1]

Sister Angela says:
    It's still true, after all,
A woman who's arrogant
    Always gets everything
The way that she has done.
    This convent as it seems   5
Exists for her alone.
    But I desire to have
A little fun with her.

Sister Hippolyta:
    Ah, wait a bit and see,
We are two malcontents!   10

---

1. There are no known extant editions from the fifteenth century. The earliest known edition (though perhaps not the oldest) is that of Florence, 1554.
There are six other Florentine editions of the sixteenth century: 1554, 1570, 1585, and four undated, and another in Siena. Seventeenth-century editions include three in Florence: 1617 and two undated (one of these also in Pistoia); and two in Siena: one of 1614, and one undated. D'Ancona notes that Torquato Tasso borrowed the holy quarrel between Theodora and Eurialus for the Olinto and Sofronia episodes in *Orlando Furioso* (D'Ancona, 2.323–24). The plot of *St. Theodora* appears in the story of Saints Theodora and Didymas (martyred 303). Pulci sets the story in Antioch, Syria, rather than in Alexandria, Egypt, where the historical events occurred. She also renames some of the characters. These facts suggest that she knew the story in a form other than that which appeared in ancient martyrologies. For an English version of the story as the martyrologies told it, see S. Barring-Gould, *The Lives of the Saints*, vol. 4 (Edinburgh: John Grant, 1914), 359.

I have my mind so full
Of wrath and of disdain,
   That I must be confessed.
My lines I'd like to shred,
   For they don't make good sense.   15

Sister Angela:
   You'll have a thousand reasons;
There are seven or eight of us
   That have some lines to say;
But they want to dress up
   Just three or four of us   20
In costumes that are nice;
   But, touching you and me,
We two will be ill-dressed,
   And then be ridiculed
By all the convent's nuns.   25

Sister Hippolyta:
   If I stay in this mood
It's them I'll ridicule,
   For they will stay to watch
And give me the delight
   Of turning up my nose at them;   30
I want to mock them all.

Sister Angela:
   I'm not so sure of this;
I am a bit afraid
   The prior might be enraged.

Sister Hippolyta:
   Don't get excited, Angela;   35
That doesn't matter much;
   Our poor old man will stay
Close by the fire and won't
   Trouble his brain about
Whatever we may say.   40

Sister Angela:
   So be it; as you wish:

We are resolved that we
    Will not speak in this play;
Don't let them pressure us,
    For they will waste their time;   45
And they will only earn
    Their just desserts from us.
But over there I see
    Your sister coming near.

Sister Hippolyta:
    If she comes, let her act;   50
I will not change my mind,
    I'm not about to bend.

Sister Daniella enters and says:
    Well, aren't you coming now?
You seem to be confused:
    You see that it is night,   55
And all the people have
    Been crowded in the hall.

Sister Angela:
    You go and do the show—
We do not wish to come;
    Don't waste time talking,   60
For you can go perform.

Sister Daniella:
    O my dear sisters, why
Are you behaving so?
    I'm sure your staying here
Will bother everyone.   65
    Now you must not delay
In coming to get dressed.
    Then I won't have to say
That you've been obstinate.

Sister Hippolyta:
    They've treated us so well   70
In sharing costumes out!
    They've tricked us a thousand times,

Taken the best themselves—
        The golden necklaces,
The chains, the rings as well,   75
        The big wigs and the hats,
They've taken everything;
        They've left us nothing but
A bunch of ragged sacks.

Sister Hippolyta:

        They say I should become   80
What I wear on my back!
        I'd have been coarse, indeed,
Had I obeyed in this.
        If I ever I get dressed,
Let it be said I've sinned.   85
        What they have got for us,
They found in bags of rags!
        I don't fear anything;
I'm not about to dress!
        You'll get tired talking to me.   90

Sister Daniella:

        My tidy little one,
There is no shortage here
        Of clothes and necklaces.
To dress old women up
        We have a lot of things;   95
We'll seem like serving girls,
        You'll seem like mistresses;
What will the people say,
        To see us look so bad?

Sister Hippolyta:

        Oh, everyone will blame   100
Our teachers, because they
        Are not at all prepared
To furnish what we need.

Sister Angela:

        I've been supplied with rags,
I've just a bunch of scraps;   105
        How *lovely* I shall be!

Sister Hippolyta:
       In sum, Sister Daniell',
  We do not wish to come.

Sister Constance enters:
       Alas! What do I hear?
  Have both of you gone mad?   110
       Already all the folk
  Are gathered in the hall.

Sister Angela:
       A babbler's all we lacked!
  You, Sister Constance, go:
       Enough of talking now;
  And no more sermons, please;
       They seem no good to us!
  Go do it your own self!
       You aren't the abbess,
  The prioress, neither, you.   120

Sister Constance:
       Come on, let's hurry up—
  Tell me the reason why
       You are so furious;
  You know, like sisters I
       Have ever loved you both.
  Don't be the ones, I beg,
       To ruin the holiday;
  And don't be obstinate,
       For you're in charge of it;
  I know, if you desire,   130
       All will go on just fine.

Sister Massima:
       Such grievous pain I feel,
  I think my heart will burst;
       It's getting late,   135
  And we're not dressed; alas,
       That you won't come for this!

Sister Hippolyta:
       O, Massima, don't try

To grieve or wheedle us,
    The two of us at once.

Sister Constance:
    Such hardness in their brains
They have created that
    They believe with certainty
That costumes are shared out,
    And they take much offense,   145
Maintaining that the best
    And all the lovely hues
We've taken for ourselves.

Sister Massima:
    O my, how wrong you are!
I want you now to come   150
    And pick out from them all
Whatever you like best,
    And as we all are friends,
We shall not mind at all,
    If quickly we can go   155
To start the show at once.

Sister Angela:
    If this is what you'll do,
We like the wind will come,
    And truly I repent
For having said those things.   160

Sister Constance:
    It's just a little sin;
Let's speak no more of it;
    Let's say that for a jest
We've joked among ourselves;
    But, pray you, let us go   165
For we are at the hour!

Sister Hippolyta:
    That tunic, may I have it?

Sister Massima:
    Yes, and a golden cap.

But I see those who've dressed
    Already coming out.
But hurry, let's make haste,
    The play will have begun.

They go inside to get dressed, and the woman who will give the summary enters and says:

Be silent, listen: once at Antioch
Indeed, a virgin, Theodora, dwelt,
Who of such ample beauties was possessed,
The Roman Consul fell in love with her;
And, every good thought proving fruitless, he
Sought at every moment to corrupt her;
No other spouse but Jesus wishing, she
Rebuffed him with her actions and her speech.   180
    The tyrant burned, and found no moment's rest—
Now wrath would put the spur to him, now love.
The virgin Theodora, keeping still,
Showed aged wisdom in her youthful flower—
Prepared to die both joyful and content
Before she ever would offend the Lord.[2]
Conducted to the place of prostitutes,
She came thence glorious and happy, chaste.   188
    Euralius, the Christian, seeing her—
A little lamb caught by the wolf's fell paw—
Came to her there and in this manner spoke:
"Exchange your clothes with me, O virgin young,
And from this place make haste to flee away;
For I'll stand there reclothed in what you have
Upon your back; and do not be afraid,
For your virginity will be quite safe."   196
    On hearing this, the dreadful Tartar sent
That young and pious fellow to his death.

Says Theodora, shouting out aloud:

With no excuse, I am that woman whom
Your master wants to suffer misery,
Not him, for he's committed no offence.'

---

2. *die . . . content:* compare Petrarch, *Rerum* 296.14, where the poet is prepared to die happy
of wounds inflicted by his idol, Laura.

The young man says: "Permit me now to die;
And with my martyrdom don't interfere."   204
    The tyrant, midst this pious war of theirs,
Orders first one and then the other slain;
Thus, one near the other fallen here on earth,
In triumph up to heaven together they go.
You know that, sometimes, someone makes mistakes;
We pray you that you'll pardon us if we
Commit some error inadvertently,
We're young girls with not much experience.   212

Two young women, Daria and Clarice, enter, and Daria says:
O my Clarice, if you wish, I'd like
Us to go see this comedy today
The consul's putting on—and I don't mind
That both of us have garments rich to wear,
For it's a sign that with our husbands we
Remain at peace, in happiness and joy.
Our emperor, they say, today was born,
Therefore we are obliged to honor him.   220

Clarice:
O Daria mine, I am as happy now
As I have ever been in all my life.
But ere I feel this happiness, indeed,
If it will not be burdensome for you,
Let's call on Theodora; right away
I'll come when I've her wishes understood;
Because she always stays alone at home,
And never seeks amusement or delight.   228

Daria:
How "if I'd like?" It's not my custom to
Refuse the company of anyone,
Especially hers—a veritable stream
Of every virtuous deed and every grace;
And of her life the light so brightly burns,
That, more than my own person, I love her.
But here is she who seems to be a sun;
Happy will this day be, if heaven wills.   236

Saint Theodora enters and says:
> Where are you going—if you want to tell,
> And if you can reveal it openly?

Clarice:
> We shall immediately fulfill your wish,
> And we desire to take you with us now.
> The entertainment we shall go to see
> That the proconsul, people say, will host;
> O Theodora mine, come on with us,
> Then later I'll accompany you home.   244

Saint Theodora:
> As you know, I've left the nurse at home,
> Alone and indisposed. It does not seem
> To me that I'd be right in leaving her,
> Nor do I also think you'd want me to.
> You go, and happy come again to me,
> And tell me all about how fine it was.

Daria:
> Since you are occupied, we'll go along,
> And then come back to tell you everything.   252

Two of the consul's young men enter, and on seeing Theodora, say:
Faustus to Crispus:
> My Crispus, tell the truth; what do you think
> Of that young lady, beautiful and fair,
> Who's standing talking with those others there?

Crispus:
> With such an arrow, Faustus, she's hit me,
> That I can think of nothing now but her,
> Nor will her memory part in haste from me.

Faustus:
> I've thought to point her out to Quintian,
> For he would find her pleasing; that I know.   260

They go to the consul, and Crispus says:
> After we had gone forth from your sight,

We met a woman fashioned in the sky
And not created here midst us on earth.
Her face was chaste beneath her snowy veil,
More lovely nature has not made, nor will,
Since earth it heat has proved, has tried its ice;
If you upon her lovely face could look,
You'd say that she'd been made in paradise.[3]   268

Consul Quintianus:

You have my heart so thoroughly aroused
With your fine speeches and your winsome style,
That I would have her brought before my face.
Go to her, please, and, using humble speech,
Tell her that she must not fear anything,
Nor judge her coming to me a low thing;
For, by the holy gods, I swear to you,
That if she pleases me, she shall be blest.   276

Faustus:

We are not very sure which house is hers,
Nor know her name; yet let's get on our way,
Because I well know where she stayed behind.

They leave and as they're walking, Crispus says:
[The goddess] Venus is my every hope;
She won't allow our quest to be in vain,
And she'll be found wherever she may be.

Faustus:

Ah, Crispus, look a moment, do I see
Aright? Do I perceive those women there?   284

Crispus:

Go! Jove is on our side, we've found her trail!
For those two women are the very ones
Who spoke with her by that old palace there.

---

3. This octave is filled with Petrarchan echoes. The motif of fire and ice as characteristic of the lover pervades *Rerum*, and the notion of a woman's seeming to have been born in paradise recurs frequently. For fire or heat and ice see *Rerum* 105.29, 134.2, 206.22, and 220.14. For Paradise in this context, see *Rerum* 126.55, and 348.8.

Faustus:

> Should I thank men the most or thank the gods,
> Because I see that I've not worked in vain,
> And that my plans are working out, I see.
> Let them a little finish up their chat,
> And then about her we'll make inquiries.   292

When Daria and Clarice have returned from the entertainment, Daria says:

> I don't know if you liked it much, Clarice,
> The entertainment we have seen today.
> Ah, tell me how well done it seemed to you.

Clarice:

> If we'd not other pleasure gained from it,
> I'd be apologetic that we went,
> And I'd return sad, angry, and worn out
> By the awkwardness of those who spoke;
> Alas, void of delight it seemed to me.   300

Daria:

> Did you see those lovely wives who were
> All plastered with cosmetics and white lead?
> So many necklaces and precious stones
> That they were wed to goldsmiths, as it seemed.

Clarice:

> I know I'll tell you they were graceful with
> Their noses big and bawling little mouths!
> And I could judge, if remember well,
> Not one was there who did not have some flaw.   308

Crispus:

> Kind ladies, where does she reside nearby—
> She whom you spoke with earlier today
> Before you had come back here once again?

Daria to Clarice:

> I think it's Theodora that they want,
> The one you spoke with earlier today.
> Knock at this door, and she will come right out.

They knock at Theodora's entrance, and Clarice says:
>   These, Theodora, want to speak with you,   ‾
>   And therefore we have had them call you forth.   316

Faustus:
>   Our proconsul, noble Quintianus,
>   Requests that to the palace you will come
>   For your gentility; it is not far,
>   And we shall guide you there reliably,
>   And you shall see a noble Roman. Please,
>   There's nothing wicked that you need to fear;
>   Just for your good he wants to talk with you,
>   And as you're worthy, wants to honor you.   324

Saint Theodora:
>   I don't know why your lord has sent for me;
>   A poor young woman; I, however, of
>   His honor have no need. And certainly,
>   I don't believe that I'm the one you seek;
>   Be careful lest some error you have made.

Crispus:
>   No need to fear, for if he speaks to you,
>   Your present tears will turn to laughter then;
>   Resolve yourself, therefore, to come with us.   332

Saint Theodora to Clarice and Daria:
>   My sisters, ah, take pity on me for
>   My sad and sorrowful fate; my virtue, now,
>   I give into you care. Be pleased, I pray
>   To keep me company up to the court.

Clarice:
>   Now don't you know our friendship cannot be
>   Split up by anything except for death?
>   So do not doubt, we shall accompany you
>   And soon we'll bring you safely home again.   340

Saint Theodora:
>   Since with me you will come, I am content
>   To go and be obedient to your lord,

Although I'm dreadfully afraid to go.
O God of heaven, give me courage great,
So that to this man's ill I'll not consent!

Faustus:

O Crispus, go along to Quintian
To tell him less than half an hour will pass
Before he sees his lovely Theodora.   348

Crispus goes and finds the proconsul and says:

Sir, faster than a gallop I have come
To bring the good news that I have for you;
Look there afar, it will not be too long
Till Theodora comfort brings for you—
Nor is there risk of any stumbling block.

Quintianus:

If not all shortened has my eyesight grown,
I see her, and my heart longs, yearns for her,
For who can't see the sun is blind indeed.[4]   356

Saint Theodora arrives, and Quintianus says:

O you are welcome here a thousand times!
I've sent for you that I may treat you well,
So that you may stay by me, rich and blest;
Don't fear that you will suffer any pain,
Or any shortages of worldly goods.
Who was your father? Who's responsible
For taking care of you so I can speak
With them and seal with them a pact?   364

Saint Theodora:

My father Theodore was citizen
Of Antioch, and he lived in this world
With honor great, but by my destiny
He and my mother both lie 'neath the earth;
And, missing them, I live with wretched heart,
Because their memory my heart seals up.

---

4. *sun ... blind:* though here the force of this image is proverbial, in this context it
echoes Petrarch, *Rerum* 248.4, 325.89, and 338.2.

A nurse of mine is she who cares for me—
With her I live my life secure and chaste.   372

Quintianus:

Your father of the Roman people was
A great friend ever, and for love of him
I shall be kindly and benign to you,
And shall such honor do you in the world
That, almost, you'll touch heaven with your hand;
And know I've fallen so in love with you
That if you will consent to be my wife,
Above all else I shall love you alone.   380
　　　To Rome I'll take you, and your loveliness
Shall Rome observe, and you will look on her,
And all my riches great you shall enjoy.
You shall be pleasing both to men and gods,
Dwelling always in triumphs and in joys.
Now answer me, if you will be content
That I your spouse and you my goddess be,
And happily forever live with me.   388

Saint Theodora:

Know that I cannot take another spouse;
For to a husband I'm already wed;
United with him my heart is—every sense—
Nor from him may I ever be divorced;
So you must make another match, my lord,
For I am so belovèd by my spouse
That I'd endure each torture rather than
Be gone a single moment from his side.   396

Quintianus:

There isn't anyone to equal me—
I, Asia's ruler and a Roman too—
And you know I can boast about myself.
None but the emperor great takes precedence;
Of my great wealth, I do not wish to speak,
My worth surpasses that of any man.
Therefore, then, leave the husband that you have,
And in delights with me you'll always dwell.   402

Saint Theodora:

These goods of yours are wholly temporal;
Those of my husband are eternal goods.
His are stable, yours are weak and frail.
You do not discern this, do not see
How often so many evils follow them,
For fraternal loves are not secure,
And when a man considers himself blest,
Sometimes in just an instant he is ruined.   410
    So wealthy is my spouse, lord, that the earth
And heaven and everything therein are his,
So noble is he, he's the son of God;
Observe how your wealth is surpassed by his!
And everything conforms to his desire;
See which of you two is the richer one!
I'd suffer any cruel death before
I ever would agree to part from him.   418

Quintianus:

I do not understand this childish tale:
You will at once tell me your husband's name,
And watch that with your mouth you don't mislead,
For I'll tell you what we'll do otherwise:
If any anger overwhelms my heart,
I'll make your life both sorrowful and sad.
I gravely fear lest you're a Christian girl;
Therefore elucidate these thoughts of mine.   426

Saint Theodora:

I am a Christian, and my spouse's name
Is Jesus, who is Lord of everything,
To him my heart I've wholly yielded up,
And such great love sincere for him I bear,
That I've forgotten everything but him,
Nor do I fear your fury or your threats,
For my love's so tenacious and so strong
That I'm prepared to suffer death for him.   434

Quintianus:

Now look at what a goal I've taken aim!
That all my love should have been staked on her!

I'll make you suffer such great pains that you
Will disavow your God despite yourself;
And with such chains I'll cause you to be bound
That your delight will into weeping turn,
And if you with her there are Christians too,
These pains and greater shall you undergo.　　　　　442

Daria:

O Quintianus, Christians we are not,
And willingly we would be pleased to see
Each Christian die a miserable death!

Clarice:

O Theodora, see your foolishness
Has snatched such happy fortune from your hand,
You can't recover ever from this loss.

Saint Theodora:

Except for Jesus there's no fortune, fate—
For him I am prepared for any death.　　　　　450

Quintianus:

Go you in peace, and leave her in my hands
In pieces to be torn, for I shall make her scream
Such dreadful shrieks of woe that she will wish
That she had not been born into this world.

Going, Clarice says:

Alas, more dear than my own eyes to me,
O, where have I left you, Theodora?

Daria:

Let her cope. If she wants ill, she'll get it.
I'd say let mad dogs fight among themselves.
458

Quintianus:

I'm very sorry for your loveliness
And for your youth, so flourishing and green,
And sad to see your obstinate mind will lose
That foolish youthfulness of yours. You could

Position high have held, enjoyed great wealth,
And now your madness yields you this reward;
If yet you will repent, I am prepared
To love you once again as I have loved.   466

Saint Theodora:

You still know what I said the other time:
That, but for God, I can't love anyone;
And though you call me foolish, call me mad,
My heart will thrill at being mad for him
When from my body my soul shall be snatched,
For then will my desire be satisfied.
So with my body do what pleases you,
For death eternal peace will bring to me.   474

Quintianus:

I won't stay here to argue more with you,
For I can see you will be obstinate;
Of these two choices, choose which you prefer:
Either remain a Christian and be raped,
Or else renounce your God and virgin stay—
One consecrated to the goddess Vesta.
You answer not; say which one you will choose,
And what you wish is what I then will do.   482

When Saint Theodora doesn't answer Quintianus, he says to Crispus and Faustus:

Well do I know the fame that Christians have—
I've put their resolution to the test.
You could first turn a river from its course
Before you'd alter any one of them.
Their blind hostility won't see the light.
Since she her heart has hardened so in this,
Take her down to the house of ill repute;
Invite all men to violate her there.   490

Crispus:

Since you the bad have sought, you'll get the worst.
Come on with us, since you won't give consent
To Quintian; of that you shall repent.
You're silent still, and nothing wish to say.
You still have time, if you will but obey,

And still you can unsay what you have said
In following your foolish thoughts. You were
For one alone; you'll be for many now.   498

As they go, the Christian Eurialus meets them and says:
Good day, companions, and where have you caught
Such lovely prey, and where are you taking her?
And she, why is her visage so disturbed?

Crispus:
This is a Christian, and so stubborn is
Her crazy will that for a spouse has she
Rejected the proconsul, and inflamed
His cheeks with wrath; therefore we lead her where
We shall invite all comers to corrupt her.   506

Eurialus:
Oh happy that day upon which I was born,
Because I have encountered you and since
I didn't keep my mouth shut but inquired.
I'd like, if both of you are pleased, and if
Whatever I have done pleased you before,
To be the first that of her fruits may taste,
And afterward let come for her who will,
For no one can take that grace away from me.   514

Faustus:
We're happy to do what pleases you in this,
And we shall accompany you in every way.

Eurialus:
I thank you; go in peace, however, for
Here company is not required. I shall
Go home, get dressed, and then shall rapidly
Come back again my fortune to enjoy.

Crispus:
Go in good time. Ungrateful woman, you
Remain right here so you can suffer pain.   522

They depart. Saint Theodora alone says:[5]

Eternal God, why have you granted that
Your miserable, unhappy spouse may be
Penned up in an unholy place like this? 525
    I, who solitary as the phoenix was—
Who on a man's face wanted not to look—
Am now led here to be a prostitute. 528
    The tyrant, harsh and cruel still, could have
This breast run through by iron if he were
Against me to direct his [vengeful] wrath. 531
    O truly by the cruel beasts let me
Be torn, or otherwise within the flames
Pray let my miserable flesh be burned. 534
    Ah me, unfortunate, I do not know
Where I can flee to save my modesty,
And danger creeps up one step at a time! 537
    O cruel tyrant, [governor] unjust,
Two such dilemmas you've put in my heart—
And both of them filled with iniquity. 540
    You either want me idols to adore—
Become a virgin pledged to Vesta—or
Make me become a Christian girl corrupt. 543
    With tears I bathed my garments and my face!
In silence was I to that pigsty led
Where unchaste women [ply their trade] and dwell. 546
    Yet usually you grant a humble prayer;
Lord, shelter me in my great injury
That I may not before you be judged vile. 549
    My limbs do not have any other help
If not from you alone; ah, be not cruel,
For they, without you, don't know how to live. 551

Seeing Euralius coming, Saint Theodora says:

Lo, more than fell, my bitter enemy,
Behold, the thief of my virginity,
Ah, Jesus mine, preserve my troth to you. 554

---

5. As Theodora begins this prayer, the poet shifts into terza rima—the verse form of
the *Divine Comedy* and that considered by Dante in *De vulgari eloquentia* to be the highest
of the vernacular verse forms.

O, help me, Lord, in such necessity;
Have pity on me, O young man: I don't
Beg life, but that you, with ferocity   557
    Will pierce this miserable breast of mine.
You're yet a man and not a cruel boar—
Ah, please with some respect regard my tears.   560
    You've come to force me, if I do not err;
But never shall your will be satisfied,
Unless you wish to have me when I'm dead.   563

Eurialus:

Don't let my visit bring you anguish and
Do not believe my piety extinct,
But rather turn your ears to my advice.
I don't want you to yield to sin with me.
To Jesus, though, let your good will be turned,
And do not fear, for he'll make you content.
I am a Christian, and by him I'm sent
That you might be preserved, and not to sin.   571
    I'm the same size as you are, as you see,
Nor is my face yet covered with a beard;
If you then will escape from your great ill,
In all haste flee forth from this place:
You take my clothes; it matters not to me
If, saving you, I die a cruel death.
Your garments I'll put on; you flee at once,
And let me stay here in this place unchaste.   579

Saint Theodora:

If I thought I could flee my dismal fate,
And that I was not being mocked by you,
I would be fleeing urgently and fast.
Yet too ungrateful would it seem to me
If I were the occasion for your death;
I shall think my death a blessing if
I can die a virgin and be chaste,
Not be corrupt, inimical to heaven.   587

Eurialus:

You're in great danger; get away at once.
Change clothes with me and leave this wicked place,

And leave it then to God to guide the rest;
To him have I committed all my thoughts.
If it's his wish, then I won't be aggrieved
To suffer for him, and willingly my soul
Would from my body be released for him,
Provided your virginity weren't reft from you.   595

Saint Theodora:

Who'd ever think that one would want to kill
Himself to save another human being?
Sweet Jesus, if your pleasure it should be
That my chaste body on the fire be placed,
Or ever that for me this young man die,
For whom I once again renew my tears,
Let's clothes exchange, and do what you think best;
For your action may God you reward.   603

They go inside to change their clothes, and two women enter. Madam Minoccia says:

It is a fine thing still that from my hen
I cannot even taste a single egg,
Because my neighbor woman's stealing them!
So hardened is she in her thievery
That she deserves to be the queen of thieves.
If only she could drown for once and all.
I know that I am not defaming her,
Since everyone today calls her a thief.   611

Madam Acconcia:

Madam Minoccia, what you say's a lie,
Because she doesn't lay eggs; don't you know
That brooding hens come always to their nests?
If you're not getting work enough, now heed:
Wash from your face so much encrusted grime.
But if I start to speak, you'll something hear
That will make you abandon your desire
For so much croaking, make the woeful grieve.   619

Madam Minoccia:

I know that you're with your old vices filled;
You well know that, when I was combing flax,
Five spindles, maybe six, you stole from me.

Madam Acconcia:

> You must have had far too much wine to drink,
> For every morning, long before you're dressed,
> You always swill a half a jug of it,
> And often you're so feverish with it
> That you can hardly stand firm on your feet.   627

Madam Minoccia:

> You well know how gluttony draws you on.
> I spy you from my window oftentimes,
> With your head revolving here and wandering there.

Madam Acconcia:

> I know that you must have much worse to say,
> Because the awful truth enrages you.
> But only this grace do I ask of God:
> Whichever one of us is lying, may
> She burst right in the middle of the street.   635
>   Come, if you wish, and search through everything;
> I'd have you open all my cupboards wide;
> And if you can find anything that's yours,
> Take everything, so that you cannot say
> That you've discovered that I stole your spools.
> But, trust me, I will make you take that back,
> You filth, you ugly, vicious, dirty slut!
> Oh, great's the shame that you've not been destroyed!   643

Madam Minoccia:

> You think you'll scare me with your bluffing, but
> If I should seize you by your little hood,
> You wouldn't feel so bold or so secure.

Madam Acconcia:

> When your hen comes into my house, I swear
> To you, I won't be guileless or be pure,
> But I'll see that she graces my cuisine.
> Say I'll do this, and you will speak the truth;
> I'll eat her without giving it a thought.   651

Madam Minoccia:

> Don't do it, Madam Acconcia; I repent

Of having quarreled with you about the eggs;
I'd die of hardship if I should lose her.

Madam Acconcia:

Come now, I'd have you be forgiven;
But if I ever hear you say such things
Again, you won't be pardoned for such sin.
Let's not waste time; let us go now to spin,
For I know drink will teach you how to eat.   659

*They leave and Saint Theodora enters dressed as a man and goes into the house, and
Faustus and Crispus enter and Faustus says:*

I do believe he must have gone to sleep,
Since, Eurialus, he delays so long.

Crispus says:

Or maybe he is waiting to be called.
Or maybe he has taken the wrong road
Because he has made such a great delay.
It would be well if one of us went in,
To make him come out here, if it may be,
Because so many others want to come.   667

Faustus:

I'll go; wait here and don't you go away
Because in just a moment I'll return.

He goes inside and comes back out and says:

Who ever heard of such a case as this?
I'm almost terrified just telling it.
Into a woman is Eurialus changed,
For I was inside there and looked on it.

Crispus:

If this is true, the consul we must tell,
And then go do whatever he thinks best.   675

They go to the consul and Faustus says:

O best of consuls, Theodora we
Have taken to the place you told us to,
And on the way we chanced to meet a youth

Of habits chaste and honest in his deeds
Who instantly on going in to her
Became a woman, and her garments wears.
And I spoke not to him, but fled away,
Afraid that I'd become a woman too!   683

Quintianus:

This rarity is much to be admired;
Bring that man here, for I intend to make
Comparisons and tests in all such things.

Faustus:

Though stupefied and trembling, I shall go;
Yet often among Christians it is found
That they from men make women, as I've heard.

Quintianus:

Go both of you, and do not fear,
And that man bring to me here, right away.   691

They go and knock and Eurialus comes forth clad as a woman and Crispus says:
Or man or woman or what else you are—
The way I ought to greet you, I don't know,
And my imagination is confused—
Know, we must lead you to the consul now.

Eurialus:

I'm ready; let's be on our way because
What I shall say will clear up everything,
And going to him gives me great delight,
Nor can I be afraid of anything.   699

When they arrive, Quintianus says:
Are you the man who's had the audacity
To take a garment from a woman and
Against my will to make her run away?
I shall severely chastise your offense;
Yes, I shall have you punished bitterly.
Say instantly where you have made her go,
And if you are a Christian and from whence,
And tell me what you have to do with her.   707

Eurialus:

 I am a Christian, and I'm from this land,
 And, but for faith, have naught to do with her;
 But, seeing that your mind so greatly erred,
 I pity took upon this virgin so
 She could her freedom gain from war unjust—
 So she'd not be the heiress of your vice.
 I took her clothes, and she has fled away;
 Now you can have her sought where she has gone.   715

Quintianus:

 So, you've been made a woman from a man;
 O brazen rascal, what a faithless mind
 And wicked in this act have you revealed.
 So very bitterly I'll have you die
 That you'll be an example for them all.
 You vile and worthless man, tell this to me:
 Are you a man or to a woman changed?
 Have you and Theodora names exchanged?   723

Eurialus:

 Not Theodora, I am Eurialus
 And what I've done to save her modesty
 I don't repent, and I'd do it again.

Quintianus:

 You traitor false, filled with iniquity!
 Lead him away, for I'm devoured by wrath.
 For such great malice have him punished soon;
 Take him at once outside the country and
 With iron let his flesh be seared away.   731

*They bind Eurialus and are leading him to his death, when Saint Theodora enters and
says:*

 Stop! You're mistaken! I, I am the one
 Who ought to die, and not this innocent
 Who wanted to preserve my chastity.
 And if your lord intends that I must die,
 Because, in loving my God I adjudged
 The consul's riches worthless, set him free,
 And let the iron be turned in me instead,

And with it let my body be transfixed.   739

Eurialus:

Leave, Theodora, and do not desire
To stay my martyrdom and victory.
Ah! permit me to possess the martyr's palm;
Don't take from me my triumph and my glory—
Let me with martyrs up in heaven rejoice!
My memory inscribed do not erase;
Do what your lord there has required of you,
And here, ah, rather let my blood be shed.   747

Saint Theodora:

Do not, for any reason, slaughter him;
For I am she your lord so greatly hates,
For he, with all his ingenuity,
Seeks to convert my laughter into tears.
Ah, cause me to die with iron, or else with wood,
And let my soul slough off this paltry cloak;
If you should spare my life while killing him,
You certainly will soon repent of that.   755

Faustus:

These are events both marvelous and rare,
For neither of them is afraid of death;
And pains are to the one and the other dear,
Contending over who'll first suffer death.

Crispus:

I want to lead them to the consul—both.
As he may wish, let sharp iron be one's fate,
Because we also might have reason to
Repent if we should have them murdered now.   733

Faustus:

You've spoken well; together let's consult,
And to the consul let's return at once.
Since neither of you is afraid of death,
He can content you both without delay.
He both your hopes at once can satisfy:
You see that he is present here with us;

About who must give up the soul, contend,
And who will gain by death the glorious palm.   741

He continues speaking to the consul:
We went to execute him, as you said,
To take away his life from him when she
Arrived and with shrill weeping and with cries
[Most piteous] our journey did obstruct.
I believe stupidity leads her to death—
She wants to leave this world at any rate,
For she says that his death would be unjust,
And so, to make fate fair, she ought to die.   749

Quintianus:
You, foolish Theodora, what say you?
Why would you suffer such a cruel death?

Saint Theodora:
O consul, listen somewhat to my words:
He shouldn't suffer this dark death obscure
For having plucked me from that horrid place
Where my virginity was jeopardized;
For I am she who has belittled you.
Let me be killed, and let him be set free.   757

Quintianus:
Eurialus, your reasons tell to me,
Defend your side against her [argument].
Which one of you should I have put to death?

Eurialus:
I ought to die, I who revealed the means
For fleeing from that place. I was the first—
Nor here is needed argument nor briefs;
Then, I deserve death and I want to die,
And beg that you won't let this interfere.   765

Quintianus:
If the god Jove you'll worship, then shall I
The one and other of you liberate.
And ere you leave to go elsewhere I shall

See that you marry one another too.
Because such friendship rains down in you two,
From my own goods I'll dower Theodora;
Now answer if this pleases both of you,
So that you may a long time live in peace.   773

Eurialus:
If to pollute my body I had wished
I never would have liberated her,
Nor dug her from that evil, wicked place,
Nor your idols ever worship, for
I only wish to worship my own God
From whom I'll never separated be.
Do what you want to, do not waste your breath—
Except for Jesus, none my heart desires.   781

Saint Theodora:
You know I want no peace or truce with you—
Beyond this nothing else in question stands;
From you as far as possible my heart
Shrinks back. How little did your faith perceive
In believing I'd pursue your wishes sad,
And how unsteadily it guided me!
I want no spouse, don't wish to worship Jove;
So treat me now as may seem best to you.   789

Quintianus:
O cruel, obstinate, and cursèd race!⁶
You're thankless, and every torment harsh deserve!
Have each of them tied up immediately.
Them torture in a fashion that my scorn
For them, their pain and woe, be satisfied;
They are not showing any sign of fear;
Remove them from my sight, and quickly go
To do to them what I have told you to.   797

Bound and singing as they go, Saint Theodora and Eurialus say together:
Blessèd be thou, O Jesus merciful;
Look on your servants who in your name go forth

6. That is, Christians.

To die with happy hearts and joyful minds   800
    Since they have overcome the tyrant cruel
And, following in your footsteps, they have burst
Perpetual damnation's awful bonds.   803
    And laughing we return to you at peace,
And in our martyrdom and bitter grief
Rejoicing, for hope nourishes our hearts.   806
    Our triumphs here have been equivalent—
This cruel judgment, both of us have won.
Because of your love, torture's dear to us.   809
    Our sacrifice, O Jesus, now accept.

They go within and are executed, and afterwards are thrown into the fire, and then the person who made the summary enters and says:
O happy, glorious and blessèd souls,[7]
For with spilled blood you bore away to heaven
In triumph and victory your martyrs' palms!   813
    They were not terrified by death;
Rather it seemed they made a rivalry
Of who would first make red the sword with blood.   816
    How wonderful it was to look on them!
Theodora giving Eurialus thanks
That he, for Jesus' sake, prized not his life.   819
    Then she bade him farewell with pious grace,
And on her knees she offered low her neck
And with her blood appeased the [thirsty] earth.   822
    A hard stone would to pity have been moved,
To see her loveliness fall down in death.
The youth next took his way along that path   825
    And said: "O my sweet escort, wait for me,
For, as together we have won the war,
So let's together enter heaven's gate."   828
    And then he fell to earth upon his knees,
And, never having any fear of death,
Under the cruel iron closed his eyes.   831
    So did they both achieve the victory,
And climb together to the highest sphere
Where one can everlasting love enjoy.   833
    Let us then seek, indeed, this good alone:

7. *glorious and blessed*: echoes Petrarch, *Rerum* 264.59.

That we the crooked path and way desert,
And raise our minds in flight to heaven instead.   836
  This mortal journey is so very brief
That in but little time we shall grow old—
Today is man alive, tomorrow dead.   839
  We, women young, now give to you our thanks,
For your welcome and attentive audience;
We ask that you our errors pardon us;   842
  Now you may take your leave, and go in peace.

[THE END]

THE PLAY AND
FESTIVAL OF ROSANA

Attributed to Antonia Pulci

The angel heralds the festival:[1]

To the praise and glory and to the peace
Eternal of that Lord who reigns and made
All things: let all keep still, be silent, if
You please. Enjoy this fine play. Pluck good fruit
    You'll hear about a truthful virgin who,
Trusting in Mary, issued forth from woe,
So that you will have great bliss for your souls
If quiet, humble, and in peace you stay.   8

King Austerus says to his barons:

Beloved barons, my dear company,
Within whose arms this reign of mine rests safe,
A melancholy have I in my heart
That gnaws me so I never can find rest
Thinking about who will succeed me in
My lordship since my spouse has born no fruit.
And I believe for Romans it's a shame
That some seek haven in the Christian's lands.   16
    Please be content, therefore, to counsel me

---

1. The earliest known edition is the now lost volume 5 of the fifteenth-century Magliabechiana collection. D'Ancona lists twenty-one sixteenth-century Florentine editions: 1526, 1544, 1553, 1557, 1569, 1572, 1576, 1581, 1584, 1587, and the rest undated; and one in Venice in 1574. Seventeenth-century editions appeared as follows: Siena, 1608 and 1626; Florence, 1601; Venice 1600, 1606, and 1629; Orvieto, 1608 and 1611; Treviso, 1660; and Lucca, undated.
The story comes from the French romance *Floire et Blanchefleur* via Boccaccio's *Filocolo* (D'Ancona 3.361–62).

About how I should manage in this case.
I would not want to wander from your will—
My subjects I wish always to console—
Thus every hour I think, but know not what to do
To set in order both the realm and state.
Where duty lies, please, therefore, counsel me,
For to perform your will I am resolved.   24

A counselor says:

O sacred crown and our great lord, when we
Consider all that you have said to us,
Both woe and sorrow in our hearts increase,
That there is danger for us and the state.
I'll tell you what seems best to me to do
For fleeing such great doubt and such a fault:
Have recourse to the temple of sacred Mars,
And you will be consoled in everything.   32

The second counselor speaks:

Great lord, what he has said, this I confess
And I affirm to be the better course.
The gods will raise you out of danger and
From sorrow and annoyance set you free.
Go now, therefore, put this plan in effect
For going to Mars's temple fervently,
For he from sorrows great will raise you up,
And he will grant your having children too.   40

The king says to the queen:

O my belovèd spouse, I am resolved
To pay the gods a visit at their shrine
So what may be required of me I can
Fulfill, for I would never disregard
Their counsel, and from trouble to be freed
I want to go at once, for I'm in doubt,
Much troubled. Therefore set your mind and heart
On coming with me to fulfill the vow.   48

The queen says to the king:

There never was as sad a woman as
I am with such great sorrow, or such pain,

Nor could one have a greater happiness
Than I if I could only bear a son.
And I am pleased to have Mars's friendship, and
I am resolved to follow in his train;
The only thing that grieves me is delay,
To his place, then, let's go; I am content.   56

The king says to a page:

Come here, young page, you go on my behalf
So that the temple priests may be prepared
With gold, with silver, every fabric fine,
And with most solemn chanting, most devout
That can be done, for with my barony
I want to turn to Mars, fulfill my vows.
Let us set forth, wife, for all is arranged;
You go ahead, and what I've told you, do.   64

The page goes to the priests, and says:

O priests, to you the king has sent me, for
You are specifically commanded that
The temple shall be splendidly prepared,
For he will come to see it with his court.

A priest says to the page:

The temple of the god, Mars, is prepared,
And humbly we stand waiting for him here;
Return in haste, our answer give to him,
For he has left, and comes here to his place.   72

The page returned, the king goes to the temple and says to the idol:

O god, high, famous, and formidable,
Who guides and rules the world from pole to pole,
Who can our every longing satisfy,
And lift us up from sorrows, pain, and woes:
I pray you, lord, beneficent and kind,
That you will grant that I may children have,
Who will deliver me from pain and woe,
And I shall have you cast in solid gold.   80

The idol answers and says:

Austerus, O thou famous King of Rome,

In what you ask for, you'll be made content.
Not one of your requests will be in vain,
But I consent that they will come to pass
In full, and in a few days, be assured,
Great torment shall be taken from your heart;
Depart now, and have perfect faith in me:
Your own heir will succeed you in the realm.   88

The king addresses a priest and says:
O worthy priest, please be content to pray
And to have prayers continually said
For me, enough that I'll be freed from pain,
For such discretion I shall leave to you.

The priest says to the king:
O, do not be alarmed, our lord, because
The god will keep his promises. You may
Believe that firmly, for he'll give you help—
Our duty you may leave to us to do.   96

The king returns to his throne, and a courier comes and says:
O great, exalted, high and famous king,
I bring you letters from your captain, who
Is most desirous that he honor you.
The land of Cesarea by his hand
Submitted has to you, O glorious lord;
Through hill and plain you must rejoice for that,
For thus may you be called a happy lord.
Now read here what this letter clearly says.   104

Having heard this news, the king says:
This news is cause for celebration great.
For this news that he's brought by word of mouth
Let him be given instantly a robe,
For I wish to repay him for his pains;
O chancellor, approach and read this out,
And please speak up and make the meaning clear
So all may grasp the sense of the dispatch.

The chancellor says:
It will be done at once, my noble lord.   112

The chancellor reads the dispatch and says:
>   Exalted crown, victorious and great,
>   Glory and triumph of the Roman race,
>   Whose fame resounds through all the world and by
>   Whose power we've indeed acquired the realms
>   Of Aragon and of Navarrre, and with
>   The spoils and captives we return to you
>   With revelry and joyful triumph great,
>   O happier king than any in the world!   120

Having heard this, the king says to the barons:
>   You've understood that which our chancellor
>   Has from our captain read to you, and how
>   He's won through mountain and through plain, and how
>   He makes our power feared. This causes me
>   To call to mind my own peculiar case,
>   Considering who should possess these realms,
>   Of my not having yet obtained from Mars
>   That which he promised us. All time is lost.   128

The queen Rosana says to the king:
>   O my belovèd spouse, and my sweet lord,
>   O pillar of your people, peace, support;
>   That I've no children so distresses me,
>   Myself and my own life I hold in scorn.
>   At every hour on my misery
>   I think, for after us there's no one who
>   Will guide the realm. Physicians, idols, baths
>   I've tried, but nothing helps me, finally.   136
>   Since we are sterile, then, and thus alone,
>   I wish that elsewhere we may set our hands.
>   I want to make a vow to him who guides
>   And rules all spheres—that is, the Christians' God—
>   That if he grants us children, then shall we
>   Him follow, and not idols vain. I want
>   To send for a Christian holy man; give me
>   Permission, for I don't want to delay.   144

The king answers:
>   My dear companion, my belovèd spouse,
>   I feel a torment very grave in this,

And if I should believe that Mary's son
Could give us children, I would be content
At that; therefore I yield my will to yours.
Do what you wish, I give you my consent;
Since children I so greatly want to have,
My every means shall be at your command.   152

The queen calls a servant, and says:
Gianetto, faithful servant mine, come here,
And what I say to do, at once perform,
And secretly accomplish my desire,
And I'll reward you handsomely for that.
Seek out some Christian devotee of God,
And bring him to me here without delay—
A hermit, priest or friar. Now, depart.

The servant answers:
So, Lady, shall I do. I'll go for him.   160

The servant goes to the hermit, and says:
Accompany me, hermit, to the queen,
Who wants to speak about the faith with you.

The hermit thanks God, and says:
O Lord supreme, O Grace divine, who gives
Aid always to whoever believes in you,
Give me valor, wisdom, doctrine, strength
So that she will request to be baptized.
And you, sir, servant noble, trusted one,
Let us at once depart; let God be praised.   168

The servant and the hermit go to the queen and the servant says:
Behold, my lady, a Christian hermit who
Most willingly has come to call on you.

The queen says to the hermit:
For an important cause we've sought you out—
I wish to ask a secret thing of you.
If this wish of ours should be fulfilled,
To baptism we mean to follow you.
Now, it's needful that your prayers should move

Your God and that great trial be made of him.   176
     For ten years I've been with my husband, but
My womb has never brought forth any fruit.
I have tried doctors, baths, and every thing
With herbs and medicines, for all things have
The idols promised, but I remain still mocked,
Whence in myself I've built a groundwork new.
If, with your God, you'll promise me a child,
My spouse and I will believe and be baptized.   184

The hermit answers:
There is no need Christ Jesus to assay,
But to beg grace and mercy, if I can,
For he is always ready to forgive
A person who requests his grace, and asks.
That he will give a child to you, doubt not;
Be sure that you have perfect faith in him,
And fix your hope here—your desire as well—
And only believe that he's the son of God.   192
     Believe that he's the Word of God incarnate,
And that he died so we might be redeemed;
Believe that on the third day he arose;
That he can save you, also firmly believe.
Then you, queen, and your precious spouse shall I
Baptize, if you desire to follow us;
Thus shall you children have from Christ,
The true Redeemer, and peace after death.   200

The queen asks the hermit:
Your words should please me very much, since a
Good outcome ought to follow from this thing;
Thus I believe the king would give consent,
Since having children would so gladden me.
[My spouse,] you understand the hermit's wish
By what he's frankly and so clearly said.
To bring us out of this woe, I'll consent;
Fully, though, express your will in this.   208

The king says to the hermit:
Come near, O Christian, for I'm here resolved
Never to quickly trust in those who speak

So they'll decide to tell the truth to me,
For errors I am always keen to flee.
If from your God I gain such great relief,
I shall come forth from suffering and woe.
But if I'm not assisted in this wish,
What must I do with you if I'm betrayed?   216
    O king, henceforth, if you've to Jesus turned
Your every hope, and don't have children and,
What's more, don't save yourself, your lady, and
Your realm at once, then I shall be content
To suffer every torment, every pain
As much as can be, for my mind fears not;
Still firmly trust: who hopes in Jesus Christ,
On earth is glad, in heaven has true peace.   224

The king says to the hermit:
If the God you speak of is so prized,
What shall we say of Jupiter, of Mars,
Of Vulcan, Saturn, Neptune all enraged,
Apollo, who shines forth on every side,
Who have the heavens ruled, and earth as well
(As one can read in many a book and page).
Take care how you support your argument,
For you don't deal with naive women here.   232

The hermit says to the king:
These gods of yours, that you "undying" call,
Are wretched beings to the inferno damned;
Who in the world were bestial, arrogant,
But now are suffering torment for their sins.
And never accomplished anything but ill,
And those who believe in them are also damned.
Whether of gold, of lead, of rock, of iron,
It's by the wish of Satan that they're made.   240

The queen says to the king:
Will you, my lord, see if he speaks the truth?
For Pantaleus pledged, but can't produce.
It's better, then, to hold another belief
And trust that God in whom this man believes.
That God's our refuge both in life and death,

And is the rest and welfare of your folk,
If you wish happiness, my Lord, believe;
Ah! be content, and what he tells you, do!   248

Being reduced to penitence, the king says:
God's servant, spiritual Father, you
Have with your words so captured me, so bound,
That I believe—bewail my grievous sin.
I'm only sorry I delayed so long.
Let your desire become our will. It seems
To me a thousand years of being cleansed
In soul and body. I'm at your command.

The queen says to the hermit:
And, Father, as you wish, so do for me.   256

The hermit says to the king:
Since you, my lord, are of such valor great
That you desire to make up for lost time,
Come with me to the temple and I shall
Make you see what you've foolishly believed.
And from his mouth shall I make known to you
The order, the way, the style, that he has kept
For tricking you with his false governance,
And to fill up infernal vacancies.   264

The queen and the king go with the hermit to the temple, and the hermit says to the idol:
O Pantaleus false, you I command
By this God who was nailed upon the cross,
Who banished you from his supernal realm,
That you exhibit with a perfect voice
How, where, and when you men deceive who are
On earth, and show how your false game
And your idolatry does its inhabitants
Great harm, and where your realm is, where your place.   272

The idol answers:
I'm one of those who fell, indeed, from heaven,
By sentence of that One who sees all things.
I place a veil now upon mortals' eyes,
And what I say, that everyone affirms,

Believes; and false is all I show to them,
For neither mercy nor pity rules in us,
And filled with springes is our government,
And we remain with Satan down in hell.   280

The hermit says to the king and to the idol:
King, you have heard with what deceptions great,
With how much blindness you have lived, indeed,
Here in this world for many, many years,
For you were lost in body and in soul,
And ever did you seek to do us harm,
To render tribute up to Satanas.
You [idol], I command to change your place,
Return to hell to stay midst fire and flame!   288

The idol collapses in ruins, the hermit raises the cross on high, and says:
As in your folly you, O famous lord,
Have seen their certain trickery, indeed,
Do you believe now in the son of Mary?
Now will you see a miracle most clear?
This is the place the true Messiah died;
Behold, the Lord has suffered in this place;
Behold the faithful Christians' vessel, for
Now you must worship it with praying hands.   296

The king adores the cross and says:
O holy cross, O thou support of Christ,
O cross on which the highest Good was fixed,
O sacred wood, exalted, glorious,
On which the veins of Jesus shed his blood
And made me worthy, by his sacred love,
By that with which the Scriptures are all filled:
On my transgression, Lord, have mercy, for
A thousand times a day may you be praised!   304

Addressing the hermit, the king says:
And, O my Father sweet and cherished, since
Only to save me have you led me here,
Be pleased to gratify my wish, and with
Your own hand here baptize me, to block off
The highway of the demon wicked, cruel,

Who tries his utmost, always, to trick me.
The false faith of those gods I now perceive.
They're damned, and all those persons who
Believe in them are wickedly deceived.   312

The queen says to the hermit:
Have mercy, lord, I trust myself to you,
Have mercy, and assist me in my woe,
For this fault was I cast aside by heaven;
Therefore, outside the Lord's grace did I come,
Adoring these false gods who stripped me of
The highest honor. Them I here renounce;
I flee from them and their dominion leave,
And ask you, in Christ Jesus, baptize me.   320

The hermit says:
O king, fear nothing, nor must you, my queen,
Because God will forgive the humbled heart.
You will escape the infernal ruin, for
Your hearts and bodies you have given to God,
And baptism will be the medicine,
For hell he's given you heaven in exchange.

The king says to the hermit:
Our wills you've greatly kindled, Father, now
Delay alone torments and weighs on us.   328

The hermit has them kneel and says:
Each one of you kneel down upon the earth
So you can cleanse your souls and cleanse your hearts.

The hermit takes the water and says:
Lord Jesus, who because of primal sin
Wished from the virgin human flesh to don,
Who from the dead raised Lazarus to life,
Who made the man born blind receive his sight,
Thus do for these for every sin and flaw,
Whom I baptize to praise and honor you.   336

The king and the queen together say:
O Jesus sweet and good, you took indeed

228 Antonia Pulci

For our salvation human flesh; you were
For three and thirty years a pilgrim in
This valley perilous and strange, and you
Have with your faith illuminated us,
For we were following the way both false
And vain. O grace and courage lend us, strength
And love, that we shall have to do your will.   344

The hermit says [to the king]:
Because you've been an enemy of Christ,
And have on many Christians judgment passed,
Now is it not enough to be baptized,
But you must now do penitence as well.
You'll have to journey to the sepulchre
With your wife and in solemn reverence
On foot, and everyone must, without pomp,
On all those holy places pay a call.   352

The king says to the hermit:
As I am here, I want to press ahead,
And do that, hermit, which you've told me to.
May God keep all this company in health.
May God go with you; I shall act on this.

The hermit says:
For company, you'll saints and angels have;
I now entrust you to blest Jesus' care.

The queen says:
Make us perfect with your blessing, Father.

The hermit gives them his blessing, and says:
May you be blest and may you be at peace.   360

The king returns to his throne and says:
Before we can depart from Rome we must
Give orders that two matters be arranged;
First, viceroys for the realm we must appoint,
Then armored troops we must prepare to lead,
For Cesarea we shall have to cross,
And much cause to oppose us has its king,

For we have conquered many lands of his.
Therefore, we must not go with foolish folk. 368
    Rise up, O seneschal, hear my command,
And see that all the soldiers are prepared,
And bring them quickly in my presence, for
It's necessary that I march afar.

The seneschal answers the king, and says:
    What you have said will be put in effect,
For in a flash they'll be at your command,
And in a moment, Lord, I'll go for them,
So that they may perform their every skill. 376

Addressing his counselor, the king says:
    You, first among my counselors, rise up
And heed my order with your ready wit;
Here recently I've hit on an idea:
Till I return, you'll have to rule the realm;
With love perform it and with willing faith,
And be the pillar and support of all,
In such a way conduct yourself till my
Return that they shall prize you; I as well. 384

The counselor answers:
    High crown, and my great lord, what you've assigned
Me as a duty is too great a weight
To put upon my shoulders,[2] yet I'll do
It willingly if you are pleased. Command
Just what you wish; so shall it be, for I
Am ready to obey and glad as well,
And if I have not prudence governing,
I'll do it still with diligence and love. 392

The king says to the counselor:
    Because you are most venerated, take
My pendant and my sumptuous array,
And on your finger place my secret ring,
And set my royal crown upon your head;

2. *weight . . . shoulders:* compare Petrarch, *Rerum* 20.5–6: "But neither weight that's suited to my strength / Nor work for my file's polishing I find."

With rigor punish those who've fallen short,
While holding in joy and fest those who do well.
And I command you all to honor him,
And what he tells you, do it properly.   400

The king having given him the tokens of office, says:
Because I know you're wise and circumspect,
You well will rule my vassals and my realm,
And at all times keep justice in your mind,
And treat widows well, and minor wards.

The counselor says to the king:
Though I am negligent, rough, ignorant,
I'll leave your subjects happy and serene.

The king puts him on the throne, and says:
And thus perform until I have returned,
And sit right here, for we must take our way.   408

King Austerus departs, and a baron of the King of Cesarea goes before his king and says:
There in the plain, lord, is a great brigade
That comes from Rome, and "Austerus" they shout.
They are deployed, and all their people armed,
And all are bent on pillaging your land.

The King of Ceserea says:
Well, this is a peculiar embassy;
Up quickly, each of you, go forth in arms,
For every design of theirs I wish to foil;
They'll meet their deaths seeking to steal my realm.   416
    Against those Romans come with me: I want
To occupy the passes and the roads;
And if an armed encounter should ensue,
See that not one escapes and none is left.

The King of Cesarea sets his soldiers in ambush and says:
We'll stay here secret, silent, quietly;
You lie in ambush there until it's time,
And when I shout, then everyone charge forth,
And see that every one of them lies dead.   424

King Austerus arrives at the pass and says:

> We've entered into Cesarea's realm,
> A place of peril where we must take care.
> We are a people great, armed very well,
> We march united, with fraternal love,
> For if, by any chance, we are attacked,
> We'd wish to die for blessèd Jesus' sake
> Before we'd ever from a battle flee.

The King of Cesarea reveals himself and says:

> Aha, you traitors! Now you'll have to die!   432

They attack the Romans, they slaughter them, and the King of Cesarea says:

> Rise up! Kill all the scoundrels, for
> I don't wish a witness to remain;
> Come on! Let's see how well my sword will cut,
> And if each coward here is skillful still;
> Let everyone win armor and victuals.
> Ride every person down! So shall you pick
> The fruits of your discomforts, for there is
> Booty enough to make all of you rich!   440

Austerus being dead, Rosana throws herself on his corpse and says:

> O my sweet husband, oh, where are you now?
> O queen, alas, where are your followers?
> Your courage, where? What longer can you hope?
> What is your life if it's not sorrowful?
> O realm, O people mine, what will you do
> When you shall hear sure news of such a rout?
> O husband dear, my comfort and my hope,
> Together with you, at least, I might have died!   448
>   Ah, here will be the honored sepulchre
> You'd hoped to have, if this be honor great,
> If cruel iron in this dark wood without[3]
> A servant to keep watch, nor any lord.
> O thou Redeemer of all human kind,
> Who governs everything with love, receive
> Among your saints this pilgrim, and give me
> The strength to do what you may want me to.   456

---

3. *dark wood:* see Dante, *Inferno* 1.2: "I found myself in a dark wood."

A soldier of the King of Cesarea takes Rosana, and says:
> What are you doing, lady, all alone
> Here? Why do you bewail the death of these,
> Enemies of my king and of his sect?
> Why do you seek to feel the final throes?

Rosana weeps and says:
> I sorrow greatly for this vengeance done,
> But that I'm not among them, more I grieve;
> My grief, I know then, you will want to end,
> So I may with my husband here remain.   464

A soldier says:
> I would not do you harm for anything—
> Who'd strike a woman shows great cowardice,
> For how to fight with weapons they don't know;
> Instead they're used to making war with tears.
> I will inform the king about this case,
> Nor will I strip or otherwise abuse you.
> Fear not; come with me, for he's merciful.

Rosana is led away a prisoner and says:
> Let's go, for only death can bring me peace.   472

The soldier brings Rosana before the King of Cesarea and says:
> Being entangled in the forest, lord,
> And seeking to earn silver and gain gold,
> I saw her with a dead man in her arms,
> And she was making great lament for him.[4]

The King of Cesarea says to Rosana:
> The penitence will follow from the sin.
> Who was that man who with such torment great
> Was in that fatal conflict done to death?

Weeping, Rosana answers:
> Austerus was he, my afflicted spouse.   480

The king says to Rosana:
> Since you alone midst many have escaped,

---

4. *dead man . . . lament:* a buried image of the *pietà*.

I do not wish, O queen, to take your life.
I rather wish that you should honored be,
And in my house you'll be revered by all.

Rosana says to the king:
Unfortunate, afflicted, sorrowful
Am I because my people and my spouse
Have perished; I'm with child, and, lord, your slave.

The king comforts her and says:
Fear not, you will be treated honorably. 488

A man brings the news of the victory to the Queen of Cesarea and says:
Dear lady, your belovèd husband went
Against the Romans, as you know, and when
He at a certain narrow pass arrived,
Above the plain he hit them furiously
And put such fear and terror into them
That in our hands they were but smoke from straw;
The queen alone was captured from the troop,
And joyful we return, and each one rich. 496

Joyfully the queen says:
Nothing could more welcome be, nor could
Another thing more joyful make me than
This news that you have brought to me; I am
Consumed with happiness; therefore I wish
To travel with my entire brigade to see
My husband and without delay. Come with
Me everyone now instantly. We shall,
With all our people, celebrate [this news]. 504

The queen goes before the king and says:
How good that you could win a victory
So great! Dear spouse, you're very welcome home!
This is the glory and triumph of your realm!
One acquires state, fame, and honor too!
A great reminder this will always be
For Rome; thus are they given penance for
Their sin—when you kill them in such a way,
You take away their courage and their strength. 512

The king gives appropriate honors to the queen:
>   Didn't I tell you, if they intended to
>   Deprive me of my realm, I'd take their lives?
>   And so the case has wholly fallen out
>   And they've not even given us a wound.
>   All are dead with Austerus their king,
>   And his queen, whose life was spared, is here;
>   Tell me what I must do—I promise you
>   That I leave her entirely in your hands.   520

The queen takes Rosana and says:
>   If none but this lady has escaped from there,
>   I want her to become my prisoner.
>   O precious queen, [pray tell me,] what's your name?
>   Be happy; don't fear any villainy.

Rosana answers:
>   Unfortunate Rosana is my name,
>   And it's to my disgrace that I'm not dead.
>   Yet Heaven may want me dead with greater pain—
>   A satisfaction I shall thank it for.   528

The queen says to the king:
>   We now must give a chamber to her—one
>   That will befit her noble station—and
>   She must have maids and servants, household staff
>   Enough so she'll be like a queen at home.
>   And treat her kindly, as our custom is,
>   In dealing with a person of her rank.
>   And after the birth, with honor great we'll send
>   Her back to where her husband was the king.   536

The queen leads Rosana to bed, and says:
>   In this chamber take your rest until
>   We can arrange for your delivery;
>   Pages you'll always have, slaves, household staff,
>   And everything you ask for, what you will;
>   And after the birth, to Rome you shall return,
>   And at your pleasure, live within your realm.

Rosana answers:
>   My pain and sorrow overcome my strength;

I can do nothing else; I am content.   544

The queen departs, and Rosana entrusts herself to God's care:
    Ah, fortune's deprived me of my every good;
    Where is my spouse? My realm and power, where?
    Eternal God, your goodness be acclaimed;
    In patience make me constant, make me strong.
    Just as each good must be rewarded, so
    Must one do penitence for each ill deed.
    My failures merit this—they merit worse,
    So for eternity let God be praised.   552

An angel appears to Rosana and says:
    Rosana listen well to what I say.
    God says: "Within three days you will bring forth
    A daughter wise and chaste and beautiful
    Who will endure much suffering in the world,
    But in the end she'll be a maiden glad.
    But once she's born, the next day you will die,
    And you will go to heaven to feast anew
    There where your husband dwells now with the Lord."   560

The angel disappears. Rosana thanks God and says:
    Eternal God, thou spotless and most high,
    Who has lent grace to me, and fortitude:
    To have left the evil demon harsh
    And come, O Lord, unto your gentleness
    Most sweet, thanks be to you, and grant that I
    May your beatitude receive; the baby that
    Must issue forth from me—O lend her grace,
    That she may always heed your will for her.   568

Rosana addresses her chambermaid:
    Now has the end of my confinement come;
    Come all you women, find the [needful] things;
    O virgin Mary, pray you, lend me aid.

A chambermaid says:
    Dear lady, pray, do not become alarmed.

Rosana has the baby girl and says:
    O Lord in heaven, I have lost my strength;

O sisters mine, do not abandon me!
O virgin Mary, Mother heavenly!

A chambermaid takes the baby:
　　Run hither! She has had a little girl.　　　　　　　　　　　576

A groom runs by, and the chambermaid says:
　　Where are you running, groom, in such swift flight?

The groom answers:
　　I'm going to tell the king about the queen
　　Who's given birth and had an only son.

The chambermaid says:
　　Tell him Rosana's had a baby girl.

The groom goes to the king and says:
　　Your wife has borne a handsome son to you,
　　And this same morn Rosana's had a girl,
　　For almost at the same time came their pains.
　　And you are still together, man and wife.　　　　　　　　584

Rejoicing, the king says:
　　Groom, this is splendid news! For from my wife
　　I've had an heir—a male especially—
　　And that she's also healthy! For three days
　　Already I have greatly feared for her.
　　I must go see Rosana and her girl,
　　Because her misery has troubled me;
　　Let's go and visit her—pass onward, groom,
　　For kindness to strangers is a courtesy.　　　　　　　　592

The king visits Rosana and says:
　　Noble Rosana, to congratulate
　　You on your giving birth I've come to you.

Rosana thanks him and says:
　　As I am able, I give thanks to you,
　　For in your coming you have honored me;
　　I must commit my daughter to your care,

Because in a few hours I must die,
And with my hand I wish to baptize her,
And I should like to give her the name Rosana.   600

The king comforts her and says:
Why make yourself so melancholy? Whence
Proceeds so great a suffering? I shall
Send you again to your dominions, and
There you your own intentions can pursue.

Rosana says to the king:
Believe that brief my life shall be, and so
You must for me have great compassion and,
If you desire to set my mind at ease,
Concede to me the grace that I have asked.   608

The king says to Rosana:
Your sadness sorrows me, so great a weight,
That I must do that which your tongue requests.

Rosana baptizes her daughter and says:
In the Father's, Son's, and Holy Spirit's name
I baptize you, and leave you the faith, in pain,
Rosana doleful, and in tears; within
The arms of God, who looks on everything,
I leave you, for to the good road will he
Direct you, my dear, sweet, beloved child.   616

Rosana calls a servant:
Come here, my trusted servant Candidora,
For in my need you've always served me well;
With me, here, you're the only one baptized,
And all the other people here are doomed;
So I give my Rosana to your care,
And she'll be reared by you and nourished well.
Show her that Christ in heav'n sheds so much grace
That, in a great church, she will be in Rome.   624

The servant answers:
By that faith which you took at baptism, I

Indeed affirm and swear and pledge my faith,
To teach her the way of Christianity,
And always her companion to remain;
If she should go to Rome, to that same place
Will Candidora always go with her,
At least until she reaches fifteen years.

Rosana says to the servant:
Go, may God reward you for your pains.   632

Rosana addresses the king and says:
I would desire to beg a grace from you.
When I am dead, my daughter, will you please
Dispatch to Rome and to her relatives,
That she to her dominions may yet return?

The king answers Rosana:
Like my own daughter I shall have her reared,
To you I swear this and my faith I pledge.

Rosana speaks to the king and dies:
I thank you; and, my daughter, you remain
In peace, and may God [always] be with you.   640

With Rosana dead, the king says:
I cannot help but feel surpassing grief,
For this poor woman and unfortunate;
In tears her life she ended, and in pain,
For she was never comforted at all.
What sort of man can boast—if he has well
Considered her affliction and how much
Her adverse fortune seems to touch her—that
He could ever [once] restrain his tears?   648
    See that she's carried to the Christians' place,
And bury her according to their rites;
This baby to the nurse then send along
With my own son until they have been reared;
Up, seneschal, come over here, take her,
Take my own, too, and have them suckled well.
To my golden castle have them brought;
When the time is ripe, I'll send for them.   656

A Roman who was with King Austerus, having been wounded, rises up, and says to himself:

> O haughtiness, O envy curst, O pride,
> That cannot ever any good fruit bear,
> What injury produced revenge so great
> That the king and all his folk should be destroyed?
> O wretched realm that vainly waits the king's
> Joyful return, you weep, [realm], and you mourn.
> O humble Christians, exercise great care;
> The king is lacking nothing but a tomb.   664
>   What am I doing here? I should not part
> Until I first have buried all our dead;
> But if I stay, I shall be put to death.
> Since all the rest are done for, shall I go?
> Or stay? I don't know what to tell myself,
> For either option is a bitter choice;
> Best that I go to Rome with great dispatch
> To see there's vengeance done for such a wrong.   672

The same departs to go to Rome, and says:

> In my parting I have taken on
> Much pain, and tears, and troubles, sorrow great;
> I can't go on, and I am so dismayed
> That I've not got the heart left for one step.

Two Roman grooms come, and one of them says:

> What does this mean? Who thus has wounded you?

The wounded one says:

> Alas! For there is worse about our lord!
> Help me to go to the lieutenant now,
> For every one will weep at what I'll tell.   680

The grooms lead the wounded man to the lieutenant, and he says:

> Lieutenant of a sorrowful domain,
> I come to bring you sorrow infinite.
> The King of Cesarea has us disdained;
> He came and he attacked us on our road.
> He targeted Austerus and his troop,
> And he has bereft them all of life,
> And wounded I have fled, and I've escaped;

I know that no one else of them remains.   688

Sorrowing, the lieutenant says:
O wretched and afflicted reign, now fall
In ruin and widowhood; what will you do?
Your king, where is he now? and where your queen?
Alas! How will you, justice, be maintained?
Dear brothers and you wretched people, here
Must be avenged much woe and much disgrace;
Let each of you with care prepare yourselves
To be revenged by one year from this day!   696

Now addressing messengers he says:
Go, take this letter to Burgundy; you,
To France, to England, and to Hungary;
To Germany go you; you, to Gascoigne;
You go to Brittany—announce the war.
You, Spain and Ascalon; you, Saxony—
That each may guide the people of his land,
And let each with his legion come to Rome
To march on Cesarea to seek revenge.[5]   704

Now an angel speaks the epilogue, and says:
O people wise, good, pious, and benign,
Because today so kindly you have stayed
To see how evil so displeases God,
And that he always pardons people who
Repent, whoever wants to grasp the rest,
Tomorrow we shall warmly welcome you,
Each one, for God saves everyone from sins,
And with our thanks you're licensed to depart.   712

THE END OF THE FIRST PART

5. This octave echoes Petrarch, *Rerum* 28.31–40. In this famous *canzone*, Petrarch calls
on Cardinal Giacomo Colonna to provide leadership for the crusade of 1333 against
Islam. The Roman call to arms against Cesarea mirrors that summons.

THE SECOND PART OF THE FESTIVAL
OF ULIMENTUS AND OF ROSANA
Attributed to Antonia Pulci

The angel heralds the play:
  The peace of him who has created us
  In bliss and charity, in joy and love,
  Preserve you and from worldly sin protect,
  From death defend you, and from sorrow's pain;
  O fathers, mothers, children gathered here,
  In our Lord's [holy] name, keep silent while,
  Bearing heaven always firmly in mind,
  We carry on the story we began.   8

On his throne, the King of Cesarea says:
  There's no one stronger or more powerful
  Than I. I made Austerus gentle grow;
  From East to West I must be reckoned with,
  For I discretely govern well my realm
  With wisdom, diligence, and I attend
  To it, restrain those who won't keep the peace.
  Who wants to keep the people faithful, he
  Must ever watchful be, and must be cruel.   16
      It's fifteen years since I sent off my son
  To have him reared, and I've not seen him since.
  Rise quickly, seneschal, depart in haste,
  And, with Rosana, lead him here to me.

The seneschal answers:
  I'm going with my troop to get them, lord.
  Before you here you'll have them right away.

O barony courageous, come with me,
And what the king commands, let it be done.   24

The seneschal brings the children to the king:
Your own son, sacred majesty, behold,
The girl whom I took to be nursed as well.

The king looks at his son and says:
You're very like a lily, my sweet son;
My wife belovèd, how does he strike you?

The queen says to her son:
He's fair and blond, so fresh and rosy hued;[1]
I'd never have him leave me; him I'll kiss.
How are you—you who are my labor's ease?

Facing Rosana, the queen's son Ulimentus says to his mother:
At Rosana's pleasure, I'll be fine!   32

The kings says to his son Ulimentus:
Take pleasure at your will, my cherished son,
And in your fashion through the wide world go;

Ulimentus says to Rosana:
Come on, Rosana, let us go to see
The temples and fair castles step by step,
For when I'm with you, I seem always pleased,
And when without you, I'm downcast and sad.

Rosana:
Let's travel where you will, for I've confirmed
That, if I'm not beside you, nothing's right.   40

Ulimentus and Rosana depart, and the queen says to the king:
Our son, O my sweet husband and my lord,
Is so enamored of Rosana that

---

1. *fair . . . rosy hued:* images like these in similar contexts are very frequent in the works of
the poets of the "sweet new style" (*dolce stil novo*) whose first generation appeared just
before Dante. Poets who wrote in this style included Guido Guinizelli, Iacopone da
Todi, Guido Cavalcante, Dante himself, and others.

[I fear] we'll see him perish before long
Unless this matter soon is remedied;
It would be well to make him journey far,
In France to study, or some other clime;
O, call him to you, send him far away;
If not, he'll soon be taken from our hands.   48

The king says to the queen:
Where would you have me send him, so cast down?
Can someone there reprove him for his faults?
Indeed! For we are always in his heart,
And that's what we must make him understand.

The queen says:
And she'll much deeper enter in his heart
Than you would wish, and that you can't fend off.
Let's therefore do what I have said and find
Some way to send him far away from here.   56

The king and the queen speak, and Ulimentus comes:
My son belovèd, I have thought about
What course of action would be best for you:
You're young, good looking, you have wealth and rank,
And, but for martial skill, you nothing lack.
With your mother I've concluded, then,
To make your limbs grow firm and forceful, that
I'd like you to consent to go to Paris,
And there learn jousting, dancing, tournaments.   64

Ulimentus answers and says:
My dearest Father, and my mother sweet,
I'm happy to, but want to take Rosana.

The king says:
About this fantasy, don't even speak!
As long as you are there, she'll be far off.

The queen says:
Ah, lift this foolish notion from your heart,
For such an enterprise is shameful, vain!

Ulimentus says:

> If I shall go or not, I won't now say;
> Tomorrow, though, I'll clearly answer you.   72

Ulimentus goes to Rosana and says:

> Alas, Rosana, I feel myself grow weak
> Because of what my father has just said.
> He want me to study in Paris to perfect
> Myself in arms, in jousting and in dance.
> How can I ever be without you there
> When, thinking of it, my heart leaps from my breast?
> Clearly and frankly, tell me what you think—
> To go or stay, I'll do what you desire.   80

Rosana answers and says:

> Why is your leaving as abrupt as this?
> Is there no one to teach you in your realm?
> Some other cause provokes this trip of yours;
> God grant us grace that it's some good design.

Ulimentus says:

> I've almost lost my mind because I know
> That they'd just have me hold you in disdain.
> My father's surely foolish in this, blind;
> Though body leave, my heart will stay with you.   88

Rosana says:

> Three favors, first, I have to ask of you,
> And then you'll be made perfect, pious, kind.
> The first thing is, I want to baptize you;
> The second is, I want you to fear God;
> The third: your father and your mother honor,
> And in all things obey what they desire.[2]

Ulimentus says:

> Baptize me now; a thousand years 'twill seem
> For issuing forth from troubles perilous.   96

---

2. The admonition to obey as a means of honoring one's parents, besides being one of the ten commandments and prominent in this section of the play, was a regular emphasis of youth confraternities in late fifteenth-century Florence.

Rosana baptizes Ulimentus and says:
> You I do baptize in the Father's name,
> The son's, the Holy Spirit's—one sole God
> In perfect Trinity—and at the same time I
> Do raise you up from curst idolatry.
> Go where your father likes in joy and song,
> For Christ will ever show you the right way.
> And chastely live, for so I also shall.

Ulimentus says:
> God be with you; thus I plight you my troth.   104

Ulimentus returns to his father and says:
> Belovèd Father mine, I am content,
> Resolved, and firm to do what you have thought.

The king says:
> At your convenience, leave, as you may like,
> Take servants as you wish and money too.

Ulimentus points out the servants that he wants and says:
> With gold and silver I'm well furnished, and
> For company I have each one of you;
> To your safekeeping, Mother, I entrust
> Rosana—my body's heart, my life as well.   112

The queen says to her son:
> Rosana will remain in our embrace,
> And more than a daughter she'll be loved by us.

Ulimentus says:.
> I'll go then to perform what pleases you;
> Give me permission, Father, to be gone.

The king admonishes him and says:
> That sorrow bear with joyful countenance,
> Lest every insult be avenged on you.[3]

---

3. The idea here seems to be that a melancholy countenance might give offense and start fights.

Ulimentus says to his father:
> So shall I do, and I shan't cease to strive.

The king grants him his leave and says:
> Go now, my son; God bless [and be with] you.   120

Ulimentus turns to Rosana and says:
> Ah, dear Rosana, cherished soul of mine,
> Before I yet must take my leave of you,
> Until I reach the gate accompany me;
> Together we've a thousand things to say.
> I know not how or where I go, or am;
> Though I'm alive, 'twill seem that I have died.
> My mother doesn't mean to take you from me;
> What does me ill, she thinks will do me good.   128

Rosana says to Ulimentus:
> Because your father is so obstinate
> That you must go away despite your wish,
> Don't seek the reason that he's ordered it,
> But take the course your father's told you to—
> And know that I'll be always at your side,
> Because I'll ever have you in my heart.
> Let's pray to God, who every secret knows,
> That he'll preserve us happy, well, and glad.   136

Falling to their knees, Ulimentus and Rosana say together:
> O Lord supreme, O perfect Jesus who
> Our humanity put on to save us,
> And did not upon worldly pleasure gaze,
> Who in your faith has brought us to the light,
> Protect us, us defend from malice cruel,
> As Israel from Pharaoh you set free.

Ulimentus arises and says:
> Do you wish something from me? Take my hand.

Rosana gives him her hand, and says:
> Go, may God give you peace, and keep you well.   144

Ulimentus departs, and the queen says to the king:
> Belovèd husband mine, I am afraid

That I shall see my son expire for love;
Rosana will enter in his heart so deep
That in the end I'll see him die for woe.
Because of this I have a firm intent
To see that, secretly, she's put to death,
For she so vexing has become for me,
That, come what may, I mean that she should die.   152

The king says to the queen:
I wouldn't want her dying by my hand,
But I've a method good: a better way
I've found, for merchants of the sultan come
Who willingly would purchase her; I shall
In secret have them sent for, and we shall
Give her to them at a high price, and when
Our Ulimentus comes, in voices hushed,
And tearfully, we'll tell him that she's dead.   160

The queen says to the king:
Let these travelling peddlers be sought out,
If we'll pursue the course that you've proposed.

The king says to the seneschal:
Go, seneschal, and seek out merchants and
Have them quickly come before me here.

The seneschal says to the king:
O sacred majesty, I go now for them all,
And I shall see they come and they obey,
And without saying why, the chance, or cause,
They at your dwelling all will soon arrive.   168

The seneschal goes to the merchants and says:
O worthy merchants great, our sacred king
Has had me seek you out, and I believe,
In frankness, that he will reward you well,
For weighty matters he'd discuss with you.

The first merchant says:
Let's go see what he wants, companions, for
Tomorrow must we travel on our way;

For one who wishes to arrive at wealth
Will not come by it sleeping or at ease.   176

The seneschal leads the merchants to the king and says:
I have gone to the market, sacred king,
I've found these who are anxious to depart,
For they're prepared to go to Babylon,
But I have had them stay and come to you.

The king descends from the throne and says:
O merchants, I have sent for you because
I have a secret great to share with you,
For I will sell you certain merchandise,
That much will yield you and be of great use.   184

Leading them aside, the king says:
How would you like to buy a lovely girl?
A virgin, beautiful and nobly born?
I've reared her from a tot in cradle, and
She has no peer, she's chaste and well behaved.
But I don't wish that anyone should know,
And I'll want a good price from you for her.

The second merchant says:
I would not set a price nor pay one if
You don't at least let us see how she looks.   192

The king says to the merchants:
Come with me, I shall speak to that young girl,
Because to her my son has greetings sent.

And then he brings them to Rosana and says:
Rosana, my son is scourged on your account,
And you must go to be with him in France.

The king pulls the merchants aside:
You merchants, look, is she not beautiful,
Wise, noble? Well, what think you of her, then?

A merchant says:
If she's a virgin, as you'd have us believe,

Take what you want, for she well pleases us.   200

The king says to the merchants:
    I swear to you upon my crown that she
    A virgin is—as pure as she was born;
    Of gold a thousand doubloons is her price,
    And you can take her quickly to her fate.

The first merchant says:
    We don't perceive the manner nor the way,
    Nor how from these walls we can issue forth.
    For if she goes outside, she will be seen,
    And everyone will recognize her too.   208

The king says to the merchants:
    I've thought about the details and the way:
    Outside, tomorrow to your hands she'll be
    Delivered. With my lady she shall go
    Into the garden and you'll gag her in
    Her presence; for the journey hide her face,
    And then without delay shall you depart.

The second merchant says:
    Take the cash and send her forth to us,
    And do not be afraid that there'll be noise.   216

Having paid the money, the merchants conceal themselves, and the king says to himself:
    Alas, to what has my faith been reduced!
    In such a folly shall I take a part?
    Both faith and justice call to me each hour,
    My scepter and my royal throne to which
    I'm raised; but if I do it not, the queen
    Will grumble, she'll complain, shout, always stew—
    For those who have the brains of butterflies
    Must always have their way in everything.   224

The king returns to the throne and says to the queen:
    My darling wife, the matter is arranged;
    I have received the money for the girl.
    Tomorrow take her to the garden where,
    On your arrival there, those evil folk

Will seize and gag her in a trice, and then
In all haste they will carry her away.

The queen answers and says:
I understand the fine points of this thing;
Leave all to me—I'll take her to the garden.   234

The queen goes to Rosana and says:
Rosana mine, I think you're half distraught
Because you have ill color in your face.
Into the garden I would like to go
To pick some flowers, yellow, white, and red;
Come too, and you shall have your braids bedecked
With lilies and with jasmine—violets.

Rosana answers the queen:
A moment wait, I'll get my small prayer-book,
And to the garden gladly go with you.   240

Rosana goes for her little prayer book and says:
Mother of Christ, O holy Virgin Mary,
Keep me, for your mercy, in your hands,
Safe from the evil spells of wicked folk,
For I can't guard myself without your aid.
Although this queen so pious seems today,
Yet I'm as wary of her as can be;
Who'd much caress me, when it's not her way,
Has either tricked me or will soon deceive.   248

Rosana returns and the queen says:
Observe what air, what weather, what nice sun,
For everything to heart and sense brings joy,
And we must always go at times like this
Through gardens lovely, picking fruit and flowers;
Enter within and gather violets,
And flowers from which all the dew has dried.

Rosana goes in the garden; a merchant assaults her and says:
In company with us you'll have to go.

Rosana screams and says:
O give me aid, O Virgin Mary—woe!   256

The merchants take Rosana, and a friend of Ulimentus says:
> Ah, that's Rosana, and this one is the queen,
> Who for despite is sending her away,
> O orphan sorrowful, O wretched girl,
> And there is no one here who's on her side.
> If Ulimentus ever knew her ruin,
> He'd die of melancholy and of woe!
> Such sobbing as this I cannot hear and live—
> Oh, come what may, I'll write to him of this.   264

The queen returns to the king and says:
> Don't ask me if the thing's accomplished, for
> I sent her in the garden by herself.
> When she arrived, they gagged her so that she
> Could utter not a solitary word;
> Out of my sight, you see, I've got her; now
> My son can come back home from school, for I
> Am certain that he'll never see her more.

The king says to the queen:
> Don't speak of it, for much worse that will be.   272

Ulimentus' friend gives a courier a letter and says to him:
> Come hither, courier, go as far as France;
> Find Ulimentus, the king's son, and give,
> On my behalf, this letter to him there.
> Go secretly and do not tell a soul.

The courier says:
> In just a few days you will have been served;
> The road is good, and I have sturdy legs;
> Before you know it, I'll have done your task,
> And will have brought an answer back to you.   280

The courier departs, and the merchants arrive [at an inn in the east], and the first says to the landlord:
> O host, we have arrived for lodging here,
> And so this girl can have a little rest,
> For she is weary, tired from her long trip;
> She's eaten nothing for three days, indeed.

The host says to the merchants:
> I'll have my wife look after her, for she
> Will willingly devote her time to this.

The second merchant says:
> While we go to market, make her well,
> And pamper her, and we shall pay you much.   288

When the merchants have departed, Rosana says to herself:
> Woe, Father, O my Mother sweet, alas!
> Why in an evil hour was I born?
> O cruel king, O impious, wicked queen,
> Where was the faith you to my mother swore?
> Redeemer of the world, Messiah true,
> Your handmaid whom you have created, save;
> Except for you my every hope is lost,
> They sold me—they who should have shielded me.   296
>   Well could I grieve because of fortune, and
> Amidst the afflicted luckless count myself;
> But I don't know what else my Lord may wish.
> Mother of Christ, O be forever praised.

The wife of the host comforts her:
> Weep not, my daughter, be happy rather that
> In but a little while you'll be restored.

Rosana answers:
> Why don't you want me to bewail my woe?
> For I'm a slave; my father was a lord.   304

The merchants go to the sultan:
> O sultan great, we have a woman young
> Bought from the King of Cesarea; she's
> A virgin, chaste and lovely as she's born—
> A daughter of the royal blood of Rome.
> If you should wish to take look at her,
> We can, for her, make you a bargain price.

The sultan says:
> Let her immediately be brought to me;
> If she is what you say, you'll profit much.   312

The merchants return to Rosana:
> Rosana, our departure is prepared.
> At dawn tomorrow morning, if you please,
> The lord of this land has commanded that
> We go, because to see us is his wish;
> See, therefore, that your body is adorned,
> And come to do our duty to the king
> So that, tomorrow, you may be set free.

Rosana goes with them and says:
> O Virgin Mary, be my help today.   320

The merchants go to the sultan:
> This, sultan, is the one we've told you of;
> Does she seem to lack anything I said?

The sultan says:
> It's fact, if clean and pure her body is.

The first merchant says:
> Make every test and all comparisons.

The sultan says to them and to Rosana:
> I shall do so right now, I promise you;
> Now something of your own condition tell:
> What, young Christian woman, is your name?

Rosana answers:
> The sorrowful Rosana is my name.   328

The sultan says to the butler:
> Now if she's pure and chaste I want to see;
> Give me the wine, O butler, that's prepared.

The butler says:
> Here is the wine, lord, do what pleases you,
> For I believe that she will pass the test.

The sultan gives the cup of wine to Rosana, and says:
> Only a virgin, chaste and pure, can drink it;
> Who spills it on herself has been defiled.

Now take and drink this; if you pass the test,
The merchants have made good profit from their voyage.   336

Rosana empties the cup, and the sultan says:
To its last drop you've drained the cup, therefore,
Butler, come here and pay these merchants who've
Transported such good merchandise to me,
And give to them ten thousand ducats gold.

The butler says to the merchants:
Here, all your money I have counted out;
Behold in one small sack your treasure great,
Would you like to recount them differently?

The first merchant says:
We trust you fully, and we are content.   344

The merchants depart, and the sultan says:
Alisbech, trusty servant, come to me,
And, with your circumspection, take this one
And lead her to the harem all enclosed.
See that the others do her reverence;
Be careful that with her no one should speak,
And at the right time I shall send for her.

Alisbech says to the sultan:
On pain of death, my lord, it shall be done,
And you, young woman, come with me in joy.   352

He leads Rosana to the harem, and says:
Within here, enter; you shall honored be;
Our lord says all of you on pain of death
Must her respect as your superior,
And all must love her, all must her revere.

The first girl of the harem answers and says:
We're ever ready at all hours and
To his will we shall be obedient;
Enter with us the garden to enjoy,
And we are at your pleasure in all things.   360

Rosana enters within, seats herself alone, and says to herself:
>My liberty, alas, now you are lost!
>O Father, Mother, rulers, relatives,
>O my virginity, you have been sold.
>Where now, Rosana, is your happiness?
>A princess once, you've now been sold a slave,
>In pain, tears, sorrows, suffering and woe.
>But I don't wish to grieve, because my sin
>Deserves much worse; let God be ever praised.   368
>   Mother of sinners, Virgin merciful,
>Support for the afflicted and forlorn,
>Defend, please, my virginity, and don't
>Consider the transgressions that I've made;
>And pray your Son, the true Messiah, that
>He'll lift me from the unbelievers' hands,
>And if that cannot be, then make me strong,
>So I can die before they ravish me.   376

An angel appears to Rosana and says:
>All your prayers, Rosana, have been heard,
>By our Lord's Mother, merciful and kind,
>And, so your sorrows may be at an end,
>She wants to assuage this woe of yours.
>You shall, alive, be happy once again,
>And with your virgin honor be preserved.
>The sultan soon shall catch an illness grave:
>Be glad, therefore, I'll always be with you.   384

On his throne, the sultan says:
>Alas, this fever has assailed me so
>That I feel all my senses weakening,
>So feeble both my body and my soul,
>That I can't any longer stand upright;
>Alas, take up what I have finished, and
>Put me to bed so I can get some rest,
>And let me be, with no disturbances,
>And let nobody come to pester me.   392

Ulimentus returns, and goes to the house of the friend who has written him:
>Alas, belovèd, cherished friend of mine,
>What's this you've written me about my hope?

O Father wicked, curst, iniquitous,
How could you bring yourself to do such wrong?
I promise you, and swear now with my heart,
That I shall never enter in your room
If I don't find her. I must search for her;
To find her, I would go to Babylon.   400
The friend, named Eustorgius, says:
    I do not know what injury, what feud
With her your mother had to make her come
Into the garden all alone with her,
Where many stifled her and led her off,
Restrained and bound, so it's a pity just
To hear it spoken of, and great regret
I felt at that outrageous deed, and so
I sent the servant to you with all speed.   408

A baron sees Ulimentus, and goes to the king:
    O mighty King, your son is back again
In mourning dressed and in great suffering,
And he is staying at Eustorgius's house,
And says that, where you are, he will not come.

Disturbed, the king says:
    Ah woe is me! What treacherous seas I'm in,
For how can I excuse myself to him?
What can I say? A fool is he, indeed,
Who women trusts; I'm brainless, faithless too.   416
    O woeful me, alas, what can I do,
Because my son's so much enraged at me?
My counselors, what do you think of this?
How can I ever get him pacified?
What I have done, I can't again undo,
But I would give my state to call it back,
And children I'd prefer to never have,
For having them is such great pain and woe.   420

A counselor says:
    Although you may, my lord, have erred, you can
Make reparations, always, for your deed;
Let us go seek him there where he is lodged,

And we can civilly converse with him,
And offer money, goods, and rank, and we
Can see if we can ransom his Rosana.
Let's go to him; indeed I think we may
Lead him to do what we desire of him.   428

The queen says to the king:
I want to go to see my son with you,
For if he sees me, he'll forgive us both.

The king says to the queen:
You are the cause of all this sorrow, wife,
And he'd be stupid, mad, and foolish to
Believe you; I'd best go to him alone,
I think. Perhaps he'll credit my words more.

The queen says to the king:
I'm wholly bent on going there with you.

The king answers:
If you wish to; let's go now to his place.   436

They go to Ulimentus, and the king says:
O my sweet son, what is this that I hear,
That you won't come to rest in your own house?
For you know that the realm is yours, the gold,
The silver; you I always seek to praise,
Though you so grievously torment my heart
That I shall waste away before my time.

A counselor says:
Son, his desire and his will follow, for
It is God's precept fathers to obey.   444

Ulimentus says to his father:
O Father, listen, heed well what I say:
Since you have sold my hope, I shall hold you
My mortal enemy forever, nor
Shall I turn up wherever you may be;
I shall go poor and begging through the world

Alone to seek her, with no company;
And now I shall depart with pain and woe—
Where you may be, no more shall I return.   452

The queen seizes her son and says:
Stay where you are, my son, do not depart;
Rosana's dead, you couldn't find her now.
Entombed with my own eyes I saw her, and
I wept because you would not that believe;
Will you then leave your father in such pain?
For I know well you would not leave us so.
Forget her, come and celebrate, be glad,
For you'll have women at your beck and call.   460

Ulimentus says to his mother:
You did not suffer anything for me;
No longer do I think you gave me birth,
Because I think you my prime enemy,
So that you're wasting time in flattery;
You sold her! You'd not have me speak of her;
Go you with God; two wrongs don't make a right,
For my mind's been so poisoned, that I'd not
Be much concerned if I should lose my life.   468

The queen departs and says to herself:
You women will take pity on my fate,
For you caress them in their infancy:
Who would have children, may God grant them some,
And grant them large, as many as they wish,
I have but one who chases me away,
And wrings my heart with sadness and great woe,
When I had hope for solace in old age;
A child is that which seeks to burn me out.   476

The king turns to Ulimentus, and says:
Of all that has happened to Rosana, son,
Your mother is the cause, so if you have
Set out to follow her, it's my desire
That you go forth the right way and in ranks;
Be furnished well with money and with men—
By these is one esteemed throughout the world.

Believe me, too, for what I say, you'll do;
Beyond a doubt you will recover her.   484
  I want no counsel and no seeming more,
For poison just like sugar tastes to me;
I want to show my power with the sword,
So greatly that the body's breath shall fail.

A counselor says:
  To get her back will be an easy thing
If you will do what we advise you to;
An old man man's counsel is esteemed, you know,
As has been proved by many trials and tests.   492

The king says to his son:
  You see, son, in a moment she was gone.
If you still wish to try to buy her back,
Take up my realm, my goods, my very life,
If you will go to find her in Babylon,
For there the merchants were to make their voyage
And said they'd sell her to the sultan there.
We shall take arms, son, if you so desire;
You'll have her back, with counsel and with cash.   500

Ulimentus says to the king:
  O faithful servant, I am deeply moved,
And I indeed ask pardon for my fault;
I see that your advice will bear good fruit,
And so in full I mean to follow it.
In grief and tears let Mother stay alone;
Where she is, there I never mean to go.

The king takes him by the hand and says:
  Now, in a moment, come on home with me,
And I shall orders give to gladden you.   508

They go home, and the king says from his throne:
  Up, seneschal, admit of no delay,
And get my soldiers lined up, every one,
Because my son will lead them far away;
See that they all are instantly in arms.

The seneschal answers:
> They all will be in order at my call.

The seneschal says to the soldiers:
> Step forward, men! Behold, they are prepared;
> That they'll be worth their hire I clearly see,
> And if they must do ill, they'll do their worst.   516

The king, having reviewed the soldiers ranks, addresses his son and says:
> By three means are dominions governed, son;
> By treasure, counsel, and by force of arms;
> For force of arms, take you this barony,
> And for good counsel, take these men along—
> It's their advice that rules me. Take much gold
> For spending—silver too—for that's
> The way to do each task—flee woe and strife.   524
>   Soldiers, now go forward with my son
> And what he tells you, do it properly;
> Keep him, you counselors, from grief and woe,
> Advise him in his need; and, [son], to you,
> Alone I give this treasure, it's enough
> To more than keep you happy for ten years.
> And over all else that may come to pass,
> Be careful as you can be, making war.   532

A soldier says to everyone:
> Behold us here in arms with all our host,
> Ready to leave when he shall want us to.

A counselor says:
> We both are ready to assist him, too;
> With deeds we mean to help him, and with words.

Ulimentus requests permission to depart, and says:
> You all shall be rewarded well by me;
> Now let's be gone, for I'm grieved by delay,
> And always, Father, I'll remember you.   540

The king gives license to go and says:
> Go yet with God; God give you victory.

Ulimentus leaves, and in that same moment, Rosana says to herself:

I think that gate will never open up,
Indeed, though I won't say, "Rosana, this
Is it for you"; but God knows I would die
Before I'd fall into the hands of him
Who holds me here. Lord Jesus, strength you
Give, and courage to whoever loves and serves
You with good will, O Goodness infinite,
Your handmaid save; save me, or take my life.   548

Ulimentus arrives with his men at arms at a wood, and the counselor says:

From here to Babylon will take three days,
And we'll do well to pause to make a plan;
Do we wish with so many men in arms
To go, or think the sultan we can force?
It better seems to me that we wait here,
And one with Ulimentus ought to go
Alone into the land to seek the means
And way to get her back—that plan pursue.   556

Another counselor says:

He speaks the truth. One only take with you;
Let the other with your troops stay here.

Ulimentus says:

Who then will wish to keep me company,
While others wait to answer to my call?

Another counselor says:

Konrad will go; he has a clever mind,
And in all things he's practical and smart.

Ulimentus says to Konrad:

Come, Konrad, let's go reconnoiter troops,
And hidden in the woods, you wait for us.   564

One of the girls of the harem garden says to the others:

Companions mine, this new young woman is
So very sorrowful and full of doubt,
She is not pleased with any company;
We shall not do what Alisbech has done,

We'll ask her if she'll dance, and we shall see
If she will take delight in anything.
For if we keep ourselves away from her,
The sultan will find fault with us for that.   572

Another girl says:
You know him well, for if she will not speak,
It will be bad for you, for she's too proud,
Because I see she thinks herself so fair,
That she esteems us not and keeps aloof.

Another girl responds:
It seems she has a thousand daggers[4] in
Her heart, for harsh and bitter is the life
she leads. Let's all go keep her company,
And draw her forth from idle fantasy.   580

They go together to Rosana, and one says:
Our sister, we are wondering why it is
That you don't ever come with us at all—
Unless we firmly judge that you disdain
Us as unworthy of your loveliness—
And for this reason, we invite you to
Perform a dance, and, we entreat you,
Don't deny us this, as seems but rational,
For one who's pleasant is more beautiful.   588

Rosana answers:
My sisters, do not wonder that I take
No pleasure with you, no delight, for I
Flee everything that you are searching for;
What pleases you, annoys and vexes me,
And if I've erred in this, pray pardon me,
For what I know, I know, I promise you;
To be alone still much more pleases me.

A girl speaks to Rosana, and they depart:
Comport yourself your way, and be at peace.   596

---

4. daggers: Ital. *quadrella*—a particularly insidious sort of dagger with points so sharp its wounds were hard to close.

The girls depart, and Ulimentus arrives at the inn, and he says to the host:
    Good morrow, host, I want to stay with you
    With my companion and this company;
    Are you supplied to treat us royally?
    For we have cash enough to throw away.

The host answers:
    You could not happen on a better place
    For wine, beds, viands, hospitality.
    I know the price that's right for everything—
    The host is at your pleasure, and his inn.   604

Ulimentus says to the host:
    Host, bring some wine and give us some to drink,
    For we are tired and weary from the road,
    And do not fear, I'll treat you as I ought,
    And you'll do well for lodging folk like us.

The host brings something to drink, and says:
    Here is your wine, sit down, especially
    Because I have two capons fat for you;
    Request, though, anything you hunger for,
    For I'm provided well with everything.   612

Ulimentus gives presents to the hostess and her daughter:
    In lands where I am used to travelling,
    It is my custom and my habit to
    Be very courteous in giving gifts
    To everyone according to his rank,
    And therefore, hostess, you will pardon me;
    I take the liberty to give this jewel
    To you; please take this necklace, then,
    And wear it round your neck to honor me.   620

The host's wife says:
    Your bearing makes you seem a proper man,
    Your courtesies are without peer; but how,
    Pray tell me, can I pay you back for this?
    Because I know how costly these things are.

The daughter of the hostess says:
    For these gifts that you have given me,

I thank you, for I think them good and dear.

Ulimentus says:
Pray God that he'll protect me from distress;
If I leave happy, you will stand to gain.   628

The hostess says to her husband:
Belovèd spouse, this foreigner is not
A man who's tossed by wind and wave;
He is an ark, of pleasure he's a fount;
Look what a lovely gift he's given me.
But he's revealed he has much on his mind,
And says: "If I'm content, you'll stand to gain."

The host answers his wife:
Do not inquire about his purposes,
But as we can, I wish to give him aid.   636

Ulimentus calls the host:
O host, you seem to me discreet and wise,
And much accustomed to achieving things.
My secret I would like to share with you,
But tell me first, can I in you confide?

The host answers:
As God may keep me healthy, joyful, glad,
Say what you wish, for that I shall conceal—
My lady will as well—and if there's help
Or counsel we can give you, that we'll do.   644

Ulimentus answers the host:
In my home country, not a year ago,
A sister of mine was kidnapped, and we think
That they have brought her here; and it is said
That she's been purchased by the sultan. Host,
If you know anything of this deceit,
And find a way she may be brought from there,
I will behave so graciously toward you,
That you'll no longer need [to run] the inn.   652

The host says to Ulimentus:
This girl, the sister of your flesh, has stayed

Three weeks or longer with us here, for she
Was very pampered, beautiful and chaste.
And our great sultan bought her, finally;
He has secluded her; her none may see,
For he guards her more closely than his eyes.
My wife alone is suited for this task;
Except for her, no person *there* can go.   660

The hostess says to Ulimentus:
Because your sorrow makes me pity you,
And for you kindness, I'll shall go to her,
And I shall take a dress of taffeta,
And tell the Moor I want to show her that.
He knows me, and he's never kept me out,
So I can let her know of everything,
And I can bring her message back to you.

Ulimentus answers:
My lady, go, and do it as you will.   668

The hostess goes to Alisbech and says:
O Alisbech, I want to pass within
To see your ladies, show this gown to them,
For usually they will buy from me,
And by this means I'll give them pleasure great.

Alisbech says to the hostess:
Some day, O hostess, you'll endanger me
With all your passing to and fro. Go, hurry back;
Except for you, none outside comes in here,
Though it might be the sultan's child, indeed.   676

The hostess goes to the young women, and says:
You lovely girls, [look], I have brought with me
A gown of silk that I would like to sell,
And for it I can make you a good price
If such a purchase you should choose to make;
And it has not been worn a dozen times,
For it is new, as you must understand.
Now look it over closely and then speak
Your minds if that is what you want to do.   684

One takes the gown and says to the others:
>   This lovely color really pleases me,
>   Because I know 'twould please my lord as well;
>   And if I buy, I'll take it for his love,
>   So I can have more favor from him then.
>   But still, I would not want to err in this,
>   Therefore, each one must tell me what she thinks.

A girl answers:
>   That you don't want it, make the hostess think,
>   Then, if the price won't break you, buy the dress.   692
>   Be sure it's not some gown that's been remade,
>   Recarded by some seller of used clothes,
>   So that you won't be thought to be a fool,
>   Or that her coming be a double ill.

The girl says:
>   She's brought it, surely, from some house,
>   I've checked it very closely in the light;
>   Be sure of price, if it includes the sash;
>   And do not buy unless you're fond of it.   700

Another girl says:
>   Look closely how the silk has faded here,
>   Already through the puddles it's been worn;
>   Still, let us settle firmly on a price;
>   What do you want, in sum, that I must pay?

The hostess says:
>   It's from a worthy man who now has failed;
>   The price no less than fifty lire is,
>   For new he made it, perhaps a year ago—
>   He doesn't sell the lining or the sleeves.[5]   708

The girl answers:
>   No less than twenty patches, I'd have said;
>   You think you're dealing here with idiots?
>   Had you just now agreed to take but ten—

---

5. In the Renaissance, dresses were made separately from sleeves, which had to be tied on.

I wouldn't want it if you gave it free.

The girl says to the hostess:
>   Inquire if someone else may care for it,
>   Indeed, I wish Rosana you would find;
>   Take it to her, for she has lots of cash;
>   If she is pleased with it, you'll sell it soon.   716

The hostess goes to Rosana and says:
>   My lovely daughter, you are happily met;
>   I am the hostess where you used to lodge,
>   And good news for you do I bring today—
>   The best that you will in a decade hear:
>   A man who calls himself your brother is
>   At my house, in the same room where you stayed.
>   To you he's sent me—says he's set his heart
>   On dragging you out of here by force or love.   724

Rosana reveals that she's amazed:
>   I do not know who this may be who can
>   Come here for me and come all by himself.

The hostess says to Rosana:
>   Fear nothing, my young lady, he's the son
>   Of Cesarea's mighty king, and he
>   Has with him a great company and wants
>   To liberate you from such sorrow great.

Rosana reveals herself to the hostess, and says:
>   O you poor boy, to what have you set yourself!
>   Speak soft, O hostess, for it's really he!   732
>   To my belovèd brother thus report:
>   That I'm a virgin, and I chaste remain,
>   And that with fever the sultan lies abed,
>   For he fell ill the same day I arrived;
>   Say that the blessèd angel said to me
>   That Christ is ever with me, is my help.
>   Thus to my brother, everything report.

The hostess answers:
>   That I shall do, and may God be with you.   740

The hostess departs, and says to Alisbech:
> With the women I've left the merchandise—
> It pleases them, but they're grieved at the price;
> You've helped me, and to you I am obliged,
> And ready am for you at every task.

Alisbech says to the hostess:
> By that freedom the king has given me,
> Against your courtesy I shan't contend.
> Except for you, no one can visit her.

The hostess answers:
> I'm certain of it; I'm at your command.   748

Rosana says:
> O you poor boy, unfortunate and plagued,
> Who suffers such dire hardship just for me,
> I fear much more that you may not be found,
> For life and death content me equally.
> Lord Jesus, who art always at my side,
> Defend him from vexation and from woe,
> As I know that he has firm faith in you,
> Have mercy on your servant; pity him.   756

The hostess returns to Ulimentus and says:
> O noble youth, I have come back again
> From visiting the sister of your flesh,
> And I your message gave to her, indeed,
> That you are here and try to find her so
> You'll get her out, and she is glad of that
> And she is also yearning to see you.

Ulimentus rewards the hostess and says:
> This money take as a down payment, for
> You have, indeed, a greater bonus earned.   764

Ulimentus addresses the host and says:
> Just speaking with her, host, is not enough,
> For we must now think how to get her out.

The host answers:
> Of one way I have thought that ought to work:

    Corrupt her guards with money; Alisbech
    Seek out, and speak well manneredly with him,
    For he is haughty, and honors he prizes much,
    Above all, though, he's miserly and poor;
    Go speak alone with him—he'll be impressed.   772

Ulimentus goes to Alisbech and says:
    Into this land it happens I have come,
    Far through foreign lands and countries strange,
    And I've asked for a man discreet and wise,
    With whom I could consider certain thoughts;
    At the Sword's Inn, the host has praised you much
    And said you were a fountain of delight;
    Jewels do I have, and have much money too,
    And willingly with you I'd counsel take.   780

Alisbech answers:
    What you may be and whence here you have come,
    To speak with me instead of anyone
    In court, I do not know, but you may hold
    It certain that I'll keep your secret to
    The death; my counsel's trustworthy—unless
    You want to step inside these gates. That I'd
    Not grant, and I would let you go away.
    Now speak; I am prepared to counsel you.   788

Ulimentus says:
    I am the King of Cesarea's son
    And I have outside many troops with me;
    My father has suffered pain and woe a year
    Because one of my sisters kidnapped was,
    And here into your company was brought
    The sultan's slave, and you have her locked up;
    If back to me you'll give her, I'll give you
    High rank and wealth and honor for that breach.   796

Alisbech says:
    The state and honor that is asked of me
    Is what must be considered loyalty;
    The man who can't be trusted in this world's
    A broken flower the wind will blow away.

Don't speak of it; today I'll not agree
Such folly against reason to commit.

Ulimentus says:

You can't deny the reason, for you can
Much profit if you'll let her go from there.   804

Alisbech says:

This proposition you have made to me—
It seems to you that this thing could succeed.
Don't think it—the opposite can befall,
From which would follow endless woe for us;
Don't speak of it, for my mind is made up
That I won't do this thing, since I fear for my life.

Ulimentus answers:

I have here many troops to shelter us,
And there's no doubt that you can do this thing.   812

Alisbech answers:

I never would commit a fault like this,
For I'd be thought a traitor if I did.

Ulimentus says:

Is it so fine to be a vassal, then?
To be a slave when you could be a lord?

Alisbech answers:

That's true and sure; let's go! let's do this thing,
For, while I can, I'd give up servitude;
Go, get all your troops together at the host's,
And then return to spirit her away.   820

Ulimentus departs, and Alisbech says to himself:

O cursèd avarice perfidious!
O desire for honors in the world,
Every justice, money will corrupt,
And everyone would be of higher rank;
Today I do a great iniquity,
But when one errs with many, error's less;
To have a realm and treasure, liberty,
Will bear comparison with any pain.   828

Ulimentus goes to the host and says:
> O host, would you like to come home with me?
> Because this very night I must depart;
> I'll have my sister in my company—
> Alisbech too; so will you come as well?

The host answers:
> That God in whom you believe be with you, go
> In peace; for me, I do not want to leave.

The hostess says to Ulimentus:
> Give greetings to Rosana, if you please.

Ulimentus rewards her and says:
> Bide here, my lady, and remain in peace.   836

Ulimentus returns, and Alisbech says:
> We are in fearful peril for our lives,
> Therefore let none of you make any noise.

Having entered the harem garden, Ulimentus says:
> My beautiful Rosana, where are you?

Running to him, Rosana says:
> Right here am I, O my beloved lord.

Rosana embraces Ulimentus and faints, and Alisbech says:
> Do you not see how she has swooned? Away!
> Put her upon my back, we must make haste,
> For if within these gates we should be seen,
> We shall, with reputation none, be dead.   844

Alisbech takes her on his shoulders, and they flee, and someone sees them and goes to the sultan and says:
> O mighty sultan, from gate I come;
> I found Alisbech with three men at arms;
> He bore away Rosana on his back; they ran
> Pell mell, and outside they've already passed.

Enraged, the sultan says:
> Go quickly with your escort, seneschal,

Bring them all captive here, and bind them tight,
For each one will be flayed alive for this.

The seneschal says:
So shall I do.

The sultan says:
Get going; no more words.[6]   852

Ultimentus reaches his companions, and the counselor stands before them and says:
Our lord and brothers, you are welcome back,
And here's Rosana; matters will go well.

Ulimentus says to Alisbech:
Observe, Alisbech, here are those in arms
Who will from pain and suffering you defend.

Alisbech looks back and sees the sultan's people and says:
Look here his troops come, we have been attacked;
Each one, to arms, and let me lead the fray,
For I have broken faith; I stole the girl,
And now I shall lay down my life for you.   860

The seneschal sees them, and from afar he says:
O traitors, you no longer can take flight
Because your crime has been discovered and
You must before the mighty sultan come,
And he will punish you as you deserve.

The counselor says to his men:
Here must we gain the victory or die,
For there's no hope of having any aid;
Engage, you barons, with all their champions.

Ulimentus addresses Rosana and says:
And, in the meantime, pray to God for us.   868

6. This is the only broken line in any play attributed to A. Pulci. The action demands
haste, and the broken line reinforces that action.

*Rosana falls to her knees, and the battle rages; the sultan's troops are killed, and
Ulimentus says:*

> Are all these dogs snuffed out and dead? Is there
> Not one of them who from this place will go?
> Who'll be the one to carry back this news?
> You shake your heads, will no one volunteer?
> Well, since each one supports his fellows, we
> Must travel to our home again—both you
> And our Rosana here in company,
> And praising the Virgin Mary we shall go.   876

A baron goes to the King of Cesarea and says:

> Your son is coming, King magnanimous,
> Singing, with Rosana and many troops;

The king says:

> Now shall an end be put to all my pain,
> Up quickly—let us go to meet him now.

Grieving, the queen says:

> Unless you'd have me always sorrowful,
> Make peace among us as is just and right.

The king says to the queen:

> Leave this to me; to satisfy you more,
> I shall request from him this lofty grace.   884

The king goes and meets his son and says:

> You're welcome home again, O my sweet son,
> And you, Rosana, you are welcome too.

Ulimentus embraces his father and says:

> And you, belovèd Father, are well met!
> And are you well and happy in your realm?

The king answers:

> If you will pardon our past sin, then will
> Your mother and your father be content.

Ulimentus says:
>And if a gift from me will make you glad,
>Be reconciled forever with me now.   892

The queen arrives and says to her son:
>By all the pains that I endured for you,
>O son, from you your pardon I implore.

Ulimentus answers his mother:
>If with my father you'll do as I say,
>You of your every failing will be cleansed;
>But if you won't, you'll never see me more,
>For I shall make my dwelling place in Rome.
>That you'll leave paganism, false and vain,
>And baptism receive—that's what I wish.   900

The queen, joyful, says:
>Since you're so gracious in forgiving us,
>I'm pleased to be baptized just as you wish.

The king says:
>And I too am prepared, and very good
>The reason is that I have to consent.

Ulimentus thanks God, and says:
>Eternal God, be thou forever praised;
>Let's go, for I am tortured by delay,
>And, Father and my Mother, may you have
>in Jesus perfect faith forever more.   908

Ulimentus says to Alisbech:
>And you who've loved me more than Father has,
>Pray tell me, what life would you call your own?

Alisbech answers:
>Accompanied by these I wish to be,
>And baptized in the name of Mary's Son,
>For long I have already yearned for it,
>And to pursue the right and holy way.

Ulimentus says:
>I thank you for this gift—the other too;

Let's to that font where every [thirst] is slaked.   916

They go to the font and Ulimentus says:
    O just and clement God, whose blood has saved
    Us from the wicked demon's hand, who with
    Your faith most holy has illumined us
    And each desire of ours has satisfied,
    These persons are here baptized in your name,
    With pious hearts, benign and temperate.
    O Father, the water and the prayer are not
    Enough for you, you must perform good works.   924
        Send forth your proclamation through the land
    That idols and their temples are extinct.

The king calls a herald, and says:
    Go, herald, and on my behalf proclaim
    To all my subjects a decree that they
    Must heed precisely, for I thus command:
    That none to Jove or other idols yield,
    For all within three days must be baptized;
    The gallows' pain for all who stray from this.   932

The herald makes the proclamation and says:
    The king commands this edict be enforced:
    That Jove and all the other gods be burned.
    Within three days you must go be baptized
    At Christian churches that have been prepared;
    And woe to him who will not do this thing,
    For he will for his sins reap punishment;
    And those who go, I say, will comfort have,
    And those who won't go will be seized and killed.   940

The king on his throne says to his son:
    My dear son, now that I have been baptized
    With all my realm, and with my lady too,
    I want to give myself to God, give up
    My state, and give my kingdom all to you,
    And this is the reason I have reared you up,
    To give the land and rule into your power,
    The crown as well, and new arrangements make,
    Giving myself repose, for I am old.   948

Having been crowned, Ulimentus says:

Since I have been appointed in your name,
The first thing that I mean to do is this:
To compensate that one who served me [well].
I couldn't pay him though I gave the realm.
Come here Alisbech, I have made a vow
To pattern myself just on your design;
Let Aragon be yours, as it should be;
As my prime minister here with me stay.   956

Alisbech answers Ulimentus:

I'm very much obliged to you, my lord,
Though I don't think I'd compensation seek
That's worth more than the sacrament you gave
To me—beyond all else the treasure of
The world. As you desire, I'll ever stay
Beside you, set to do your every task.
I'm satisfied and glad to do your will,
And ever give you thanks for all you've done.   964

Alisbech sits down, and Ulimentus says:

My subjects, countrymen and citizens,
And you who always would be friends with me:
The thieves, the rascals, wicked rapists—they
Are rebels exiled in great iniquity;
The orphans, widows, churches, hospitals,
Let them be justly treated and with right.
This is my will; this my intention is,
Now let us play, and sing, and celebrate.   972

THE END

INDEX